# Tactical Portfolios

Founded in 1807, John Wiley & Sons is the oldest independent publishing company in the United States. With offices in North America, Europe, Australia, and Asia, Wiley is globally committed to developing and marketing print and electronic products and services for our customers' professional and personal knowledge and understanding.

The Wiley Finance series contains books written specifically for finance and investment professionals as well as sophisticated individual investors and their financial advisors. Book topics range from portfolio management to e-commerce, risk management, financial engineering, valuation, and financial instrument analysis, as well as much more.

For a list of available titles, visit our web site at www.WileyFinance.com.

# Tactical Portfolios

*Strategies and Tactics for Investing in Hedge Funds and Liquid Alternatives*

BAILEY McCANN

with contributions from
Opalesque Editors

WILEY

Cover image: top: © Fanatic Studio / Jupiter Images
bottom: © Photodisc / Jupiter Images
Cover design: Wiley



Published by John Wiley & Sons, Inc., Hoboken, New Jersey.
Published simultaneously in Canada.



*Library of Congress Cataloging-in-Publication Data:*
ISBN 978-1-118-73162-8 (Hardcover)
ISBN 978-1-118-73158-1 (ePDF)
ISBN 978-1-118-73163-5 (ePub)

Printed in the United States of America
10 9 8 7 6 5 4 3 2 1

# Contents

# Introduction

In just one decade, stocks have halved two times. After reaching a new high in the first quarter of 2000, the MSCI World stock index found a bottom in September 2002 following the dot.com crisis. The index, which captures large and mid-cap stocks, lost over 48 percent while hedge funds (as measured by the HFR Weighted Composite Index) were up net of fees 2.1 percent. When the global financial crisis took stocks down over 50 percent from their tops in early 2007 through October 2009, hedge fund investors were reaping over 6 percent during the same time.

Helped by floods of quantitative easing, many global stocks have reached new highs in 2013.[1]

You would think that investors would now "hedge their bets" and move to hedge funds to protect their assets and establish a meaningful diversification. The "smart" money has done this, maintaining a significant allocation to hedge funds.

## INVESTORS EXIT HEDGE FUNDS AT FASTEST RATE IN FOUR YEARS

"Investors exit hedge funds at fastest rate in four years", says a Reuters headline on January 13th, 2014. The article refers to the SS&C GlobeOp Capital Movement Index which calculates monthly hedge fund subscriptions (in-flows) less redemptions (out-flows). With −3.56 percent, December 2013 showed the biggest drop since September 2009. The article continues that "while the end of the year period usually sees a pick-up in redemptions as investors look to move money around their portfolio ahead of the New Year, December's reading is notably high. In the same month last year the index measured minus 2.61 percent."[2]

For 2013, SS&C GlobeOp's Hedge Fund Performance Index was up 12.32 percent, which is about half of the return of the MSCI World Index. So, hedge funds have performed well, but maybe not good enough?

Today (January 14th, 2014), as I write this introduction, another interesting story: "Global stocks fall on concerns about earnings"—is angst coming back to the markets?[3] Right now, we don't know what will happen and may soon enter an environment where investors wish they had invested more in hedge funds and absolute return strategies than in long-only equity.

Alexander Ineichen, one of the most well-known researchers on hedge funds globally, offers the following advice: "Equity investors have been dancing on thin ice and might continue to do so. It's difficult to say how long the ice holds. I'm quite certain though, that at one stage a hedged approach will reveal itself as more intelligent than a long-only approach. Again. To stick with the metaphor: A long-only investment style is like dancing on thin ice, while a long/short investment style is like dancing on thin ice wearing swimmies: it might look odd at times but it's safer."[4]

## LEARNING FROM YALE: 51 PERCENT ALLOCATION TO ALTERNATIVE INVESTMENTS

Yale's $20bn endowment has included alternative investment strategies for over 20 years now. The so-called "endowment model" aims to achieve superior returns by shifting a significant portion of investments away from traditional stocks and bonds into carefully selected alternative investments like private equity, hedge funds, real estate, and others.

While the global financial crisis also managed to drawdown the value of Yale's endowment 24.6 percent in the fiscal year ending June 2009, the endowment model is still regarded the most viable proposition for long-term investors. How does Yale invest? For 2014, Yale's investment targets include a massive 51 percent allocation to alternatives, while only 17 percent is reserved for international and domestic U.S. equities.[5]

Yale's investment team, made up of 26 experts, are of course, not the only institutional investors who look to create tactical portfolios using alternative investments for both return and diversification goals. Ninety-four percent of institutional investors surveyed by Russell Investments said they already allocate to some form of alternatives, on average 22 percent of total assets. This already represents a significant allocation, which over time will only continue to go up. In the last three years, alternative mandates accounted for over 40 percent of all institutional hiring activity made during this period.

## HEDGE FUNDS, EMERGING MANAGERS, LIQUID INVESTMENTS, AND MANAGED FUTURES

With an average allocation of probably in the single digits, private investors, together with a lot of their investment advisers, stand on the other side in this game of investing. There is a lot to catch up, and like in sports, a good start is always to look at the rules, and how the other players play the game.

When I started to research and publish about hedge funds and alternative investments in early 2003 under the umbrella of my company Opalesque, little did I know that hedge funds would grow from around $600 billion at that time to close to $3 trillion. Still, compared to endowments, family offices and foundations, hedge funds and alternative investment are largely underrepresented in the portfolios of insurance companies, private and public sector pension funds, sovereign wealth funds, and, of course, of private investors.

Liquid alternatives are one of the fastest growing sectors of the financial industry globally. Depending on the respective regulatory framework of the funds, liquid alternatives are mostly offered in a mutual fund format. They often have smaller minimum investment thresholds, making investments in alternative strategies easier for many investors. The investment options for professional and retail investors are growing rapidly, but still, the number one requirement when selecting any alternative investment is to understand the strategy.

In this respect, managed futures are probably among the least understood investment strategies, even for many institutional investors. On the other hand, managed futures have been around for decades, and many programs have been going for long periods during which they have proven their value of adding true diversification to a portfolio during periods of market stress and crisis.

We wrote this book to help you to better understand and utilize the new options tactical portfolios of alternative investments are offering you. Myself and the editorial team of Opalesque are at your disposal—you can email us any time your questions, suggestions and feedback at tacticalportfolios@opalesque.com.

Matthias Knab
Founder and CEO of Opalesque

## NOTES

1. MSCI World, www.msci.com/products/indices/performance.html.
2. www.reuters.com/article/2014/01/13/us-hedge-funds-data-idUSBREA0C1GK20140113.
3. www.livemint.com/Money/t9gCdLJUksAnPkDPca2EUP/Opening-Bell-14-January—Global-stocks-fall-on-concerns-abo.html.
4. www.opalesque.com/RT/ZurichRoundtable2014.html.
5. http://news.yale.edu/2013/09/24/endowment-earns-125-return.

# Preface

*Tactical Portfolios* is a book designed to help investors, investment advisors, and anyone interested in alternative investments understand what hedge funds and liquid alternatives are and what they do. The book attempts to show different strategies hedge fund managers employ and how they work in a portfolio. We also walk the reader through the various service providers and regulations impacting the industry in the wake of the financial crisis.

The book closes with a discussion of what diversification and hedging really are in an effort to help investors avoid the potentially fatal flaw of exposure risk. I hope you find the text valuable and easy to read.

I would like to thank all of the managers who have been generous with their time and expertise, as well as the Opalesque editors, Opalesque Publisher Matthias Knab, and Olivier Blanchard, who gave me great starting advice for this book. Finally, I'd like to thank E'lona McCann for her advice and support.

Bailey McCann
January 2014

CHAPTER 1

# Hedge Fund Strategies and How They Work

Until recently, most investors maintained a traditional portfolio construction of 60 percent in stocks, 20 to 30 percent in bonds, and the rest in cash. That 60 percent was managed passively, using the buy and hold method, with bets placed only on the long side of the trade. That means that investors' only hope was for equities to go up in perpetuity, which as we all know, never actually happens. Markets correct, outside events force sell offs, companies go bust. This is where alternatives come in, helping some of the biggest players in the market mitigate losses during those tough times.

Another term for hedge funds is *absolute return*, meaning that hedged strategies are designed in order to provide a return instead of 0% and/or mitigate losses in the event of a market correction. The way this works in practice is, if an individual invests in a mutual fund, that fund will likely return 3 percent a year in a positive market. In a down market, that mutual fund could potentially go to zero return and post losses. This is because mutual funds typically place bets that the market will go up.

Hedge funds, on the other hand, have plans in place for both sides. They'll take the view that the value will go up (going long), and also have insurance bets in place in case the market goes down (going short). Sometimes these bets are made together, other times the manager reacts dynamically to a change in market conditions. In a positive market, a hedge fund could post a 10 percent return over the year, in a market that is going down that return might be slightly less, say 6 to 9 percent, because of the fund's ability to react and move into short positions. Only in extreme market movements like 2008, where sell offs hit depression levels, did we see a significant number of hedge fund strategies fail to post positive returns for the year. This gives them a competitive edge over mutual funds, which can go negative in a year that is only marginally bad, relative to crisis years like 2008.

In this chapter, we will examine at a broad level how this plays out by highlighting the differences between the most common strategies, and why it is important to understand that allocating to hedge funds as though they are an asset class may not be the best way to reap the rewards of absolute return strategies. Instead, learning the role of each individual strategy can lead to more optimal portfolio construction and better returning allocations.

## INVESTOR EVOLUTION

In terms of investing, hedge funds are still a new kid on the block. They've been around since the 1950s, but they didn't really pick up steam until much later. High net worth investors and family offices got into hedged strategies first, relying on in-house expertise and big tick allocations to gain access. The biggest banks and richest family offices quickly learned how to effectively allocate to hedge funds, and pensions and endowments followed. Each year, when rankings come out about the size of Harvard's endowment, for example, you can thank hedge fund investing for much of that.

For other, less well-resourced investors, before 2008 the trend was often to allocate generally to alternatives or hedge funds, subscribing to a few blue chip names or a fund of funds claiming to offer access to best-of-breed managers. For a while, this generic allocation became a trend, a means of diversifying portfolios by somewhat passively adding hedge funds and hoping for the best. During the crisis, many of those investors realized that without fully understanding how their portfolios were constructed, different investments were actually heavily correlated to each other, resulting in greater exposure risk and broad-based losses.

Perhaps surprisingly, after 2008 investors started looking at hedge funds more than they have in the past. A number of factors contributed to this, including a lack of diversification in portfolios, even lower returns from long-only vehicles in a low-growth/low interest-rate environment, and improvements to investor education following large losses. Let's unpack these drivers and look at how investors are evolving on hedge funds and what it might mean for the industry.

The biggest hedge funds, like their mutual fund counterparts, have a quality reputation and good brand recognition. As such, these funds attract assets easily. Think of it like the crowded restaurant rule, if one restaurant is packed to the gills, and the one next door sits empty, more often than not, people wait for a table at the crowded one. However, it is precisely because of this trend that those blue chip funds lose a bit of their edge over time. As we will learn in the emerging managers chapter, as funds grow they lose the ability to be reactive or take advantage of small wins. A stampede of elephants is still slower than a pride of lions.

Bigger funds tend to group into the same positions, like going long Apple or GE. These trades are safe, and their capacity allows big funds to deploy big blocks of investor capital. This is also true for many of the largest mutual funds, because they need a surer bet. So, if an investor blindly allocates to both types of funds and thinks they are diversified, in reality they only doubled their exposure to the "surer" bets. In that instance, during a correction investors will still see less of a loss from the hedge fund allocation because it will also have a different loss-mitigating short position. Enough to account for double exposure? That's unlikely.

At an oversimplified level, this is what happened to a number of investors in 2008. When correlations went to one (meaning everything tanked together), not only did diversification have limited mitigating effects, any redundant exposures were magnified. Since then, there has been a growing trend among accredited investors to take a step back, become better educated, and bring in professionals to help them ensure that their portfolios are actually diversified and durable. Hedge funds have benefitted precisely because of the diversification and durability they offer to qualified investors.

Since 2008, markets have started to recover, but very gradually. Savers are being punished with low interest rates and investors are being punished with equally low yields on equities. In this environment, hedge funds can provide enhanced returns because they take uncorrelated long and short positions. If you are a public pension and you have to make an 8 percent return each year to meet obligations, hedge funds will look intriguing right now, as an 8 percent return seems like a dream from a bygone era. Hitting that benchmark moves back into the realm of the possible with a mix of alternative investments that could include hedge funds, private equity, and real estate.

With this renewed interest the hedge fund space itself is changing. The largest hedge funds are starting to resemble more traditional asset managers; some are even offering hedged mutual funds to retail investors. New regulations aimed at driving perceived risk out of the marketplace are also forcing some changes in how these funds operate, making them slightly more vanilla versions of their former selves. While the go-go days of hedge funds may be behind us, they can still provide better returns and more diversification than traditional portfolio structures. Next, we will break out the major strategies and how they work in a portfolio.

## MAJOR FUND STRATEGIES

Hedge funds can take on a variety of trading strategies and styles, with each manager offering his own variation on some archetypal trading themes. We offer an explanation of the biggest buckets, along with specific fund examples. It would be impossible to cover all the types of funds as new variations enter the market each day, but the following provides a solid framework that can be used to inform the diligence process around a given fund.

### Equity Long/Short

Equity Long/Short funds are probably the most populous group of hedge funds. As the name suggests, these funds typically trade listed equities, taking both long and short positions. Managers will take variations on this by focusing on a particular market cap, sector, industry, whether the equity offers a dividend, or by analyzing individual securities against a set of balance sheet fundamentals.

In a pitch book, you might see phrases like *value investing* or *fundamentals-based stock picker*. These phrases are indications of how a manager picks securities. Value investors typically want securities that are sound companies at a cheap price. Warren Buffett is an example of a value investor. He made his biggest plays on being able to find those diamonds in the rough. Managers that pick stocks based on the fundamentals are going to look at factors like health of a corporate balance sheet, growth opportunities, debt-to-equity ratios, and price/earnings ratios, and then drill down to a list of companies that meet their criteria. Fundamental shops typically add an overlay like politics or other macroeconomic indicators to their secret sauce.

One example of an Equity Long/Short fund is Varus Fund,[1] from Varus Capital Management. The Varus Fund is a long/short equity fund focusing on German mid and large caps and their European competitors. In their description, the firm describes the funds as investing in pair trades and catalyst-driven longs and shorts. Investments are based on quantitative and qualitative analysis and strong competence in German stocks. With a focus on strict risk/reward thinking, trading discipline, and tight risk management, Varus Fund aims for absolute returns with low correlation and volatility.

If we unpack what that all means, basically, in addition to looking at German companies, portfolio managers are also looking for market catalysts that might cause one or both companies in a paired trade to break a certain way. To find these catalysts, the firm not only runs the numbers but also considers qualitative factors. These factors are proprietary, but they could include measures like brand equity, management team, or other overlays that aren't based strictly on the numbers.

One of the first principals of long/short equity trading is trading discipline. Essentially, this means holding true to your analysis and stock picking even as markets change from day to day. Self-directed traders, retail investors, and even some institutions can get caught up in reactionary trading behaviors, especially in markets that have been as sideways as those since 2008. Long/short absolute return strategies are meant to perform over the long haul, with rebalancing done based on pre-determined signals or on a discretionary basis as market conditions warrant.

Typically, firms that are better at discipline will trust their models and methodology in an effort to avoid behaviorally based trading changes. A good manager will employ back testing, along with other modeling methods, when building their strategy. From there, managers often start trading the strategy with their own money to build an initial track record to show investors along with their foundational research. This approach not only allows for strategy testing, but also adds a bit to investor confidence—investors like to see that a manager has some skin in the game.

The focus on risk in Varus' description is also an important change to note since 2008. In the go-go days of the 1990s and mid-2000s, funds were putting up enough in returns that few investors focused on risk. However, in the wake of the financial crisis of 2008, that viewpoint has changed considerably. Now, both investors and regulators are focused on the amount of risk taken by a manager (including leverage) and the potential losses in the event of another downturn. Taken to the extreme, focusing too heavily on the risk portion of a risk/reward profile can mean missing out on a skilled manager and unique opportunities. But, for institutions, pensions, endowments, or even just conservative investors, that may be a tradeoff they prefer. Indeed, some pension funds are limited in the amount of risk they can even consider when looking at a given fund. Given this shift, funds will often point out in much more detail than they would have before what the risks are and how they view risk.

Ultimately, when evaluating a long/short strategy, investors will have to look at both sides of this profile to determine what's right for them. The ability of a manager to go both long and short can be a risk-mitigating factor by definition, as the investor is not exposed to the long-only side of a trade.

## Macro

Funds will often classify themselves as macro or global macro. Within this bucket, funds are largely driven by macroeconomic conditions. Common strategy variations include event-driven or special situations. Both of these variations look to capture market dislocations that are the result of specific macroeconomic events.

Macro funds will typically hold both long and short positions in a variety of asset classes including equities, fixed income, currencies, and so on. Unlike the long/short funds explained above, the macro strategy isn't asset-class specific—that is, equities—instead, managers will look at various economic and political risk overlays to determine where they make investments on either side. For example, if a manager looks at Australia they may take a long position on Australian currency or in Australian equities given the overall strength of that economy and relatively low political risk. Whereas if a macro manager was looking at Turkey, they may take a look at that country's thriving private sector against its growing political uncertainty and take on more hedged positions there, going both long and short.

Third Wave[2] is a macro fund that relies on both qualitative and quantitative factors to identify opportunities. The fund looks at model-driven trades from a macroeconomic vantage point. Within that view, Third Wave uses systematic modeling to look at discretionary opportunities. The fund differentiates itself by being at the nexus of macro approaches; most macro funds are either purely discretionary or are systematic commodity trading advisors (CTAs)[3] that rely on trend following. Instead, Third Wave opts to take a little from column A and a little from column B. Along with their systematic models, they add a variety of economic and qualitative overlays to find opportunities.

Unlike other systematic shops that may rely entirely on their computer-based models, Third Wave also allows for human intervention by the manager, and this is really what makes macro strategies stand out as a separate group. Macro managers take the view that not all relationships and not all economic activity can be modeled effectively. To this end, macro managers may adjust a trade away from what a model says to do based on a change in information or economic conditions. In some cases it could also be based on the direct involvement of a fund in a specific economic activity (like bond buying) itself.

Larry Smith, Chief Investment Officer and Co-Founder of Third Wave, gives an example of how this works in practice—"Take the Australian dollar, our model loves the Australian dollar. The currency has rallied dramatically over the past six months, but the fundamentals all suggest it will go higher. There is a good reason to expect this. Chinese economic policy has been extraordinarily successful in stimulating growth and Australia is a beneficiary of that. China's focus on commodities means that they will invest heavily in Australia. So we see no reason not to follow the model with respect to this trade. At the same time, our model is not particularly sanguine on the Canadian dollar, yet our discretionary process leads us to believe that it, too, will improve relative to the U.S. dollar."

At the same time Third Wave is examining currency-based opportunities like the one just illustrated, they are also looking at residential mortgages in the United States and other credit opportunities. The options for where a macro fund goes are really only limited to the talents of that manager.

## Event Driven

Similar to macro funds are event-driven funds. Event-driven funds look for pricing inefficiencies that may occur before or after a corporate event. So, where macro funds are looking at exogenous economic or political-risk events, event-driven funds are more interested in the possibility of internal corporate activities—bankruptcies, mergers, acquisitions, or spin-outs.

Whenever a public corporation faces any of these types of events, they're going to see the market's view reflected in the stock price. Most likely it will affect the stock price of at least two companies (think of mergers and acquisitions) and depending on the players involved in the news, an event can impact the entire sector of industry. (Consider what would happen to tech stocks if Google declared bankruptcy, for example.) Event-driven managers are going to come in during these situations and start making trades based on what they think the likely outcome will be. In some cases, event-driven managers, if they invest throughout the capital stack, may also get involved in the activity directly.

In practice, you could see event-driven funds buy the stock of a company that is about to be acquired by a bigger and more competitive company. If a manager is reasonably sure that the acquisition will go forward, he stands to gain from buying that stock. Similarly, if he thinks a transaction might fail, the manager could begin shorting the companies involved.

ArbitrOption is one such firm, and in the first quarter of 2013 the fund posted a 38.97 percent return. At the time, the firm had positions in five companies—Acme Packet (APKT), Focus Media (FMCN), Penn National Gaming (PENN), Heinz (HNZ), and Robbins & Myers (RBN). Each of these companies was involved in some type of corporate event. According to Heath Winter, ArbitrOption's managing partner and portfolio manager, the fund "profited by taking on call and put options positions that were designed to provide a better return for every dollar risked than what was available through trading the common stock in these names."[4]

ArbitrOption specializes in merger-and-acquisition transactions, restructuring opportunities, corporate spin-offs and split-ups, shareholder agitation, and proxy contests. Other event-driven strategies include activist investing, credit arbitrage, distressed restructuring, merger arbitrage, and special situations.

## Activist Funds

Activist hedge fund managers are some of the most well-known hedge managers to both the general and investing publics, precisely because of their activist stances. Activist hedge fund managers like Daniel Loeb, Carl Icahn, and David Einhorn are regulars on business news channels like CNBC, but also make their way into general interest news through some of their activist activities. Perhaps two of the biggest examples in recent memory involved the public companies Yahoo! and Herbalife.

In the case of Yahoo!, activist hedge fund manager Daniel Loeb and his firm Third Point took an activist stake in the company and quickly started demanding changes to the board and upper management. During this process he wrote a now infamous letter[5] in which he revealed that both a member of Yahoo's board and the acting CEO at that time changed the degrees on their resumes.

At the time Loeb took his activist stake in the company, it was believed by both members of the board and the general public alike that CEO Scott Thompson had a computer science degree, when in fact he had a degree in accounting. The letter also cast doubt on board member Patti Hart, who was tasked with vetting CEO candidates, when it came out that she had also changed her degree from business administration to economics and marketing. While on the surface these changes may seem merely opportunistic and a little dishonest, these notes were also included in the public filings for Yahoo!, which raised compliance questions about the overall integrity of their disclosures to investors and the public.

This is the stuff activist investors thrive on if they want to see changes. Activist investors come in as champions of either themselves or a faction of shareholders who feel as though the company in question isn't providing maximum value for shareholders, which is a public company's fiduciary duty. Once the blood is in the water, activists will go looking for evidence or will challenge the board during shareholder votes to change practices. In the case of Yahoo's resume-gate, Thompson ended up resigning, paving the way for Marissa Meyer, current Yahoo! CEO. The board also reshuffled, highlighting what activists can do to the internal operations of a company.

### Herbalife

In some cases, rather than acting alone like Daniel Loeb did with Yahoo!, activists can team up or move against each other. This happened with another public company—Herbalife. For decades, Herbalife was one of those companies largely known only to housewives and consumers of health food products. The company makes vitamin supplements and protein and vitamin shakes that are sold by individual sales representatives, similar to Avon or Mary Kay. Individuals who start selling Herbalife are encouraged to invite friends and expand the business by bringing on their peers.

In 2012, activist investor Bill Ackman launched an outright activist attack on the company saying it was a publically traded pyramid scheme,[6] with shoddy accounting and subpar product to boot. Herbalife's stock price plummeted, and the company itself was working to do damage control. Unlike with resumegate, Ackman wasn't alone in the Herbalife affair; instead he got into a standoff with not one, but two other high-profile activist investors—Daniel Loeb and Carl Icahn. Both men took the opposing view of Herbalife, saying that it wasn't, in fact, a pyramid scheme and that the company's finances were sound.

Over several months this fight escalated to include PowerPoint presentations, conference calls, and a pretty heated verbal slap fight on live television.[7] As of this writing, Herbalife is still a little bit up in the air, regulators have started to take closer scrutiny of the company's practices although no official findings have been released, and none of the activists involved appear to be backing down.[8]

Some of this inevitably involves personal battles between all three men that existed well before the Herbalife trade—Ackman and Loeb had a very public falling out some years earlier.[9] Interestingly, Loeb and Icahn also found support from some smaller and lower-profile funds, based in part on a general dislike for Ackman from some corners of the industry. The players on the board were ready to set up a short squeeze on Ackman's position in the company, forcing him to take considerable losses.

Then, in October 2013, Ackman announced[10] that he'd reduced his nearly $1 billion short on the company in an effort to stem paper losses on the bet, which by that point reached into the hundreds of millions of dollars. He replaced some of that position with derivatives, but Ackman said he maintained a high conviction position on the trade. Activist investors aren't always right and sometimes whether right or wrong, they can get squeezed. Ultimately, investors that get into this strategy have to be prepared for a slightly bumpy ride.

### Value Investing

Value investing often gets a bad rap. It's not considered all that edgy, and by definition value investors are kind of cheap. They want the biggest bargain for the lowest overhead, and they'd like to do this without a lot of fancy instruments or financial magic. Even so, some of the biggest names in finance (think Warren Buffett) are successful value investors. (Even though Warren Buffett extolls the evils of hedge funds now, he ran one himself—very successfully—for a number of years.)

One of Warren Buffett's recently successful investments was a bailout of Goldman Sachs in 2008. Buffet got almost a $2 billion stake in Goldman

Sachs,[11] one of the most profitable financial firms in history. Buffett has bailed out big investment banks before, notably Salomon Brothers. That deal, covered in detail by Michael Lewis in a piece for *The New Republic*,[12] broke out like this, "For $700 million and a job guarantee for Gutfreund, Buffett was given a security that combined the juicy bits of a stock and a bond. It guaranteed him a return of 9 percent a year, established him as the controlling shareholder of Salomon Brothers, and left him with about the same opportunity for huge gain as the ordinary shareholder—without the risks. Auctioned on the open market, the $700 million convertible preferred would have fetched anywhere from $850 million to $1.2 billion. His windfall came out of the shareholders' pockets, since his cheap option dilutes the value of the existing shares." This is the type of deal value investors live for.

In one sense, value investors can be considered the meat-and-potatoes guys of investing. When it comes to stock picking they are heavily fundamentals oriented. Value investors are going to get under the hood of a potential investment in order to determine its real growth potential along with other possible upsides like dividends.

## IS VALUE INVESTING A GOOD STRATEGY?

### *Benedicte Gravrand*

To some, value investing makes complete sense, to others it is no longer a suitable strategy as the economic environment can no longer be ignored.

Alexander Ineichen, well-known hedge fund analyst, author, and founder of Ineichen Research and Management AG, describes value investing as, "Value investing is defined as investing in 'value stocks'. Value stocks are usually regarded as stocks that have been neglected by the market, have underperformed and therefore trade at low price/book ratios, low price/earnings multiples, and have a high dividend yield. Growth stocks, on the other hand, are stocks for which earnings are expected to grow faster than average in the future."

Joe Taussig, an American-born Swiss-based veteran investor, believes that, among those strategies that can lift alpha, value investing is less prone to major blowups as it limits the downside risk. "The true value investors have ridden downside risk over the long haul," he says. Value investors have less fat tails than many other strategies. Furthermore, most of the value investors he knows do not use leverage—unlike Buffett.

Taussig is a believer in value investing. "I would rather have the average value guys than the average global macro or credit guys," he says, noting 2009 was a huge year for value investors. After stocks crashed in 2008, a lot of them, especially those who were courageous and had the loyalty of their investors, bought the once-in-a-lifetime values they could get when everybody else was hitting the ATM machines.

Larry Chen, a fast-talking private investor based in London who used to work for UBS, calls himself a "keen student of value investing . . . for many years" and says the strategy makes intuitive sense as well as common sense. Value investing is gaining recognition and one of the signs that this is happening is that the London Business School, his Alma Mater, started teaching value investing about a year ago. Besides Columbia, very few schools teach it, he says.

He explains that in order to build a bridge that can withstand anything, the best way is to build tolerances, to overbuild—instead of trying to predict future events and stresses. "Similarly, in value investing, you emphasize the margin of safety. . . as a cushion." Chen believes that earning forecasts, projections, and target prices are "completely useless." Value investors do not know what's going to happen in the future—although certain companies are more predictable than others, as for example, Coca Cola.

Before buying something, he continues, one must determine the intrinsic value. "You buy the stock only when the price is significantly below the intrinsic value so as to provide you a margin of safety, and that's the whole concept," he says. "You notice that the most successful fund managers, whether it be value investors or others, are very good at looking at one side and not so much the other side. All of them focus on the risk side, protecting the downside. They are all very good at that, and that's the common denominator among all of them that I could see."

He quotes Philip Tetlock, a U.S. university professor who researched the accuracies of financial experts' predictions. "In fact, they are so useless that the more famous the expert, the worst the predictions are." Even though there is a time lag between Buffett's investments and the SEC announcements of those investments, those investors who follow Buffett would still outperform the market over time, even without leverage, he says.

A dollar invested in Berkshire Hathaway, Warren Buffett's Omaha, Nebraska-based conglomerate holding company, at the end of 1976 would have been worth more than $1,500 at the end of

2011—35 years later. Berkshire's annualized return was 19 percent in excess of the T-bill rate, more than the stock market's average excess return of 6 percent, and has a higher Sharpe Ratio than any stock or mutual fund with a history of more than 30 years.

Berkshire's Sharpe Ratio—0.76 from 1976 to 2011—is higher than all U.S. stocks from 1926 to 2011 that have been traded for more than 30 years, and higher than all U.S. mutual funds that have been around for more than 30 years. The Sharpe Ratio is a ratio to measure risk-adjusted performance, so the greater a portfolio's Sharpe Ratio is, the better its risk-adjusted performance has been. The information ratio, the researchers say, is even lower, at 0.66, reflecting high average returns as well as significant risks and drawdown. Buffett boosted his returns partly with leverage.

### The art of selecting low beta stocks

Buffett's stock-picking ability is what drives his attractive return stream, which can then be leveraged. According to Andrea Frazzini and David Kabiller of AQR Capital Management, and Lasse H. Pedersen of New York University, there are several factors that define Buffett's approach:

1. Safe picks (low beta, low volatility);
2. Cheapness (value stocks with low price-to-book ratios), and
3. High quality (profitable, stable, growing with high payout ratios).

Beta is a measure that shows the tendency of a security's returns to respond to swings in the market, and a beta of one means the security moves with the market. For example, most high-tech, Nasdaq stocks (which Buffett tends to avoid) have a beta greater than one (they are "high beta"), so they are more volatile and more risky.

Buffett's portfolio of public stocks performed better than his portfolio of private stocks, suggesting that his skill is mostly in stock selection. The report quotes Buffett as saying in his 2008 annual report: "Whether we're talking about socks or stocks, I like buying quality merchandise when it is marked down."

"Focus: Is Value Investing a Good Strategy?" *Opalesque New Managers*, www.opalesque.com/new-managers/140/focus-all-about-value-investing .html.

## Credit

Classically, a fund involved in credit means the fund is involved in fixed income. However, credit has also come to mean collateralized loan obligations (CLOs), mortgages, student debt, mezzanine loans, really anything in the capital stack. Since the crisis, credit strategies, especially structured credit, and specialty finance have gained a lot of traction with investors as new regulation created a liquidity crisis, driving more businesses into nonbank lending and specialty finance to find the liquidity they need.

Since 2008, credit has been one of the more interesting areas to watch when it comes to both funds and investor behavior. In recent years, credit has seen a significant rally across all types of products, surprisingly even mortgages, which were at the heart of the crisis. That's due in part to government guarantee of these investments as well as significant clean up in the wake of the collapse. Now, for instance, mortgages represent some of the least risky investments.

Table 1.1 below details the overall returns of credit strategies for FY2012 and 2013 through October.

**TABLE 1.1** Overall Returns of Credit Strategies for FY2012–2013 through October

| Universe | YTD Return (%) | LTM Return (%) | FY2012 Return (%) |
|---|---|---|---|
| **Securitized Credit** | **6.93** | **15.01** | **20.96** |
| ABS Focus | 8.62 | 21.24 | 26.99 |
| MBS Focus | 3.91 | 9.96 | 18.02 |
| CDO Focus | 7.19 | 15.08 | 22.29 |
| Multi-Type | 9.03 | 18.20 | 22.65 |
| RMBS Focus | 3.93 | 9.42 | 17.49 |
| Agency Focus | –2.22 | –0.70 | 8.63 |
| Non-Agency Focus | 8.48 | 17.86 | 24.07 |
| Agency and Non-Agency | 4.34 | 11.17 | 19.78 |
| **Insurance-Linked Strategies** | **3.96** | **6.17** | **5.23** |
| U.S. Focus | 4.54 | 10.77 | 18.52 |
| Europe Focus | 12.27 | 27.33 | 27.81 |
| Global | 9.97 | 20.04 | 24.09 |

*Source:* eVestment.

Elsewhere across the credit landscape new bubbles are forming that are attracting investors. Student loans are another big bubble looming on the horizon. Some funds have a short trade on these loans, which are securitized in ways similar to mortgages to make them investable.

In some ways the student loan bubble is more insidious than mortgages. Homeowners who took advantage of easy money likely knew deep down they didn't need a $2 million mortgage, and/or mistakenly believed lenders who were incentivized to give them more mortgage than they could reasonably afford. Student loans on the other hand prey on a set of factors unique to post-crisis students who face an impossible choice—trying to get along in historically high unemployment either without an overpriced degree or with both an overpriced undergraduate degree and a post-graduate degree; neither option is likely to end in a job.

Many recent graduates went back to school after 2008, as the recent graduate cohort of the economy reported the highest levels of unemployment in recent history. That trend contributed to a steep rise in student debt, and for those that still couldn't find employment after graduate school, it also added to the percentage of loans in default. This bubble is only expected to grow as the cost of tuition keeps rising, leading some credit funds to bet on its eventual burst.[13]

New York-based credit fund 400 Capital is one of these funds. "The growth in the student loan sector has been growing since the crisis. Without any new subprime mortgage origination, there is now more student loan debt outstanding than subprime mortgage," says Chris Hentemann, managing partner at 400 Capital.[14]

"The current employment environment is not absorbing the new graduates and we are seeing that borrowers are not finding the jobs needed to repay the debt. You can see a correction occurring as delinquencies and defaults rise," Hentemann said.

Sallie Mae, one of the largest providers of student loans in the United States, also provides securitization of those loans in the asset backed securities (ABS) market, similar to how mortgage backed securities (MBS) are offered. Hentemann notes that some of these loans, just like mortgages, are better than others. "We are focused primarily on the loans that are between 97 to100 percent guaranteed by the U.S. government," he said, meaning that they will be paid up to at least the point of guarantee.

While it is not possible to get outright short student loan debt, there are ways to be opportunistically positioned. "This is a market that is experiencing some distress and one where there are likely to be some changes in the landscape going forward. As a result we are trying to position ourselves to take advantage of this distress by being long the parts of the market where prices are overly pessimistic while being short through CDS [credit default swaps], equities, or other instruments, or simply avoiding securities which will be negatively impacted by changes in the landscape," Hentemann explains.

On the more traditional credit side, LNG Capital's managing partner and chief investment officer Louis Gargour is a hedge fund industry veteran in the credit and fixed income space, having merged his Taurus Investment Management with RAB Capital in 2001 and built that fixed income business to more than $1 billion from scratch. He provides a lesson into what credit investing has looked like historically.

The fund is European focused, looking for a broad spectrum of potential opportunities in high yield, investment-grade, event-driven, relative value, and special situations in Europe. His investment style relies on established on-the-ground relationships in Western Europe and the Commonwealth of Independent States (CIS). The goal of the fund is to preserve capital and post absolute returns through long and short overall risk exposures. This approach has a lower correlation to fixed income and equity risk indices compared to others in their peer group.

"We experienced the ups and downs of market cycles and pressures of growing a business," Gargour says. His team at $52m LNG Capital has worked together for 11 years, through a number of hedge fund environments. "The business risks are mitigated by the fact that we have a dedicated institutional backer, combined with our asset class experience," Gargour says.[15]

Within those more traditional credit plays, LNG is able to maintain a fairly liquid portfolio, which makes them a standout among credit funds. Before the crisis, many investors were caught up in portfolios and investment vehicles full of illiquid investments, which made them hard to unwind and thus stem losses. Gargour explains that the fund is able to maintain this liquidity through techniques including position sizing, minimizing the number of market makers, and instruments like credit default swaps. Diversification across strategies, sectors, and counterparties plays its part, and the risk limits and entry and exit points are pre-defined. The firm also uses robust real-time risk management—position limits, leverage limits, and strategy maximums.

For seasoned credit funds and investors, these are the tools of the trade. A number of them including credit default swaps (CDS) saw higher profiles in the crisis, when they moved from being primarily hedge fund tools to being used in bulk by the biggest banks. Since then, savvy investors have brought on investment advisors to help them better understand these instruments and what they can do for the credit portions of their portfolios.

### Liquid Alternatives

Liquid alternatives are new entrants to hedged investing. Essentially, they are hedge fund-like products made for the retail investor. Let's break out what that means: In order to invest in pure-play hedge funds, investors have to meet certain net worth requirements without including major assets like homes. Basically regulators have decided that given the possible risk of loss, minimum investment requirements, and overall investment understanding needed to be successful investing in hedge funds, a potential investor is going to need a lot of disposable cash on hand. This means that even some wealthy people—by an average person's standards—aren't quite rich enough to invest in hedge funds. If you meet the threshold, you're called an accredited investor. If you don't, you're called a retail investor.

Retail investors have been limited by and large to mutual fund investing, and/or self-directed investing on platforms like E*TRADE. However, in recent years demand has grown for more options in the retail space, including access to hedge strategies. Retail investment products by their nature, generally, have daily liquidity—meaning you can get into and out of an investment in the same day, or the next day if you want to.

The Investment Company Act of 1940 established the mutual fund structure. The terms of the 1940 Act lay out fairly specific requirements for a mutual fund, making them low-leverage, usually long-only, low-volatility, low-return products. Retail investors can then take solace in their ability to get out of a mutual fund at a moment's notice, and gain an understanding about how their money is being managed through the prospectus.

In recent years, alternative investment managers have found ways to implement hedged strategies inside the mutual fund structure, giving retail investors access to strategies and investment opportunities they may not have seen otherwise. The trend toward listed alternatives really started to gain traction in 2010, although until recently many market observers and some managers considered the idea a fad. Listed alternatives will never post the same returns or capture the same alpha as a traditional hedge fund.

However in 2013, Morningstar, which serves as a benchmark for mutual funds, created a category for listed alternatives, lending a newfound credibility to the space. Fad or not, investors are piling money into listed alternatives, and finding a new market segment that is flooded with product.

Listed alternatives have had a rapid evolution. Early movers in this space were faced with a significant cost to bring new product to market, along with questions over strategy. Not every hedge fund strategy fits well inside a mutual fund product. Indeed, really only equity long/short and managed futures have taken off so far. Much of this is due to the leverage and position concentration requirements governing the mutual fund structure. Some listed alternatives aren't a strategy at all per se, instead they seek to be hedge fund *replicators*, tracking hedge fund indices like the HFRX or MSCI similar to other retail index funds.

Now, as more product comes to market, costs are coming down and investors are starting to understand the nuances of these funds and the tradeoffs that they may be willing to make for that. One of the biggest reasons investors consider liquid alternatives is lower fees. Managers running a mutual fund won't get the standard 2/20 fee structure in a mutual fund that we see in hedge funds. Instead, mutual fund investors pay commissions rather than fees for performance.

Given that, it may be hard to understand why hedge fund managers are rushing to launch mutual fund products, but there are also notable advantages for them as well. Once a manager clears the initial cost of structuring a product, asset raising for a retail product can be easier than for a traditional hedge fund. The pool of potential investors is larger, and distribution channels through large platforms like Charles Schwab or even through Registered Investment Advisors (RIAs) are greater than they would be with a private placement. For the largest blue chip hedge funds, they can easily add another business line without worrying too much about the dip in performance or a loss of assets from the more expensive hedge fund product as investors migrate to the retail offering.

In some cases, the first movers in this space are now large enough to rival blue chip hedge funds in their strategy. One of the biggest names in this space is Altegris, which offers liquid alternatives for long/short equity, global macro, and managed futures. Altegris aims to provide lower volatility and uncorrelated returns by crafting products through a research-driven approach that pulls together a mix of top-tier managers in order to drive consistent returns even in choppy markets. The firm first launched its managed futures mutual fund in 2010, and that fund is already above $1 billion in assets. In all, the billion dollar firm could rival any of the billion dollar hedge funds in terms of business lines and other industry work, like their Altegris 40 Index and manager/investor education offerings.

CEO Jon Sundt affirms his firm's approach,[16] "to do it right you have to have a well-resourced company. For example, we have nine people in research. We are looking at thousands of alternatives, to do operational due diligence, investment due diligence, compliance, you need that many people and a well-resourced compliance department." Sundt and his team base their managerial choices on a vetting process that looks at trades on a daily basis as well as in aggregate to understand the full extent of a given manager's operation.

"If you really want to look under the covers it costs money and takes talent. The best hedge funds out there are going to be selective about how they pick a 40-act fund, and they should be. Just to break escrow on a fund is $50m you have to have the ability to raise that."

Some of that talent is also tracked in the Altegris 40 Index.[17] The Altegris 40 Index tracks the asset-weighted monthly performance of the

40 largest managed futures managers who report to the Altegris database. Trend-following strategies make up the bulk of that index, which not only serves as an internal performance benchmark but has also come to be a performance benchmark for managed futures outside of Altegris as well. Taken together, Altegris' activities make the firm look more like the big asset managers than just a mutual fund shop.

Emerging mangers can also find opportunity in liquid alternatives. Longboard Asset Management operates a managed futures mutual fund that grew out of the traditional hedge fund experience of its management team. Firm principals Cole Wilcox and Eric Crittenden built their careers operating a family office for legendary currency trader Tom Basso. They took their experience as allocators into the creation of their own firm and mutual fund. According to Eric Crittenden, Longboard's director of research, launching a mutual fund made the most sense because of the growing demand for product.[18]

"We saw an opportunity to enter the mutual fund space with a product—there is a high demand and limited supply," he says. "History has shown that in hostile market environments, corporate bonds, equities, and real estate can suffer tremendous losses at the same time; while managed futures can provide effective diversification when it is needed most."

Longboard launched its managed futures mutual fund in July of 2012, and Crittenden notes some of the challenges faced by hedge fund managers who try to place their strategy in the mutual fund structure—"futures contracts, forward contracts, and OTC [over the counter] derivatives were not part of the original definition of 'investment securities' and require extra efforts to satisfy regulators when they are used extensively in a '40 Act structure."

"We have to meet compliance requirements for both the Commodity Futures Trading Commission (CFTC) and the Securities and Exchange Commission (SEC), so it is double the compliance workload. On top of that, some of the things the CFTC or NFA [National Futures Association] require you to do, the SEC won't let you do. So we had to work through that," he added.

Additional requirements such as the diversification requirements for mutual funds had to be dealt with as well. Yet, Crittenden says that overall, the process was worth it. The managed futures asset class has grown 60 percent since 2008, driven primarily by institutional investors. However, retail investors and their advisors have had a difficult time accessing managed futures, as few retail products were available. For its fund, Longboard focuses on a long-term trend-following approach, using a strategy Crittenden and Wilcox have traded with for a number of years.[19]

As more of these types of products come to market, retail investors are realizing that managed futures can bring a new level of diversification to portfolios, which has prompted inflows into these funds over recent years even as the strategy saw a dip in performance during the gradual equities rally in 2012 and 2013. Managed futures seek to have a low correlation to equity markets, and can provide positive performance when those markets go down. For a retail portfolio, including a managed futures-type mutual fund can bring a diversification component that is missing from traditional portfolio construction.

Single-manager funds like Longboard typically work with RIAs as well as bigger mutual fund platforms to distribute their product and raise assets. They may also be invited to come into trusts as a sub-advisory manager.

## Trusts

Another variation for liquid alternatives comes in the form of the trust. A multi-series trust allows for the creation of what is essentially a fund of mutual funds. The trust brings together a number of managers as sub-advisors to the fund, all housed under a single fund name. Through the trust, the firms that run these funds of funds can realize cost savings and administrative efficiencies by having multiple managers under the umbrella of a single fund.

Endurance Series Trust is an example of one of these types of products. Endurance Series Trust is a multi-series trust that focuses on bringing emerging managers into a mutual fund structure. "Trusts are usually sponsored by financial institutions, or big administrators like a State Street or a Northern Trust, but after examining those models we thought they weren't as advantageous as they could be for managers new to the space," explains Endurance Series Trust President and CEO, Andres Sandate.[20]

"We thought there was a great opportunity to disintermediate the existing business model with a turnkey option," Sandate says. "We want groups that are capable of running a mutual fund and be successful at it, not just people who can pay the fees involved in launching a mutual fund and that's a critical distinction. There is a certain pedigree of manager out there that may already be running a good mutual fund-like strategy in a separately managed account, or for one client, and we are interested in those people."

The first fund launched on April 24, 2013, just a few weeks after the firm's registration was approved by the SEC on April 8. Sandate says that he is looking at all types of strategies, "We are looking for people with an established track record. A lot of our peers say you can't run a successful mutual fund with less than $50–$100 million, we don't believe that, there are guys out there that could be successful who only have $25 million."

Unlike large platforms, Endurance Series Trust plans to keep the number of managers low and offer a high-touch relationship that includes administrative services. Endurance Fund Services, LLC, an independently owned and operated fund administration company serves as the fund administrator for mutual funds in the trust. Investment advisers who form and manage their mutual funds via Endurance Series Trust are also provided with compliance professionals and access to distribution services, including introductions to broker/dealers, registered investment advisors (RIAs), fund supermarkets, intermediary platforms, and wholesaling specialists. By way of comparison, the Endurance Series Trust is providing everything that Longboard has had to source on its own. This is similar to what managers chosen by Altegris would get by becoming part of that platform.

Endurance Series Trust and Altegris, as first movers in this space, fill the same role that funds of funds historically played for traditional hedge funds. Early on in the history of hedge funds, many of the biggest allocators to individual managers were funds of funds, picking managers to bring into the pool. Liquid alternatives are evolving in similar ways, although individual managers can still bring a product to market and find assets with an arguably easier path than their emerging hedge fund-manager counterparts.

For investors, the process of choosing a single manager fund or a multimanager fund in the retail space really boils down to individual preference. With retail products, funds are required to offer more information in public disclosures, and investment advisors will help to build portfolios based on distribution relationships forged by managers. In that sense, these products really change the game more for managers, who have to decide who and how they want to sell. Selling a mutual fund is a very different business and different audience than selling a hedge fund. Transparency requirements are greater, and the number of advisors is far greater than the number of hedge fund consultants. For managers who are more comfortable relying on a secret sauce-style pitch, they may find rough sledding trying to raise mutual fund assets. For others who are okay with smaller, but stickier allocations, mutual funds may make more sense.

## UCITS

On the other side of the pond, Europe has its own version of regulated alternatives called Undertakings for Collective Investment in Transferable Securities (UCITS). Historically, UCITS have existed separately from more traditional private placements, and much like mutual funds weren't necessarily using hedges. UCITS are available to both retail and accredited investors. Unlike the United States, which has a separate distinction, money market funds are also covered under the UCITS guidelines. The first UCITS directive came into force in 1985; now, we are on our fourth

UCITS directive, each steadily expanding what is allowed in this structure and further pushing investment funds to comport themselves accordingly. After 2008, the Eurozone kicked this into high gear, making sweeping structural changes to their financial regulations and effectively legislating private placements out of existence.[21]

The role of UCITS in the investment landscape for Europeans and even parts of Asia has grown considerably, and to the surprise of some, given their historically lower performance and higher fees. Much of this has to do with the implementation of the Alternative Investment Fund Managers Directive (AIFMD), a law that came into force for the Eurozone in 2013. This law serves as a reaction to the 2008 crisis and is also a fairly broad restructuring of how investment funds are understood on the continent. Its implementation gives preference to the UCITS structure, and sets up strict rules for how both European and foreign managers who wish to market funds in the European Union (EU) must register and behave.[22]

Hedge fund strategies were first folded into the UCITS structure under the third UCITS directive, which included allowances for financial derivative instruments (FDI). The UCITS structure itself has some of the same appeal as a mutual fund—greater distribution channels, for example, are available to UCITS funds. Retail and institutional investors also tend to prefer their liquidity and increased disclosure requirements.

However, as with mutual funds in the United States, not all hedge fund strategies fit neatly in the UCITS wrapper. Funds that invest in commodities will have some difficulty setting up a UCITS fund, as they are excluded from the list of eligible assets. Current eligible assets for UCITS structures are transferable securities, money market instruments, units of collective investment schemes, bank deposits, and FDIs. UCITS funds can also gain exposure to non-eligible assets in certain ways, notably via FDIs based on financial indices, closed-ended funds, or structured transferable securities. (It is this allowance that hedge fund managers use most often to bring in parts of their strategy that may not readily appear on the list of eligible assets, including commodities through index exposure.)[23]

UCITS funds tend to exhibit a performance drag as well. Marcus Storr, head of Hedge Funds at Feri, explains this, "we conducted an empirical analysis of both the offshore and UCITS hedge fund universes. As a start we weren't taking a UCITS fund strategy at its face value based on the manager's description, we in fact looked at each single UCITS fund and defined the strategy according to what we think it is. We at Feri have hedge fund analysts for each sub-strategy, so conducting an empirical analysis strategy by strategy, we have found only one strategy where we think a UCITS wrapper makes sense. This strategy is equity long/short. All the other sub-strategies on average have an annual consistent negative tracking error of sometimes several hundred basis points between the UCITS hedge fund and the offshore version. What drives the tracking error isn't the 'official' management fee but the fact that within UCITS, you will have to use swaps, which means that you will be 'charged' a bid-ask spread whenever traded. Hence the UCITS manager could end up with a lot of additional implied costs. Most of these UCITS funds also hold 15 percent, 20 percent, or sometimes 25 percent cash, as they want to be prepared for potential redemptions due to a daily tradability of the fund. That is certainly another drag on the fund return."[24]

Investors however, may be willing to make this tradeoff because the operational risk is much lower. Again according to Storr, "the regulator looks at all UCITS funds and hence uncontrolled activity is rather limited, if not impossible. Compared to offshore funds, some qualitative elements are just as risky, like team stability and service providers, etc. However, there are a lot of hedge fund strategies in UCITS, which shouldn't be in UCITS funds. Looking at equity long/short funds and CTAs or any security, which is very liquid, makes sense for UCITS. In fact we are investing in several UCITS funds applying these strategies. So our study, which took a couple of months, showed that UCITS funds in general have a negative tracking error versus offshore hedge funds in addition to a higher risk profile measured using annualized volatility."[25]

It should be noted that the European Commission has undertaken a steady review of allowable assets and strategies within the UCITS structure, and has already raised questions about how hedge fund managers make their strategies fit within this framework. Despite those questions, prevailing regulation inside the EU expresses a clear preference for the structure (many elements of the AIFMD trace their roots to the UCITS regime). It is expected then, that UCITS will continue to evolve over the near term as these issues are worked through in the Commission. In our chapter on investing mechanics, we will break out more of these changes in detail in terms of how they[26] affect the due-diligence process when evaluating UCITS and non-UCITS funds in Europe.

Like mutual funds in the United States, the core theme of the UCITS structure is investor protection. This is the rationale behind limiting which investable assets are allowed, as well as guidelines governing position concentration, risk, and leverage. So far, with that focus and even with a performance drag, investor assets are flowing into alternative UCITS. According to the Alceda Quarterly UCITS Review for the second quarter of 2013, assets under management for alternative UCITS strategies were hovering around €104.6 billion, putting them on par with liquid alternatives in the United States.[27]

UCITS are also offered in much the same way as their other retail counterparts. Both large platforms and single funds are offered through investment management firms and distributed through their relationships.

The Dublin-regulated MontLake UCITS Platform launched by ML Capital is one example of a UCITS platform. "The trend that seemed constant was a demand for much higher regulation and a demand for fiduciary responsibility over assets after the number of scandals that the industry had seen during the financial crisis. So, we looked at different options; a managed accounts platform, QIFs [Qualified Investment Funds], UCITS. The latter became the natural choice for us for a number of reasons. First of all, ML Capital and the MontLake platform were set up to bring hedge funds to the mainstream and open up hedge fund strategies to a wider audience. UCITS was a perfect structure for us in the sense that we could talk to retail investors all the way up to the big institutional investors in Europe and also Latin American and Asia," explains Cyril Delamare, managing partner of ML Capital.[28]

Managers on the platform run their portfolios on a day-to-day basis, but ML Capital is the investment manager and promoter of the MontLake platform, which gives them a number of fiduciary duties. In addition to distribution and marketing, ML Capital also takes care of all the regulatory filings, all of the oversight, and the compliance from a UCITS perspective for the fund managers.

Instead of working with emerging managers, ML works with more established managers who already have enough assets to run their businesses and have a proven strategy that can fit inside the UCITS wrapper. Before launching a fund, ML requires that managers have between $25 and $50 million in assets under management.

"When we launch a manager we do extensive due diligence on them. Once they are on the platform, we also conduct ongoing due diligence which is anywhere from the daily risk management that we apply all the way to, on a quarterly basis, making sure that the operational structure has not changed and that there are no risks to the business," Delamare says.

For a single manager launching a UCITS fund, he or she will typically build out their own infrastructure similar to what ML offers. Bernheim, Dreyfus & Co., an asset manager based in Paris, France, runs a global macro UCITS IV-compliant fund called Carmel Global Opportunities. The fund invests in multiple asset classes across the Organization for Economic Cooperation and Development (OECD) universe, and aims to deliver steady long-term capital appreciation through diversification of investment style, alpha source, and time horizon.

Carmel Global Opportunities' assets under management at launch were approximately $60 million, backed by a seed investment from some of Bernheim, Dreyfus & Co.'s long-term investors. The fund will focus on investments in credit instruments and equity instruments within Europe and North America. The fund's tactical trading strategy will consist of capturing all available opportunities depending on market conditions. Investments will be long only.[29]

Running a global macro strategy within the UCITS structure means managers will have to deal with some limitations. Unlike traditional credit and equity funds, managers of the UCITS fund will be limited when it comes to leverage and position concentration. If a trade has big upside potential, traditional hedge funds could amass a position that amounts to 20 percent or more of their total portfolio. UCITS (like mutual funds) limit position concentration, so this kind of result is impossible.

Managers for the fund will benefit from big-ticket investor seed funds, but will have to focus heavily on distribution to keep assets rolling in. Unlike funds on the ML platform, that means managers will need to build strong relationships with distributors and investment advisors on the continent.

## AIFs

In addition to UCITS, Europe also has traditional private-placement funds officially called Alternative Investment Funds (AIFs). Allowances for these funds have been altered slightly as the AIFMD and other regulations have come into force. The goal of the new regulation and AIF definition is to capture any non-UCITS fund.

As a practical matter, the range of strategies used in Europe is the same as those anywhere else. The only real differences are regulatory, in terms of who qualifies to market and manage funds, how they have to be registered, and subsequent reporting requirements. Managers that are headquartered outside of the EU and wish to market to Europeans are also heavily impacted by these changes.

An AIF is defined as a collective investment undertaking, which raises capital from a number of investors with a view to investing it in accordance with a defined investment policy for the benefit of those investors. AIFs can be open-ended or closed-ended funds. A number of legal structures are excluded from the definition of allowable AIFs, including holding companies, joint ventures, pension funds, family offices, securitization special purpose entities, and employee-participation or savings schemes.[30]

Managers of these funds (officially noted as Alternative Investment Fund Managers or AIFMs) are licensed to participate in the activities of portfolio and risk management, as well as administration of the fund. Once a manager is examined and registered in one EU member state, he or she has the ability to act as a fund manager in all EU member states.

Emerging managers whose fund size is less than E100 million (including leveraged assets) or less than E500 million unleveraged that also do not have redemption rights for five years can qualify for a slightly scaled-back version of the registration and reporting requirements faced by their larger counterparts. Once these managers beat those thresholds, however, they will be required to meet all AIFMD requirements.

For managers outside the EU that have been marketing their funds, or running part of their funds inside the EU, they too will now have to register in much the same way. However, from 2015 onward, non-EU managers will have to go through this process and designate an EU member state of reference (essentially an EU headquarters) and a local, domestic representative that is also approved to manage and market in the EU. Even then, non-EU funds will still have to be given special consideration by EU financial regulators to be approved.

For non-EU funds, some of the regulatory burden may be lessened or at least fulfilled, if the fund can show it complies with the regulations of its home country and that home country has a tax-sharing agreement with the EU and is approved by the EU as an acceptable home country. In general, a member state of reference is determined by the EU country in which a given fund does most of its business. This could be either where a fund is physically managed or the member state in which most of the marketing is or will take place.

Just to establish a member state of reference, the manager will first have to ask the regulatory authorities of that state for the allowance. Once they get that allowance, they can file with the broader EU regulatory authority ESMA for approval of the registration.

These little details are important, as for example, the United States and European Union have been working since the crisis to harmonize financial and tax regulations. The U.S. version of this allowance comes up relative to the new Foreign Account Tax Compliance Act ( FATCA), which became law in the United States in March 2010. Under that law, the United States is seeking to establish tax information-sharing agreements with all other countries in an effort to track U.S. persons' taxable income. Funds can fall under these requirements if they are operated by U.S. persons.[31, 32, 33]

In Chapter 5 we will return to the AIFMD in terms of how these new requirements affect due diligence processes for investors. For now, this breakdown of what qualifies as UCITS or non-UCITS funds is most important, as the strategies themselves (explained earlier) vary from country to country.

## SUMMARY

For investors who want to reap the rewards of either retail or accredited investing, it is important to understand how individual strategies work. Learning how managers approach capital markets can help with portfolio construction and ensure true diversification. For retail investors, who often lack investment teams, this is especially critical as portfolio construction is usually done on a self-directed basis or with the help of a financial advisor who may have specific products to sell.

## NOTES

1. "Varus Fund Long Short Equity Strategy," Opalesque Emerging Managers Database, www.emerging-managers.com/883/Varus_Fund_Long_Short_Equity_Strategy883.html.
2. Comments taken from: "Founders Q&A: What Are the Opportunities for Global Macro Investing in the Current Highly Uncertain Environment? Third Wave's Investment Chief Uses a Combination of Quantitative and Non-Quant Tools to Identify Attractive Trades," *Opalesque Futures Intelligence*, 2009, www.opalesque.com/OFI1120/Founders_are_the_opportunities_for_investing120.html.
3. Refer to Chapter 3 for an in depth discussion about systematic CTAs.
4. "ArbitrOption up Almost 39% YTD as Event Driven Hedge Fund Strategy Generally Enjoys Positive Quarter," *Opalesque Alternative Market Briefing*, www.opalesque.com/646343/ArbitrOption_up_almost_YTD_as_event_driven634.html.
5. "Third Point LLC Letter to Yahoo! Board of Directors Regarding Discovery of Discrepancies in Educational Records of CEO Scott Thompson and Director Patti Hart," www.prnewswire.com/news-releases/third-point-llc-letter-to-yahoo-board-of-directors-regarding-discovery-of-discrepancies-in-educational-records-of-ceo-scott-thompson-and-director-patti-hart-150048865.html.
6. Ackman's Herbalife presentation, "Facts about Herbalife" (this website is hosted by Ackman's fund, Pershing Square Capital Management), http://factsaboutherbalife.com/wp-content/uploads/2013/01/Who-wants-to-be-a-Millionaire.pdf.
7. "Icahn, Ackman in Epic Showdown of Billionaires," CNBC, www.cnbc.com/id/100408608.
8. "Ackman Blasts Herbalife in Quarterly Letter," *New York Post*, http://nypost.com/2013/08/20/ackman-blasts-herbalife-in-quarterly-letter/.
9. "The Big Short War," *Vanity Fair*, www.vanityfair.com/business/2013/04/bill-ackman-dan-loeb-herbalife.
10. "Ackman Modifies Bet against Herbalife," *New York Times DealBook*, http://dealbook.nytimes.com/2013/10/03/ackman-modifies-bet-against-herbalife/?_r=0.

**11.** "Buffett Poised to Get $2 Billion Goldman Stake," Bloomberg, www.bloomberg.com/news/2013-09-30/buffett-poised-to-get-2-billion-goldman-stake-with-warrants.html.

**12.** "The Temptation of St. Warren," *The New Republic*, www.retro.ms11.net/LewisBuffett.pdf.

**13.** "Hard Times: College Majors, Unemployment & Earnings," Georgetown University, www9.georgetown.edu/grad/gppi/hpi/cew/pdfs/HardTimes.2013.2.pdf.

**14.** "The Student Loan Debt Crisis in 9 Charts," *Mother Jones,* www.motherjones.com/politics/2013/06/student-loan-debt-charts.

**15.** 400 Capital Credit Opportunities Fund LP, Opalesque Emerging Managers Database, www.alternative-alternatives.info/2197/400_Capital_Credit_Opportunities_Fund_LP219.html.

**16.** "Student Loans, Mortgages, Regulation Offering Opportunity for Credit Funds," *Opalesque Alternative Market Briefing*, www.opalesque.com/646476/Student_loans_mortgages_regulation_offering_opportunity_for_credit647.html.

**17.** "LNG's 'Small and Nimble' European Credit Fund Achieves High Teens Performance," *Opalesque Alternative Market Briefing*, www.opalesque.com/646257/and_European_credit_fund_achieves625.html.

**18.** "Liquid Alternatives Navigate Choppy Markets," *Opalesque Alternative Market Briefing*, www.opalesque.com/643533/Liquid_alternatives_navigate_choppy_markets353.html.

**19.** Altegris 40 Index, www.managedfutures.com/managed_futures_index.aspx.

**20.** "Longboard Asset Management Grows Managed Futures Fund, Sees Opportunity In Currencies," *Opalesque Alternative Market Briefing,* www.opalesque.com/646099/Longboard_Asset_Management_grows_managed_futures_fund_sees609.html.

**21.** "The Managed Futures Asset Growth Myth," Attain Capital Management, http://managed-futures-blog.attaincapital.com/2013/09/12/what-everybody-ought-to-know-about-managed-futures-asset-class-growth.

**22.** "Endurance Series Trust Launches First Mutual Fund Multi-Series Trust," *Opalesque Alternative Market Briefing,* www.opalesque.com/646610/Endurance_Series_Trust_launches_first_mutual_fund661.html.

**23.** "Revision of the UCITS Directive," European Commission, http://ec.europa.eu/internal_market/investment/ucits-directive/index_en.htm.

**24.** Alternative Investment Fund Managers Directive, European Commission, http://eur-lex.europa.eu/LexUriServ/LexUriServ.do?uri=OJ:L:2011:174:0001:01:EN:PDF.

25. CESR's guidelines concerning eligible assets for investment by UCITS, European Securities and Markets Authority, www.esma.europa.eu/content/CESRs-guidelines-concerning-eligible-assets-investment-UCITS-0.
26. Opalesque Frankfurt Roundtable, 2013, www.opalesque.com/RT/RoundtableFrankfurt2013.html.
27. Opalesque Frankfurt Roundtable, 2013, www.opalesque.com/RT/RoundtableFrankfurt2013.html.
28. "UCITS: Product Rules, Liquidity Management, Depositary, Money Market Funds, Long-Term Investments," http://ec.europa.eu/internal_market/consultations/2012/ucits_en.htm.
29. Alceda Quarterly UCITS Review, Alceda Fund Management, www.alceda.lu/en.
30. "Q&A: An Investment Manager Describes His UCITS-Compliant Funds Platform," *Opalesque New Managers,* www.opalesque.com/new-managers/60/investment-manager-describes-his-ucits-compliant-funds.html.
31. "Bernheim, Dreyfus & Co. Launches Global Macro UCITS Fund with $60m Seed Capital," www.opalesque.com/647267/Bernheim_Dreyfus_launches_global_macro_UCITS726.html.
32. Alternative Investments, European Commission, http://ec.europa.eu/internal_market/investment/alternative_investments.
33. Foreign Account Tax Compliance Act, U.S. Internal Revenue Service, www.irs.gov/Businesses/Corporations/Foreign-Account-Tax-Compliance-Act-(FATCA).

CHAPTER 2

# Emerging Managers

*Benedicte Gravrand*

Opalesque New Managers

## WHAT ARE EMERGING MANAGERS AND WHO INVESTS IN THEM?

According to the Opalesque's New Managers publication and database, emerging managers are any firm that is less than 48 months old with assets under management (AUM) at the time of inception of less than $600 million. Other analysts will provide a broader range than this, and may consider firms up to five years old as emerging managers, but, for the sake of this chapter, the definition outlined above will guide our understanding.

Within the emerging managers space, there is a diversity of funds, strategies, and personalities as broad as the hedge fund industry itself. To help understand how funds are created, we will break out some of the more common types of startup funds and provide examples of these managers. Understanding the common landscape of startup funds can also help investors establish a baseline for the type of emerging manager they might be looking for.

### Fully Vested at Inception

In the wake of 2008, the biggest banks lost their proprietary trading desks, which served as an incubator of sorts for emerging managers. As proprietary desks were broken up, a number of proprietary traders decided to set up shops of their own, trading the same or similar strategies they employed while an employee of a large bank. Typically, when these traders spin out, the bank—Goldman Sachs, Credit Suisse, or even other super large hedge funds like Tiger Capital, will give their spin outs seed capital.

Inside the industry, this is known as being fully vested at inception. Vested funds likely also contain money from their managing partners, but a big slice of the assets they start with come from previous employers. This is slightly different then the friends and family funds we outline next. Often, vested funds have an easier time attracting new assets and gaining the eye of institutional investors, precisely because they already have a bank, or a big fund backing them up.

### Friends and Family Money at Inception

As you might guess from the subtitle, friends and family at inception means that the fund has been able to start with more than just the manager's own money. Typically, emerging managers are going to try to start with more than just the personal funds of the founding team. If they aren't lucky enough to begin fully vested from an institution, the next place they go is friends and family.

### Good Pedigree

Having a *good pedigree* is a common shorthand phrase used by seeders and investors to describe the background of an emerging manager. Even if the manager isn't fully vested at inception, but has experience at major institutional banks or other well-known hedge funds, they'll be considered to have strong experience and a good pedigree. This type of resume is critical for emerging managers, as new funds come with an embedded blowout risk, and often, early stage investors are looking for some indication that a new fund will be able to ride out tough times.

An example of good pedigree is Stone Toro. Stone Toro Asset Management LLC, an asset management firm based in Princeton, New Jersey, was formed at the end of 2009 by three ex-Merrill Lynch colleagues: Mike Jarzyna, Jeffrey Russo, and Richard Jenkins. Jarzyna and Russo were also directors at BlackRock, and Russo, the PM, managed more than $14 billion in AUM as a director there.[1]

Their fund, the ST Alpha Event Fund, which was launched in January 2011, is an absolute return fund using a global multi-strategy approach to event driven arbitrage. It manages around $146.9 million and is up 0.92 percent YTD (to March 2013), after returning +2.5 percent in 2012 and +1.18 percent in 2011. It is also featured in Opalesque's EManagers database.

Jeff Russo actually started trading his strategy while at Bankers Trust in the mid-1990s, where he served as portfolio manager of global developed and emerging market index funds with assets over $4 billion. (Bankers Trust at the time was the third largest index manager in the world, managing around $200bn worth of index related assets.)

Russo defines *event* as things that are tangibly happening in the market. "So we like to look at where the world is, as opposed to the way we hope it to be or wish it was," he said.

The ST Alpha Event Fund has four distinct strategies, namely:

1. Index events
2. Merger arbitrage
3. Structural changes (or special situations, corporate actions)
4. Relative value pairs

"That's actually something that I think is a really attractive part of the strategy is the breadth of the index world and how the markets have changed over time," Russo explains. "The markets have become very passive with the emergence of ETFs. As active management on the mutual fund side has decreased in size, possibly due to active managers' long-term inability to outperform their benchmarks, and because of the tactical nature of ETFs and how people use them, that's really increased in scope and size and index Each time an index or an ETF reconstitutes itself, there is an investment that happens, and people have to react to that event. Because we have an index side, we think we are pretty good at that."

Whether it is an index fund, a mergers and acquisitions (M&A) trade, or a structural event, the managers at Stone Toro look at them from a quantitative perspective to see whether stocks react by underperforming or outperforming the market. Then they look at the fundamentals to figure out what a stock is going to do.

"It's a universe of animal spirits and people with high convictions," he notes.

"We try and take a humble approach, step back, and try and see how stocks perform and react to different events, and then position a portfolio accordingly to take advantage of that."

In periods of low events, the managers look to make money on the events that are open. They look for a ripple effect across their book this is where the multi-strategy approach creates an edge.

More typical of an event driven fund, the fund deals in global M&A. M&A "has got the headline risk, but it's a consistent strategy to have in a context of a multistrategy fund," he adds.

Within the M&A strategy, Russo explains, there is now (and over the last few years) a smaller universe of deals along with greater competition, thus decreasing the returns. However, the probabilities of deal closure have increased by 80 to 90 percent. "So you get a compressed spread, but you have more certainty."

Russo expects that those events will tend to be companies taking action. "Either a company decides that they want to buy a company or that now is a good time to sell. It's a company deciding that, you know what, we are going to take advantage of the stock market being this high, and issuing shares and then we are going to buy back debt, or we are going to buy back stock in an aggressive manner because we don't think our stock is valued properly. Or, we are going to spin off a company because we don't think it is being valued in our conglomerate structure."

Corporate action has historically followed the equity markets, Russo explains. More activity happens in up markets than in down, or when there are inflection points.

"Even in the low event environment of 2013, we tend to have over 200 different events within the portfolio over a course of a month," he notes. "So there are things happening. It's just that they have been smaller and they have been lower probability. So we have been able to put less conviction behind the trades, but all things do turn in cycles."

### Emerging Fund of Funds

Fund of fund structures, which we explained at the beginning of the book, can be a great place to pool together a bunch of emerging managers and mitigate risk to investors. The due diligence process for emerging managers is also so unique, that fund of fund teams that focus on them have been able to provide more value than some of their cohorts by specializing in this niche.

Pacific Alternative Asset Management Company (PAAMCO) is one such fund of funds. The approximately $10 billion firm has a global investment portfolio, but also focuses on emerging managers.

"Some [large] allocators are looking beyond those big multi-strategy hedge funds and expressing demand for exposure and alpha generation from emerging managers, using them as completion portfolios to their larger institutional portfolios," explains David Walter who is responsible for Asian investments at PAAMCO.[2]

His viewpoints are echoed by Edward Moon, Chief Investment Officer for Woori AbsolutePartners, an arm of the large Woori franchise that covers Asia. "We believe emerging managers can provide very attractive investment opportunities going forward—they are generally more willing to provide increased transparency and by implementing various structures, we are able to monetize the risk premium associated with investing in early stage managers. Not to mention that we have very strict guidelines indeed regarding risk taking, and our ability to redeem our capital should certain thresholds get breached."

## Emerging Fund of One

Emerging funds of one are a relatively new structure that have gained more traction with investors in the wake of the 2008 crisis. These funds are typically a separate share class tailored for one single investor. More than a managed account, that replicates the existing fund, the fund of one gives investors full control to tailor a given manager's strategy. This can be a dicey road for emerging managers who are still working to prove their flagship product, but being flexible enough to work with an investor in this way can also attract institutions early on.

A number of large institutional grade firms that work with emerging managers are providing support for fund of one structures, which require an added administrative, middle, and back office load. Much of this is driven by managers coming around to investor demands for increased transparency and greater investor rights.

"The topic of investor rights is definitely key. We have been engaged in the managed account space for the last 15 years. Within that period we saw the transformation of the managers' mentality from very opaque, very protective and secretive about what they do to today fully transparent and fully amenable to managed accounts as the new normal for 'fund of one' solution and new routes to diversify their asset base. Another way to put it, the manager community finally realizes that investors' rights must lead the way to do business," explains Nathanaël Benzaken, Managing Director, Lyxor.[3]

"We understand the concern about potential strategy reverse engineering (which is very remote to be honest). But we also have to explain the expected investor benefits of offering enhanced transparency and detailed risk exposures."

The fund of one is typically set up as a limited partnership with investments made into underlying hedge fund comingled vehicles. Unlike the $250 million or above price tag for separately managed accounts, fund of one's can come in at $50 million or above. They also benefit from having fund of funds style governance including boards of directors and CIMA.

"Everyone thought managed accounts would be the next big thing," says Peter Hill, Global Head of Fund of Hedge Fund Services at Citi. "But, what limits managed accounts is that they are very expensive and they require an entire infrastructure." Separate managed account platforms can involve monitoring tens of managers and the necessary due diligence for each of those managers.

Through a fund of one structure, investors have consultation and due diligence baked in. Rather than building that infrastructure in house, investors can access it as they would with a more traditional fund of funds structure while still retaining control through customization.

"Essentially this creates a stickier client. We've seen sovereign wealth funds for example, look at this structure over creating their own hedge fund program. Large institutions looking too—Aberdeen runs a $10 billion fund of one program," Hill says.[4]

## Seeders

Seeders are investors or funds that are not necessarily immediately related to the funds they invest in as a vesting firm would be, but do invest in emerging managers very early on. Some on the zero day, some in later stages. Seed funding is understood as a means of helping these funds get to the next level, expand and attract big-ticket investors.

One of the more famous seeders is IMQubator, Europe's largest seeding platform. Established by Jeroen Tielman, now a 25-year veteran of the global institutional industry, IMQubator offers an institutional platform where professional investors can gain exposure to emerging managers through the IMQubator multi-manager fund.[5]

Emerging managers deserve to be included by institutional investors in the core of their hedge fund exposure, Tielman asserts. Alluding to emerging managers as *speedboats* and larger funds as *supertankers*, Tielman noted, "It's clear that speedboats are better equipped to explore and navigate the unknown, uncharted waters that make up the 'new normal' of the current political and economic environment. Supertankers need a longer time to test the waters and change course, while they need to be prudent to stay in deep waters only. The present economic climate favors the quick and nimble and might punish the large, slow, and cumbersome."

The current IMQubator fund is designed to take 10 emerging managers at any one time. The firm doesn't disclose its performance beyond saying it has been in line with its targets, which includes achieving capital preservation.

The firm prefers managers who have already made a start at building their business and likes people with a two to three year track record who have started with their own money or that of their friends and family. "It might help if they already have a track record in this current climate," he says.

Sometimes seeders can also be banks and not just funds or fund platforms like IMQubator. SEB is a merchant bank headquartered in Sweden. It has been seeding hedge funds since 2003 and runs two seeding funds, and the two funds have similar structures: Manager Catalyst Fund I (MCF1) was launched in April 2010. It was open for subscription for three months, during which investors committed $280 million. SEB drew the capital as they needed it during a year and invested in seven funds. MCF1 is now fully invested.[6]

There was more demand for this type of vehicle among Nordic institutions, so Manager Catalyst Fund II (MCF2) was launched in October 2012. It was open to new investors for three months as well, who committed $300 million. MCF2 has done five investments so far and still has two or three more to do. SEB has so far divested from one of the funds, but all the others are still live.

SEB does invest in day-one deals, but prefers acceleration deals generally. The group usually invests between $25 million and $50 million in each fund, and the aim is to build a diversified hedge fund portfolio with an economic interest on top.

"Each deal we do is evaluated from several angles but generally we look at it from: 1) standalone merits, 2) portfolio contribution, and 3) economic deal," says Mikael Nilsson, co-portfolio manager of the two seeding vehicles. "All three needs to be fulfilled for us to do a deal, and if we cannot create a win/win situation for our fund and the managers, the deal is off. In the economic deal, we prefer gross revenue sharing, however we are flexible and each deal is unique in many ways to address the specific manager's needs."

According to Nilsson, just like anywhere else, it's increasingly hard for Swedish hedge fund start-ups to attract capital. (This is also true for funds worldwide in the wake of 2008.) Launching with only $10m or $20m is not enough, and investors don't view this size as viable. Besides many investors cannot have more than 10 percent in any one fund.

Many investors don't want to—or cannot—spend the time on the necessary due diligence just for a small allocation, especially if they don't know whether they can grow into them or not.

Small and new hedge funds have to deal with smaller revenues and the increasing costs of running a hedge fund. So seeders are becoming increasingly important for them.

"There are different types of seeders and I do not have any statistics on this, but maybe 50 percent have an external anchor investor or a seeder," he said. "Many managers can't find those and some do not want to give away any revenues and find micro investors without those ambitions."

Nilsson believes that the shortage of capital for new managers over time will increase the quality of the hedge fund market.

"The industry is very competitive and if funds consistently underperform or have operational hiccups, investors will redeem," he added. "Hopefully seeders like us will help to decline the managers least equipped to deal with the increased challenges ahead both from an operational and a legal perspective, but also from the strategy standpoint."

Capital may be hard to raise, but there are many investors out there who want to invest in new and emerging fund managers. They just don't do it because it is difficult for them due to the implied career risk. So they are looking for knowledge transfer, Nilsson stated.

"Knowledge transfer has been one of the benefits our investors look for," Nilsson noted. "We invite them to join us in various steps in the process. So they get to learn and they can do add-on investments themselves outside our funds. That's a selling point both for the investor and the hedge fund managers, because managers get exposed to large investors, which they wouldn't otherwise at this stage. And investors like the idea that we scan the market for them. We agree to present them with ideas and flows, and tell then what we see in the market as they might not have the time to observe or gather data themselves."

"So therefore there is a large portion of knowledge transfer in this process. We don't have many investors so we do have the time to actually speak to them as well."

Emerging managers can offer investors a broad range of opportunity but aligning the interests of both parties is important, here we look at what that means:

### NEW FUND MANAGERS AND EARLY STAGE INVESTORS: A BETTER ALIGNMENT OF INTERESTS?

#### *Bruno Guillemin, Fundana Investment Advisors, Senior Analyst CAIA*

Fundana is an investment advisor to several funds of hedge funds and directs at least half of its new investments to Emerging Managers. The investment process typically involves allocating a small amount of day one or early stage (defined as less than one year after the fund's launch) to new managers who have strong pedigrees.

The Emerging Managers space is currently in vogue. Following the 2008 credit crisis, allocators focused first on the opportunity to invest with previously hard-closed Blue Chip hedge fund managers. Now that most of those funds are hard-closed again, investors are taking another look at Emerging Managers.

We will focus on small and mid-sized fund launches (typical day one assets under management of between \$20 million and \$500 million) as Fundana does not invest in the very large new launches

(>$1 billion at launch). The dataset has been compiled from all new investments made in our Funds of Hedge Funds since January 2006, encompassing 69 day one/early stage investments in the Long/Short Equity, Global Macro, and Event Driven strategies.

For the purposes of this example, we consider two separate periods: the first period runs from January 2006 to July 2008, hence before the industry crisis; and the second period runs from August 2008 to date. The database contains 25 day one/early state investments in the first period and 44 in the second period.

### Early stage investors now get instant rewards to invest early . . .

Delving into the database, we first compile information on the level of management fees for each new fund (we will only look at the management fee of the main share class, so ignoring classes offering discounts in exchange for longer lock-ups). We also look at whether the fund has set up a founder's share class for its initial investors.

**TABLE 2.1** Evolution of Management Fees and Founder's Share Classes at New Hedge Funds

| Management Fees | Pre-July 2008 | Post-July 2008 | Total Funds |
|---|---|---|---|
| Below 2% | 28% (7) | 43% (19) | 37% (26) |
| Equal to 2% | 72% (18) | 57% (25) | 63% (43) |
| Founders Share Class | 0 out of 25 launches | 11 out of 44 launches | 11 out of 69 launches |

According to our dataset in Table 2.1, while new hedge funds charging 2 percent management fee accounted for the majority of the funds (63 percent of all early stage investments), the number of new funds with reduced management fees has increased strongly (43 percent of early stage investments post-2008 had management fees below 2 percent). We can foresee 1.5 percent becoming the new normal, which was the case in the late nineties.

Concomitantly, we saw the development of founder's share classes. These are special share classes dedicated to the first investors in a fund and are structured to motivate investors to commit money sooner rather than later. Hence they provide a discount on fees, typically 25 percent off both management and performance fees, without requiring any additional lock-up of capital. However, they are limited in size (the average founder's share class is $100 million) and/or duration (for instance only offered for the first six months). In addition, half of the founder's share classes we received enabled investors to double their initial investment at the same fees.

While we had no managers offering founder's share classes before the crisis, we participated in 11 post-crisis, and their use is spreading: six of them were from funds which launched less than one year ago. Compared to a seed deal, it is advantageous to the manager as the discount offered to early stage investors has no impact on the revenues generated by the subsequent assets raised at the firm.

**. . . which are most often offered by the wealthier fund managers . . .** To take the analysis a step further, we split the new managers in four categories based on the initial commitment of the managers (i.e., how much of his personal wealth does the PM invest in his new fund).

We look more specifically at the post-crisis period because there were few incentives pre-crisis there were no founder's share classes and, if we remove the funds seeded by Julian Robertson pre-crisis, we invested with one hedge fund with less than 2 percent management fees.

**TABLE 2.2** Details of New Launches According to Managers' Investment

| Initial Commitment from PM(s) | Number of Funds | Average Years of Hedge Fund Experience | Average Management Fee | Founder's Share Classes | Seed Deal |
|---|---|---|---|---|---|
| <$5M | 25% (11) | 5.9 | 1.89% | 27% (3) | 64% (7) |
| $5M–10M | 25% (11) | 7.5 | 1.82% | 27% (3) | 82% (9) |
| $10M–20M | 32% (13) | 8.7 | 1.80% | 23% (3) | 38% (5) |
| >$20M | 18% (9) | 11.5 | 1.66% | 22% (2) | 11% (1) |

According to Table 2.2, 18 percent of the new managers we invested in had more than $20 million of their own money at launch in the fund. We saw that post-crisis, launches for emerging managers have tended to see more experienced managers who are also wealthier. These wealthy new fund managers had an average of 11.5 years of experience working in hedge funds, which is significantly more than the other three categories.

Interestingly for investors, these managers charged management fees of 1.66 percent on average. Apparently, the wealthier you are, the more inclined to reduce fees to 1.5 percent you are. Part of the motivation comes from the fact that many investors started in the industry at a time when 2 percent was not a standard, and by not taking a seed deal (only one of them did) they are able to offer better terms to new investors.

Not surprisingly, it is the least wealthy new managers who have the highest management fee rate, at 1.89 percent on average.

### . . . and led to interesting results for the managers best aligned with investors . . .

**TABLE 2.3** Details of New Launches According to Management Fee Levels

| Management Fee | Number of Funds | Seed Deal | Founder's Share Classes | Average over Performance versus Peers after Two Years |
|---|---|---|---|---|
| Less than 2% | 43% (19) | 6 | 6 | 8.6% |
| 2.0% | 57% (25) | 16 | 5 | –0.1% |

Table 2.3 goes on to look at the outperformance of these new managers, split into two groups depending on the level of management fees charged. This shows that those charging less than 2 percent massively outperformed over the first two years of their new fund, by close to 9 percent. Their colleagues starting with 2 percent management fees on average produced the same returns as their peers.

While this result is absolutely not statistically significant, it certainly shows that top performing managers are not always the ones charging the highest levels of fees and that investing with the investor-friendly new managers during the last three to four years was the most profitable.

### Key observations

Looking at the alignment of interests of new fund managers with early stage investors, our small sample of data suggests that: Overall, investors benefit from lower management fees post-crisis. Early stage investors are receiving more discounts than ever, primarily through the development of founder's share classes.

Post-crisis, investing with new fund managers would have produced the best results if one had selected the more investor friendly new managers, partially because it encompasses a majority of the more experienced and wealthier.

"New Fund Managers and Early stage investors: a better alignment of interests?," *Opalesque New Managers*, www.opalesque.com/new-managers/123/fundana-series-new-fund-managers-and.html.

Investors will often rely heavily on the first year performance of a new fund to assess the overall ability of a manager, however this can be misleading especially if the market drops significantly soon after a launch. This was true for many funds that launched late in 2007 or early 2008.

## IS THE PERFORMANCE IN THE FIRST YEAR OF A NEW HEDGE FUND A LEADING INDICATOR FOR A GOOD INVESTMENT?

Here we will look at the performance of hedge funds in their first year of operations, how it has evolved over time, and whether it can give a good insight into the future success of a fund.

We will focus on the small and mid-sized launches (typical day one assets under management (AUM) of between $20 million and $500 million), as Fundana does not invest in the very large new launches (>$1 billion at launch). The dataset has been compiled from all the new investments made in our Funds of Hedge Funds since January 2006, encompassing 58 day one/early stage investments in the Long/Short Equity, Global Macro, and Event Driven strategies which have been operating for more than one year as of the end of April 2012.

### How has the first year's performance of hedge funds evolved before and after the crisis?

We consider two separate periods: the first period runs from January 2006 to July 2008, hence before the industry crisis; and the second period runs from August 2008 to 2012. The database contains 25 day one/early stage investments in the first period and 33 in the second period (funds with at least one year of returns, hence which started on or before May 2011).

Rather than comparing first year absolute returns between the new funds over time, which is difficult to analyze considering the volatility of the last few years, we analyze the over- or under-performance of the new hedge funds against a portfolio of hedge funds.

For the purposes of this study in Table 2.4, we look at the relative performance of the new hedge funds versus our flagship Fund of Hedge Funds (Prima Capital Fund, or "the proxy") as this is a good proxy for a blended mix of existing and older hedge funds. (See Table 2.4.)

**TABLE 2.4** Relative Performance of New Hedge Funds versus a Proxy after One Year

| Day One/Early Stage | Pre-July 2008 | Post-July 2008 | Total Funds |
|---|---|---|---|
| Number of hedge funds | 25 | 33 | 58 |
| Positive performance versus the proxy after one year | 18 | 22 | 40 |
| Negative performance versus the proxy after one year | 7 | 11 | 18 |
| Ratio of positive funds versus the proxy after one year | 72% | 66% | 69% |

It confirms our overall observations that current new launches are as successful now as they were before the crisis at delivering a positive relative performance, as 72 percent of pre-crisis launches were positive and so were 66 percent of the post-crisis funds. However, we are mindful of the problems of drawing conclusions from these statistics (firstly because of the low number of observations and secondly due to the inherent selection bias implied by an investment with a successful fund made 6 to 12 months after it launched).

In contrast, looking at the details of the relative performance of the new launches after one year, (Table 2.5) we do see a change in the relative performance of the new managers as shown in Figure 2.1. The horizontal axis shows the launch date of the day one/early stage investments in which we invested, and the vertical axis represents the relative performance of the hedge funds versus the proxy after one year. Since the crisis, we have observed that the relative outperformance of the new funds after one year has been much less impressive than those launched pre-crisis. (See Table 2.5.)

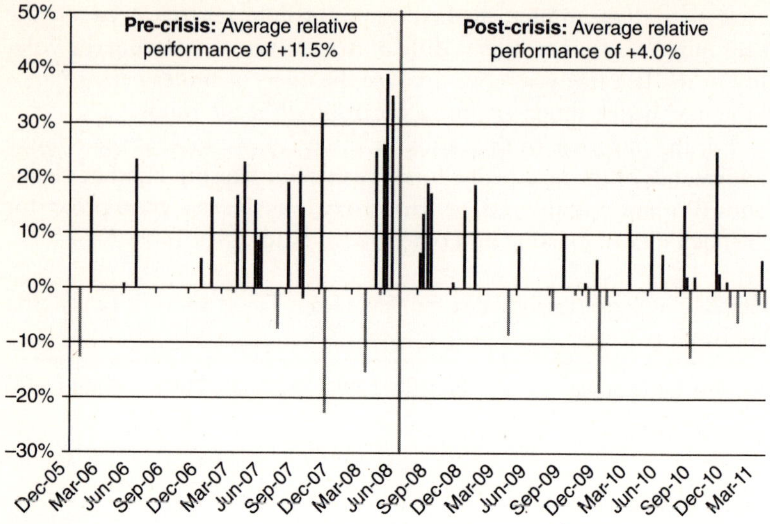


**FIGURE 2.1** Details of the Relative Performance of the New Hedge Funds versus the Proxy, One Year after They Launched

**TABLE 2.5** Relative Performance of the New Hedge Funds versus the Proxy before and after the Crisis

| Day One/Early Stage | Pre-July 2008 | Post-July 2008 | Total Funds |
|---|---|---|---|
| Number of investments | 25 | 33 | 58 |
| >10% relative performance after one year | 15 | 8 | 23 |
| <−10% relative performance after one year | 3 | 2 | 5 |
| Average relative performance after one year | +11.5% | +4.0% | +7.3% |

## What are the possible explanations for this pattern of results and what conclusions can we draw based on these results?

Several explanations exist for the change of this return pattern, all of which we have experienced over the last three years. Some are more objective, others are more subjective, but we do think they have played a role in the recent behavior of less outstanding performances from new launches:

1. A more volatile environment has pushed new managers to take longer to build the portfolio to avoid setting off on the wrong foot from the start of their new fund. Post-crisis, we often see new managers taking two to three months to build up their portfolio, compared to two to three weeks pre-crisis.
2. The increase of start-up costs (mostly linked to the institutionalization of the industry and the increasing compliance and regulatory burden) is discouraging new managers from taking more risk at the start.
3. The increase of backing by large institutional seeders and large institutions is creating a sense of less short-term business risk mentality for the new managers (through the use of investor level gates for instance).
4. Few hedge funds have been strong performers over the last few years, and new hedge funds were not immune to the more difficult trading environment.

We have drawn **five conclusions** from our experience thus far are:

1. Most successful new launches (>+10 percent relative performance in the first year) have been good or great investments, meaning they have been large positive contributors for our funds of hedge funds. For instance, out of the four successful new launches since January 2010, three managers are already significant holdings as of today, of which two were day one investments.
2. However, this early outperformance does not give any indication as to the long-term success of the managers. Some of them were good/great for just a couple of years; others generated strong outperformance for five years and more.
3. None of these successful new launches were bad investments (i.e., no large negative contributors to our funds).
4. Very few flat/negative relative performers during the first year were subsequently strong performers and contributors to our funds of hedge funds.
5. Although we took *increase or out* decisions with our new investments after 12 months of performance before the crisis, we are now

typically waiting longer as we understand that the change of the industry with its related costs, as well as current market volatility, have changed the way some managers operate during their first year.

"Is First Year Performance a Leading Indicator?," *Opalesque New Managers*, www.opalesque.com/new-managers/73/fundana-the-performance-in-the-first-year.html.

Just as the timing of a launch and first year performance can be indicators of the potential stability of a new fund, seed deals can also have an impact. The terms of the deal or the culture a seeder expects can shape how a fund does business. Let's look at this in-depth.

### HOW DO SEED DEALS IMPACT ON THE PERFORMANCE OF NEW HEDGE FUND MANAGERS?

***Nick Morrell***
***Fundana Investment Advisors, Head of Operational Due Diligence***

Seeding of emerging managers has become more institutionalized since the 2008 credit crisis, at a time when asset raising for newly launched hedge funds has become significantly more difficult.

#### Reading the data

Here, we look at the relationship between performance over the first couple of years of a new fund's life, and whether or not the fund manager accepted a seed deal. We will also analyze the same data split between two time periods: the first period runs from January 2006 to July 2008, hence before the industry crisis; and the second period runs from August 2008 to date. All data discussed below will show the outperformance of the emerging hedge funds compared to the performance of our flagship FoHF (gross of fees) over the same time period. Prima Capital Fund is Fundana's flagship FoHF offering with a 19-year track record.

In the analysis, we will focus on small and mid-sized launches (typical Day 1 assets under management (AUM) of between \$20 million and \$500 million), as Fundana does not invest in the very large new launches. The dataset has been compiled from all the new investments made in our Funds of Hedge Funds since January 2006, encompassing 59 day one/early stage investments in the Long/Short Equity, Global Macro, and Event Driven strategies, which have been operating for more than one year as of the end of September 2012. Of these, 40 have more than two year's track record. Finally it is important to bear in mind that there is some degree of bias in these results, as a number of the funds (five pre-crisis and three post-crisis) with one year of performance did not reach their second year anniversary.

### Q1. How does a seed deal impact performance in the first couple of years?

Here we will analyze all funds in our database to determine whether managers who use seed deals are able to outperform both the overall portfolio of our flagship FoHF, and also their competitors who do not use a seed deal. For this we will look at outperformance over one- and two-year periods after launch. Table 2.6 looks at all funds in the database (from 2006 to today), and compares outperformance over the first year and the first two years of our funds' existences. So for example, the 29 percent figure indicates that 29 percent of the funds had an outperformance between 0 and 10 percent in the first year when compared to the FoHF portfolio. The 7.7 percent average indicates that the average outperformance of all funds in the first year was 7.7 percent.

**TABLE 2.6** Outperformance versus FoHF Portfolio Comparison after One and Two Years

| Outperformance versus FoHF Portfolio | After First Year | Annualized over Two Years |
|---|---|---|
| <–10% | 7% | 5% |
| –10% to 0% | 24% | 23% |
| 0% to 10% | 29% | 30% |
| 10% to 20% | 25% | 33% |
| >20% | 15% | 10% |
| **Average** | 7.7% | **7.5%** |
| Median | 5.8% | 7.8% |

This shows that there is no significant difference between the two time periods, but it also indicates that our emerging managers have significantly outperformed the overall portfolio, indicating that this strategy of looking to emerging managers has been a successful one. Around 70 percent of the managers have outperformed the overall portfolio over time. Table 2.7 goes on to look at the differences between managers who used seed deals and those who did not.

**TABLE 2.7** Outperformance versus FoHF Portfolio—Comparison between Funds with and without Seed Deals

| Outperformance versus FoHF Portfolio | After First Year with Seed | After First Year without Seed | Annualized over Two Years with Seed | Annualized over Two Years without Seed |
|---|---|---|---|---|
| <–10% | 13% | 0% | 5% | 5% |
| –10% to 0% | 23% | 25% | 19% | 18% |
| 0% to 10% | 19% | 39% | 29% | 21% |
| 10% to 20% | 26% | 25% | 29% | 25% |
| >20% | 19% | 11% | 19% | 0% |
| **Average** | **7.9%** | **7.4%** | **9.7%** | **5.1%** |
| Median | 8.8% | 5.6% | 9.3% | 4.9% |

Here we can see that after the first year, there is no significant difference between funds with and without seed funding. However, after two years of operations, there is a significant difference, with annualized outperformance for funds with seeds increasing from 7.9 to 9.7 percent on average, whilst for funds without seeds the outperformance fell from 7.4 to 5.1 percent.

### Q2. What differences in outperformance can be seen before and after the 2008 credit crisis?

Looking at the same data, but split into pre-crisis and post-crisis periods, Table 2.8 shows data for all funds split across the two time periods.

**TABLE 2.8** Outperformance Split between Pre- and Post-Crisis Time Periods

| Outperformance versus FoHF Portfolio | After First Year Pre-Crisis | After First Year Post-Crisis | Annualized over Two Years Pre-Crisis | Annualized over Two Years Post-Crisis |
|---|---|---|---|---|
| <–10% | 12% | 3% | 10% | 0% |
| –10% to 0% | 16% | 29% | 5% | 40% |
| 0% to 10% | 12% | 41% | 10% | 50% |
| 10% to 20% | 28% | 24% | 55% | 10% |
| >20% | 32% | 3% | 20% | 0% |
| **Average** | **11.5%** | **4.9%** | **12.0%** | **3.0%** |
| Median | 15.6% | 2.9% | 13.0% | 3.9% |

This split highlights that since 2008, whilst the emerging managers have continued to outperform the overall FoHF portfolio, there has been a significant decrease in the level of outperformance over both the first year and the first two years. Also of note is that whilst the first year and first two year figures are in-line for the pre-crisis period, when it comes to post-crisis there has been a fall from 4.9 to 3.0 percent, indicating an underperformance in the second year post-launch. Finally, Tables 2.9 and 2.10 split the data further to analyze the impact of seed deals between the pre- and post-crisis periods, again looking at the first year (Table 2.9) and the first two years (Table 2.10) after launch.

**TABLE 2.9** Outperformance (First Year) with and without Seed Deals, Split between Pre- and Post-Crisis Time Periods

| Outperformance in First Year versus FoHF Portfolio | With Seed Pre-Crisis | With Seed Post-Crisis | No Seed Pre-Crisis | No Seed Post-Crisis |
|---|---|---|---|---|
| <–10% | 20% | 3% | 0% | 0% |
| –10% to 0% | 13% | 16% | 20% | 18% |
| 0% to 10% | 13% | 13% | 10% | 36% |
| 10% to 20% | 13% | 19% | 50% | 7% |
| >20% | 40% | 0% | 20% | 4% |
| **Average** | **11.0%** | **5.0%** | **12.3%** | **4.7%** |
| Median | 15.6% | 2.8% | 15.6% | 4% |

Table 2.9 does not add anything significant to the data in Table 2.8, simply highlighting again that the outperformance in the first year is significantly less for post-crisis new manager launches.

**TABLE 2.10** Outperformance (First Two Years) with and without Seed Deals, Split between Pre- and Post-Crisis Time Periods

| Annualized Outperformance over Two Years versus FoHF Portfolio | With Seed Pre-Crisis | With Seed Post-Crisis | No Seed Pre-Crisis | No Seed Post-Crisis |
|---|---|---|---|---|
| <–10% | 8% | 0% | 13% | 0% |
| –10% to 0% | 8% | 33% | 0% | 45% |
| 0% to 10% | 8% | 56% | 13% | 45% |
| 10% to 20% | 42% | 11% | 75% | 9% |
| >20% | 33% | 0% | 0% | 0% |
| **Average** | **14.2%** | **3.6%** | **8.8%** | **2.5%** |
| Median | 14.7% | 7.1% | 12.9% | 1.4% |

However, Table 2.10 shows that the pre-crisis outperformance was largely driven by those funds with a seed deal, with an average annualized outperformance of 14.2 percent against 8.8 percent for funds without a seed. Post-crisis, the level of outperformance is significantly lower for all funds, but again those funds with a seed deal did slightly better than there un-seeded counterparts.

### What conclusions can we draw from these results?

The first conclusion is that investing in emerging managers has been a good investment decision for us, and continues to be so—all the aggregated data are positive, indicating that these investments have outperformed the overall portfolio in our flagship FoHF. Secondly, emerging managers were able to generate significantly more outperformance prior to the 2008 credit crisis. This could indicate that on average the quality of managers was greater prior to 2008, or, more likely in our opinion, that the ability of any manager to generate significant outperformance since 2008 has been hampered by the very difficult market conditions. Finally, the data indicate that for investors looking at emerging managers as a longer-term investment (two or more years) they could be better off focusing on those who have received seed deals. However, whilst this distinction was clear-cut prior to 2008, there is much less in it today.

### Lower fees

For price conscious investors, emerging managers may also offer a way to access hedged strategies at a lower cost. As noted earlier, emerging managers sometimes offer *founders rounds* where subscribers to the fund are allowed in at a lower fee than the 2/20 common to the industry. This can mean a half percent reduction or other allowances, for investors that get in the door first.

Others, take a unique view and charge no management fee whatsoever. London-based Eschler AM is one such firm.* For the Eschler Recovery Fund, if the fund sees gains of more than 6 percent each year a 25 percent incentive fee kicks in, but fund principals say that expenses are low enough to forgo management fees.

The Eschler Recovery Fund follows an equity long/short strategy with a long bias, managed by a small, independent equity fund manager called Eschler Asset Management LLP, based in London. It was launched in October 2012 and has returned almost 17 percent since then (to March 2013).

"The strategy is focused on equities and the approach is bottom up, concentrated, and value-oriented," Eschler's founding partner, Theron de Ris explains. "My focus is primarily North America, though up to a-third of holdings may be outside North America (mostly in Europe)."

De Ris invests in two types of investments: "The first is companies with franchise qualities that for one reason or another are under a cloud or experiencing a temporary difficulty, but that have underlying asset value and strength in cash flow. The second category is holding companies or closed-end funds that are trading at a very large discount to NAV, where there is either a clear path to growth in NAV per share or a management plan to narrow the NAV discount through divesting assets and returning cash to shareholders."

*"Profiles—Eschler AM, RDA Capital Speak about Their Fund," *Opalesque New Managers*, www.opalesque.com/new-managers/199/profiles-eschler-am-rda-capital-speak.html. (The fund currently features in Opalesque's Emerging Mangers database, www.emerging-managers.com/4739/Eschler-Recovery-Fund-SP-Class-B473.html.)

### One-man band

The fund does not demand any management fee. If it exceeds gains of more than 6 percent in any given year, then the incentive fee of 25 percent kicks in. This is because the fund is small ($2.9 million in AUM) and expenses are low. Indeed, this is a one-man band, with support from Trinity Fund Administration in Dublin, and Morgan Stanley as the prime broker.

"Frankly my view is it's a bit of a myth that one needs to hire a big team, travel a lot, or even spend all day looking for investment ideas, to generate good returns and maintain sound operations," De Ris notes. "I've been running Eschler Asset Management for several years now and have kept costs very low; that has been key. On the investing side, the portfolio is concentrated and unlevered and that helps me to focus on what matters and tune out the noise."

### Why do emerging managers fail?

Why do emerging managers fail? The simple answer is because they fail to raise assets to a level that supports their business. And this failure, according to Autumn Capital, usually falls into one of three categories: (1) capital mistakes, (2) business, mistakes and (3) strategy mistakes.

Capital mistakes relate to the process of raising capital and managing investors, or to the capitalization of the management company. Business mistakes relate to the actual business of running a hedge fund management company. And strategy mistakes relate to the investment activity of the fund that the manager is running.

Autumn Capital Partners is a London-based investment consultancy firm founded in 2009, which currently advises hedge funds and institutions; it has a focus on emerging products and advises investors on early-stage hedge fund investments.

### Top 10 reasons for failure

Autumn's partners have drawn up a list of the top 10 reasons why emerging managers fail:

1. Underestimating the challenges
2. Lack of clear definable alpha
3. Inability to communicate
4. Wrong team
5. Wrong time
6. Under-investment

7. Assuming that all investors are equal
8. Lack of transparency
9. Greed
10. Fear

The overwhelming majority of emerging managers will be loss-making businesses in the first three years of their existence, according to the firm. Some of the typical reasons for failure are not curable, but many of those mistakes can be avoided.

We asked Kevin Cook, Partner at Autumn Capital, and Pierre Crama, Head of Operational Due Diligence at Signet Capital Management Ltd to expand on their own experiences of emerging managers' mistakes. Signet is a London-based fund of hedge funds house with a focus on emerging funds.

"Strategy mistakes are fewer and further between, as thankfully, managers tend to have a decent idea of what their strategy ought to be, why it might deliver alpha and why it might be attractive to some investors," he said.

"There is still an under appreciation of the level of capital, infrastructure, effort, timing, and luck that are required to launch a successful hedge fund today. Managers make very optimistic assumptions both in terms of asset growth and in terms of performance. Planning and resourcing your business on this basis is very dangerous."

Autumn Capital explains to new managers that they need to assume there will be no external assets, and that performance will be mediocre at best in the first three years. If there is enough capital to operate under such assumptions, then managers have the best chances of success. Cook suggests that $100 million or $200 million—even if raising that much is hard—is the asset level that is sustainable for those managers who want to maintain an institutional hedge fund business.

### The A team

In terms of business mistakes, underinvestment and poor allocation of resources are common, Cook notes. "Managers must have the right team, and must be clear about how they are going to resource their business. Investors really do care more today about pedigree, track record, and the team as a group, particularly when dealing with emerging managers, than they have at any point previously. They also care about proper separation of functions. So it is simply unacceptable to have a situation when a portfolio manager is also the head of sales, or the COO is trying to also act as a portfolio manager."

Cook further recommends working out the right team to put together, defining roles clearly and creating incentives, and outsourcing appropriately.

### A clear proposition

Managers will also need to be patient and focused when it comes to raising capital. They must be able to differentiate themselves from everyone else.

"They must have a clearly defined alpha proposition that they can articulate with conviction to the right sort of investors," Cook suggests.

"Too frequently, we see managers adopting a scattershot approach to capital raising, marketing a product that is ill-defined or wasting time on investors who either don't invest in their strategy or invest at their stage in their lifecycle."

### Investors: Aim for the tougher ones

Cook also has recommendations for investors. Autumn Capital, which services an institutional investor base, has just completed a detailed review of the academic and market data in this area and found that, over the last 20 years, there has been consistent emerging manager outperformance.

"If you break down those emerging managers into particular strategies," he said, "if you understand when the best times to allocate to them are, there are strong arguments for an allocation to emerging."

As a consultant, he stresses to investors that the due diligence burden is much higher with emerging managers. There are thousands of younger, smaller managers out there, all carrying a certain degree of risk. So finding a good strategy is not sufficient.

"Fundamentally, you also need to believe that that manager is set up to ride out some of the bumps in the road that will be inevitable in growing their business in this environment. You need to work harder in order to make sure that you make a right investment."

He points to a significant distinction: "We consider an emerging manager to be somebody who has gone through the start-up phase, has found an initial capital partner, has actually got themselves up and running and has started to develop a track record of at least 12 to 18 months. Whilst we believe in the value of newer managers and in our ability to identify and develop those managers, it has been very difficult for us to find the right model and to have the necessary conviction to back pure start-ups, other than in exceptional circumstances. At that level, there is a huge imbalance between the availability of product and the availability of capital which, at this point, creates too great a challenge for us as a viable business proposition."

### Golden capital

Like Cook, Pierre Crama draws attention to the Golden Rule:

"From a business angle, the management company needs to be well capitalized."

Signet always looks at the managers' business plan to see how they plan to finance their operations in the next two or three years—as this often becomes a source of distraction for the founding partners.

### Wanted: Business head with vision

Crama also comments on business heads too often being appointed too hastily and inappropriately. Managers need to pay attention to employment contracts, job descriptions; they should do professional background checks, determine whether they are likely to be stable, and if their interest is aligned with the founder partners'. He stresses: "Having a CEO with a vision about where he wants to be in five years is of utmost importance for the success of a hedge fund."

### Scale

He also mentions scalability. Indeed, new managers must have scalability in mind when building their infrastructure: "At the beginning, you may decide to run one single product, but eventually this product is so successful you are going to launch different cohorts of your existing fund, or you are going to launch a managed account structure, or you are going to launch a sister fund in a different strategy with a new team. So the scalability of the infrastructure to support the AUM growth is key."

### Understanding service providers

Crama recommends managers appoint the right service providers on day one, after a thorough due diligence—even on the big providers.

"What you really need to assess is, whether they understand your strategy, whether they fit your culture, do they have the right IT infrastructure, the right qualified team and a good reputation, and the capacity to service you when you reach your ultimate AUM," he explains. "When you switch from one provider to another, it might be for a good reason but this is usually considered as a red flag by investors. Consequently it is important not to rush the process related to the hiring of the providers."

"From previous experience, you will see a PPM drafted by lawyers that does not really reflect the terms of the fund, but which will be applied to the strategy. You need to pay special attention to remove any unnecessary language, which could prevent an investor from investing. I have come across liquidity terms or some kind of risk definitions in the PPM which were not appropriate for the strategy the portfolio manager was running."

### Investors: Feedback and amber flags

To investors, he recommends they provide feedback to emerging managers that they chose not to invest in. "Not investing in a manager without telling where they have failed, impedes their ability to get better," he noted. He also stresses on the need to adapt due diligence on every strategy and on the life cycle of the manager, whatever the size.

Investors will always find mistakes in emerging managers. But some managers have mistakes that can be rectified.

"You have to take into account that an emerging manager can have a small team with different financial resources from an established manager's, so you will need to make a judgment call and differentiate from what is a red flag and what is an amber flag." Signet sees many new managers, and expects those managers with issues to work on those issues.

"We will come back to the managers at a later stage to verify whether all the issues spotted earlier have been rectified to consider an investment," he added. "It is not black and white as you can imagine!"

"How Does Seeding Impact Performance?," *Opalesque New Managers*, www.opalesque.com/new-managers/110/fundana-series-how-do-seed-deals .html.

**"Why Do Emerging Managers Fail?," *Opalesque New Managers*, www .opalesque.com/new-managers/111/focus-why-do-emerging-managers.html.

Although new managers have a certain level of risk, their ability to take on smaller opportunities can help them capture alpha in the market that the big guys miss. The research below by Peter Urbani offers insight into what these opportunities are.

## MISSED OPPORTUNITIES BY LARGE MANAGERS

Peter Urbani is the former CIO of Infiniti Capital, a former Hong Kong-based fund of funds group. Here he breaks out the performance of equity long and short picks by the top 696 large hedge funds represented in the Goldman Sachs VIP Hedge Fund Index during Q3 2012.

Goldman Sachs calculates both Long Basket (Figure 2.2) and Short Basket (Figure 2.3) VIP Indices. Both indices contain 50 stocks. Weights in the Long Basket are proxied by the frequency with which the stocks appear in the top 10 holdings of the underlying universe of hedge funds. Weights in the Short Basket are proxied by the dollar value of the shorts. The results are published quarterly by Goldman Sachs in their *Quarterly Hedge Fund Trend Monitor*.

Here we have used the Goldman Sachs data derived from 13F filings and recalculated the results using both the above-mentioned weighting system and an equally weighted long and short basket. We assume longs and shorts are matched with both accounting for 50 percent of the overall long/short portfolio.

In addition, we also calculate the portfolio opportunity distribution (POD) for each of the baskets. The POD method is a methodology popularized by Ron Surz and can be thought of as a Monte Carlo simulation of possible portfolios and returns built from the same underlying selection universe but with random weights. The distribution of portfolio returns generated by this method represents the range of possible portfolios that might have eventuated from the same selection universe or opportunity set had different weights been used.

What the findings show for Q3 is fairly unequivocally that the long positions taken by the underlying managers were generally better than those of the broader underlying market as proxied by the S&P 500. However, most funds did not reach the potential returns that the PODs indicated were available either through a lack of conviction reflected in position sizes or poor management of their short positions.

Bearing in mind that Q3 was a particularly good quarter for equities with the benchmark S&P 500 Index gaining +5.76 percent over the period, one would expect the long basket to have outperformed, also given the more concentrated number of holdings (50 vs. 500).

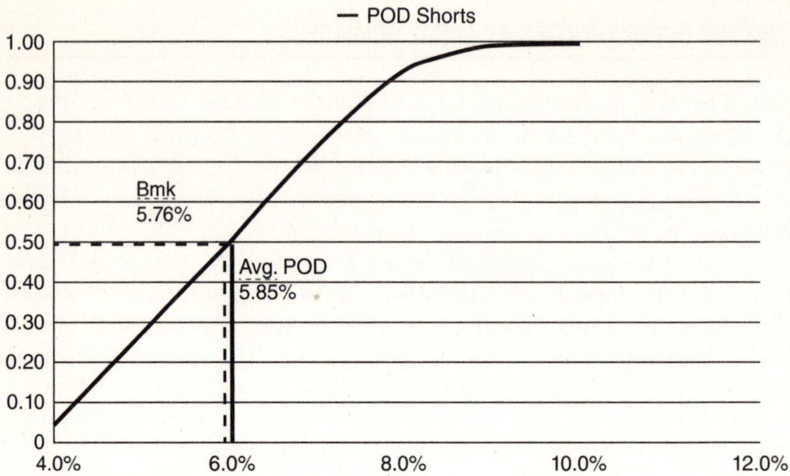


**FIGURE 2.2** Goldman Sachs Short Basket VIP Index With The POD Method

And in fact, this is what happened with the average long basket gaining between +10.62 percent and +9.61 percent, depending on which weighting method is used (proxy or equally weighted).

However, the overwhelmingly bullish trend for stocks over the period caused the short basket to return –4.24 to –5.67 percent. This

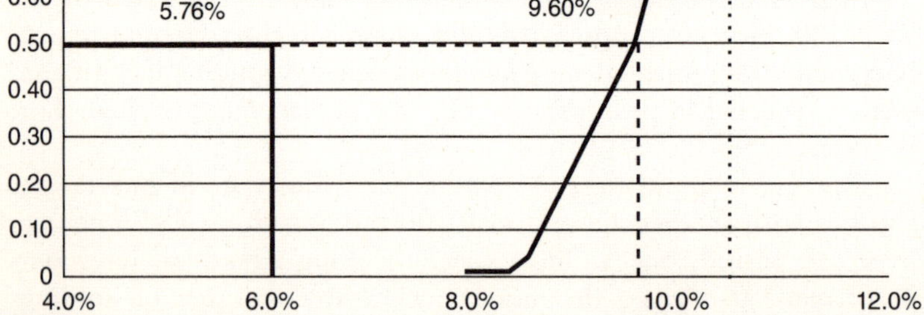


**FIGURE 2.3** Goldman Sachs Short Basket VIP Index With The POD Method

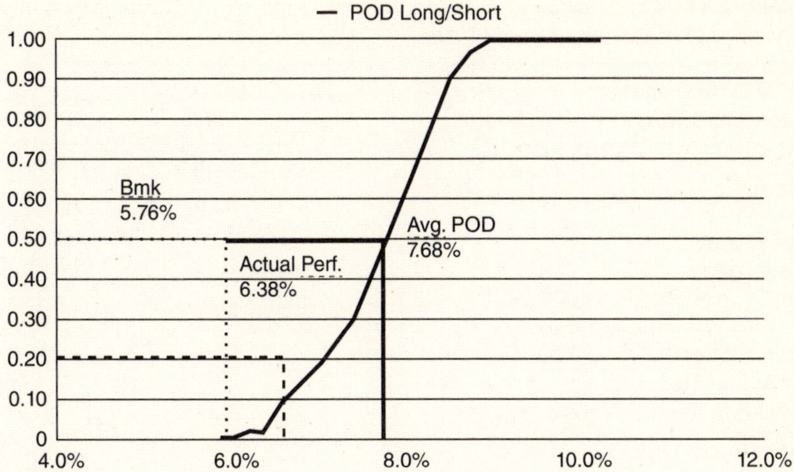


**FIGURE 2.4** Goldman Sachs Long-Short Basket Gross Returns

gives net long/short basket gross returns (Figure 2.4) of +6.38 percent and +3.94 percent, which after costs translate to net returns of +4.61 percent and +2.65 percent respectively.

The fact that the comparative hedge fund indices like the Eurekahedge long short index returned +3.27 percent and that this is closer to the +2.65 percent return generated by the equally weighted basket suggests either that the actual weights were closer to equal or that some larger managers mismanaged their short exposure thus failing to benefit fully from their generally good long picks.

This is further borne out by the POD for the short basket, which suggests that given sufficient leeway (i.e. ability to reverse shorts), an average return of roughly +5.85 percent was achievable from the same universe of short positions.

Over the same period the Emanagers Hedge Fund Index returned Table 2.11 +3.73 percent roughly 45bp more than that of the Long Short Equities Hedge Fund Index.

Some of the better picks during the quarter (Table 2.12) were as follows: Longs: 9.9 percent weight in AAPL generated +1.40 percent, 7 percent weight in GOOG generated +2.07 percent return. Shorts: –7.34 percent holding in INTC generated a +1.10 percent return, –1.88 percent holding in KO generated a +0.97 percent return, –2.39 percent in HPQ generated a +0.36 percent return.

**TABLE 2.11** Performance of Different Baskets Using Two Different Weighting Methods Weighted by No and Value

| Q3 Performance Returns (Gross) | Shorts | Longs | Net | S&P 500 |
|---|---|---|---|---|
| | –4.24% | 10.62% | 6.38% | 5.76% |
| Fixed Fees 2% | | | 0.50% | |
| Performance Fees 20% | | | 1.28% | |
| Returns (Net) | | | **4.61%** | |
| Long Short Equities Hedge Fund Index | | | **3.27%** | |
| Emanager Hedge Fund Index | | | **3.73%** | |
| **Equally Weighted** | | | | |
| **Q3 Performance Returns (Gross)** | **Shorts** | **Longs** | **Net** | **S&P 500** |
| | –5.67% | 9.61% | **3.94%** | 5.76% |
| Fixed Fees 2% | | | 0.50% | |
| Performance Fees 20% | | | 0.79% | |
| Returns (Net) | | | **2.65%** | |
| Long Short Equities Hedge Fund Index | | | **3.27%** | |
| Emanager Hedge Fund Index | | | **3.73%** | |

The major losing positions were in short positions that lost value over the period due to the strong rally in equity markets. These included: A –1 percent return generated by the –3.4 percent holding in GILD, a –0.39 percent return generated by the –2.22 percent holding in TWX and a –0.38 percent return generated by the –2.1 percent holding in PXD.

The only material losses in the long basket were from MSFT and PCLN and DG.

**TABLE 2.12** Changes in Basket Holdings Q2 and Q3

| Q2 2012 <GSTHHVIP> | | Q2 2012 <GSTHHVIP> | | Q32012 <GSTHHVIP> | | Q32012 <GSTHHVIP> | |
|---|---|---|---|---|---|---|---|
| **Hedge Fund** | **VIP Lon** | **Hedge Fund** | **VIP Sho** | **Hedge Fund** | **VIP Lon** | **Hedge Fund** | **VIP Sho** |
| **Added** | **Dropped** | **Added** | **Dropped** | **Added** | **Dropped** | **Added** | **Dropped** |
| JNJ | F | F | JNJ | IBM | INTC | INTC | IBM |
| AMAZN | BRK-B | BRK-B | AMZN | GE | WMT | WMT | GE |
| DUK | CSCO | CSCO | DUK | PM | ORCL | ORCL | PM |
| WMT | PXD | PXD | WMT | BRK-B | DUK | ISRG | BRK-B |
| ORCL | EMC | EMC | ORCL | EMC | KMI | MCD | EMC |
| SLB | HPQ | HPQ | SLB | CSCO | CBE | DE | CSCO |
| INTC | CRM | CRM | INTC | XOM | UAL | ORLY | XOM |
| KMI | WLP | PEP | DELL | COF | ARBA | CERN | CRM |
| DG | RKT | GILD | BXP | ABX | DAL | STX | ETN |
| UAL | STX | HAL | UNP | MDLZ | DTG | RRC | PEP |
| ARBA | VRX | USB | CERN | DTV | TRIP | TWC | ABT |
| DAL | BIDU | KMB | CCL | MPC | SUN | HNZ | KSS |
| SBAC | HES | ITW | AXP | OXY | CVS | MCO | UPS |
| TRIP | WMB | BHI | MCD | LLY | USB | | |
| SIX | ABX | UTX | FAST | MMM | CMG | | |
| SUN | COF | MO | FCX | MTB | WM | | |
| CVS | CPN | MYL | SPLS | SWN | KMB | | |
| FCX | DVN | | | NEM | SPG | | |
| CTRX | ILMN | | | NEE | ITW | | |
| | | | | AZO | BHI | | |
| | | | | PGR | AA | | |
| | | | | AET | UTX | | |
| | | | | MYL | HST | | |

"Missed Opportunities by Larger Managers," *Opalesque New Managers*, www.opalesque.com/new-managers/180/guest-article-does-size-of.html.

## SUMMARY

Emerging managers are often able to take advantage of true alpha in financial markets by virtue of their size and nimbleness. Much of that capability is determined by who invests in them, and when. Seeders, founders, and funds of funds can each bring their own benefits and tradeoffs, as shown above. Regulation may make it harder for new funds to come to market without a big initial backer, but the ability to capture smaller ticket opportunities in the market can make investing in emerging managers worthwhile.

## NOTES

1. "Stone Toro and Varden Pacific Talk about Their Funds," *Opalesque New Managers*, www.opalesque.com/new-managers/211/profiles-stone-toro-and-varden-pacific.html.
2. Comments made during the Opalesque Singapore Roundtable, www.opalesque.com/RT/RoundtableSingapore2013.html.
3. Comments made during the Opalesque France Roundtable, www.opalesque.com/RT/RoundtableFrance2013.html.
4. "Citi Transaction Services Responds to Struggling Fund of Funds Model with Fund of One," *Opalesque Alternative Market Briefing*, www.opalesque.com/644800/Citi_Transaction_Services_responds_to_struggling_fund_of480.html.
5. "Emerging Managers Can Offer Diversification in 'New Normal' Challenging Climate," *Opalesque Alternative Market Briefing*, www.opalesque.com/644545/Emerging_hedge_fund_managers_can_offer_diversification_in454.html.
6. "Seeders' Corner—SEB Offers Two Seeding Funds and Knowledge Transfer Too," *Opalesque New Managers*, www.opalesque.com/new-managers/165/seeders-corner-seb-offers-two.html.

CHAPTER 3

# How to Approach Investing in Hedge Funds: Investment Structures

In this chapter, we will consider the various structures and avenues available to investors who wish to invest in hedge funds. For potential investors, there are a variety of ways to access managers and each option carries with it somewhat unique due diligence requirements.

## ALLOCATION TYPES

### Single Allocation

The most straightforward way to invest in hedge funds is to make that first initial allocation to a manager. Single manager hedge funds generally have a minimum investment requirement to get started. Single allocations are typically the domain of ultra-high net worth investors or family offices who are willing to invest the time and due diligence into one person. Often, they will already know this person or come to them through a personal network. Many emerging manager allocations are done this way. For others, single allocations can take a fund from emerging to established if a manager's personal network is solid enough.

### Funds of Funds

Funds of funds are the granddaddy of hedge fund investing. In the early years, they ruled the roost when it came to allocations, outpacing family offices. Then, when institutions got into the mix fund of funds hit their peak, that is, until the largest institutions got smart enough about alternatives to invest on their own. So what is a fund of funds?

For our context, funds of funds are basically big pools of smaller hedge funds. The investment team at a fund of funds will work with clients creating portfolio solutions from a pool of hedge funds. That means they may look for a group of long/short managers, then a group of macro managers, and then a group of commodity trading advisers (CTAs). Or, they could just stick to long/short managers offering a pooled fund of handpicked long/short funds. Funds of funds in general can also exist with other asset classes; there are funds of mutual funds, private equity funds, real estate funds, and so on.

Early on, these investment teams were the first movers—looking at new and established managers and acting as kingmakers. Once a manager is chosen for a fund of funds, they get the benefit of broader distribution without much legwork. Instead, the fund of fund sets about marketing the pooled vehicle that contains them.

When big investors like pension funds, university endowments, and even some family offices were still trying to get their arms around investing in alternatives, funds of funds were an easy way to test drive that exposure. Funds of funds provided education, due diligence, and access—for a fee. Just like any other hedge fund, the principals of a fund of funds get a fee, as do the underlying managers.

BarclayHedge,[1] which provides a number of performance indices for the hedge fund industry, tracks the overall top performing funds of funds on its Barclay Fund of Funds Index. The index is simply the arithmetic average of the net returns of all the funds of funds that have reported that month. BarclayHedge also makes historical performance data available, should interested parties desire a look back.

Initially, this was a great value proposition for the manager and the fund of funds. However, as investors have become more educated and some institutions have brought in their own investment managers to oversee allocations, funds of funds have faced some rough sledding. Paying two sets of fees for hedge fund exposure in a down economy is a steep price tag for not much upside. This is especially true for investors who have teams in place in-house that understand alternatives. Still, funds of funds persist and can attract investors provided they have proven records of performance, and access to managers that investors may face difficulty finding on their own.

Gottex Fund Management is an example of a fund of funds provider. The Swiss firm creates and manages bespoke portfolios that can include multi-asset funds, funds of hedge funds, or separately managed accounts. Essentially, when they bring on a client they are going to work with them to determine how best to optimize their portfolio.

Gottex's total fee-earning assets were approximately $5.94 billion as of June 30, 2013.[2] The firm has recently made several strategic acquisitions that underline the trend of consolidation in the fund of funds space. Larger firms like Gottex are well positioned to maintain both their existing client base and scoop up smaller shops, given the range of services they offer. In

July of 2013, Gottex took a majority interest in UK-based Frontier Investment Management, which added $490 million to its multi-asset endowment business unit. The company is also moving forward with global partnerships in Australia, New Zealand, and Japan.

For investors that are considering a fund of funds for their hedge fund allocation, firms like Gottex are on pace to be the new face of the fund of funds business. Not only do they offer pooled vehicles, they create bespoke portfolios, and have the infrastructure to support newly popular structures like the fund of one or separately managed accounts. Essentially, they're an expanded fund of funds—in the early days few fund of funds offices had such a wide range of offerings available in-house. Much of this is the result of investor demand, but also business decisions—if funds of funds want to remain in business they will have to remain competitive and account for their higher price tag.

Other funds of funds are making a stand by focusing on specific niches in the industry that may require specialized backgrounds. California-based Pacific Alternative Asset Management Company (PAAMCO) could be placed in this group. PAAMCO looks at a variety of structured credit opportunities, along with emerging managers—both areas require a certain kind of specialized expertise.

PAAMCO has approximately $8.9 billion in assets under management, and is one of the older funds of funds in the business. Like Gottex, PAAMCO has a broad range of offerings it can provide to investors and the amount of assets it has under management means that it is also, in and of itself, an institutional-sized allocator. Once any investment firm enters the billion dollar club, it almost creates its own virtuous circle of fundraising. Investors like to see that firms have a lot of assets—it engenders a certain kind of trust and also preys on the fear that if they don't invest with the big shop they might miss out.

For example, PAAMCO has been involved in one of the few big break out trends since the crisis—re-investment in credit. Credit hedge funds saw a boom in investor inflows after many of the toxic assets that defined the space at the height of 2008 were unwound and sold off. Since then, credit has been one of the few pockets of yield return that starved investors could find in this low-growth environment. Credit funds saw steady inflows over 2012, and into 2013, but the pockets of opportunity are starting to dwindle. This is where the long-term investment expertise of fund of funds principals can be advantageous.

In this case, the credit portfolio manager for PAAMCO, Putri Pascualy, has evaluated many credit managers in order to decide which ones she will allocate to. The size of her potential allocation will also mean she may look at managers from emerging to established in an effort to fit them into her clients' portfolios. This is part of her role in PAAMCO, but an individual investor may not have the time or resources to do the same thing, especially when it comes to specialized credit strategies or regional opportunities.

"We like structured products," she offers as one example. "It's a relatively complex market, and an inefficient market that is attractive on a relative value basis. There aren't a lot of players in this space yet."[3] In this way, Pascualy takes a deep dive into credit, coming away with both broad market trends and specific managers who can capitalize on those trends. PAAMCO's clients gain from this view, without having to do all that legwork on their own.

Reading media accounts of funds of funds, you might expect that the pure play fund of funds offering is headed the way of the dodo bird. While they are on the endangered species list to be sure, they are adapting through specialization.

Mike Taylor, managing director and executive chairman of New Zealand boutique absolute return fund management house Pie Funds, is taking on the fund of funds space by going on a quest to find his fellow small cap absolute return funds across the globe.

Pie was founded in December 2007, and already has other, successful fund offerings in the market. Pie has NZ$100m ($85 million U.S.) under management in three funds, having started with just NZ$3m ($2.5 million U.S.) in 2007 and has, as the only small cap specialist manager in New Zealand, carved out a niche in the space. The three funds are Pie Australasian Growth Fund, the Pie Australasian Dividend Fund, and the Emerging Companies Fund. The new offering will be a Global Small Companies fund of fund.

Not only has Pie staked out a regional niche, but an operational one as well. Principals limit the amount of capital they allow in a given fund to preserve the nimbleness of each strategy. "If we removed the cap we would get significant demand from investors but it would be detrimental to returns," Taylor says.[4]

The Growth Fund is in the top 50 funds globally out of more than 180,000 ranked by Morningstar for five year returns, with a five-year return to March 31, 2013 of 27.6 percent per annum.

The idea for the fund of funds comes partly from their regional niche. New Zealand is still a relatively small market, with few competitors and a robust investor base. So far, that has equated to high quality investors and solid overall performance for Pie. However, when it comes to research, being so far removed can have its downsides.

"We would require a significant team of people on planes going out all over the world," Taylor says, so the firm is conducting its research to find other managers who look like them through data research and networking.

Ideally these entrepreneurial fund groups will come from the United States, Europe, the UK, Latin America, Asia, and the emerging markets. Taylor says: "Initially I thought it would be relatively easy to find people who look like us but it's actually quite hard." Taylor was inspired to set up a fund management firm because he found that retail managed funds in New Zealand were serial underperformers. "The funds are very actively managed because in the small company space things can change quite rapidly and we are not ashamed to admit if we get something wrong—if something changes we cut the investment," he says.

His aim for the new global fund is to have one of the lowest fee structures possible in a fund of funds, also reflecting the overall downward pressure on the industry. Yet, with a capacity of $250 million, fundraising is likely to go well. Relative to other funds of funds, $250 million is a small number and the targeted small cap focus will likely attract investors that are looking for that opportunity, versus investors looking for bottom dollar on generic long/short equity exposure.

### Fund of One

The fund of one structure is a brand new structure that has evolved out of the popularity of both funds of funds and managed accounts. Generally lower cost than a fund of funds, but with less of an administrative and trading burden than a separately managed account, the fund of one has emerged, filling the white space between these structures.

Investors in the fund of one model get much of the same control that they would through a separately managed account in terms of customization options. Those customizations are then coupled with the due diligence and infrastructure support common to funds of funds.

"Funds of hedge funds are at an inflection point," says John Mackin, Global Head of Marketing and Business Development at Protégé Partners, a fund of funds.[5] Protégé Partners was founded in 2002, and Makin says plainly that taken together, the fees and lukewarm returns in the fund of funds space has been hard for investors to swallow since 2008.

In recent years, separately managed accounts have seen increasing popularity as institutions, family offices, and even high net worth individuals use the structure as a means of test driving managers or strategies before going all in. However, separately managed accounts come with a significant level of due diligence and infrastructure responsibilities. At a minimum, this reality means an uphill climb for well-resourced investors, and is a near impossibility for middle market investors.

The fund of one is set up as a limited partnership, with investments made into underlying hedge fund comingled vehicles. Unlike the $250 million or above price tag for separately managed accounts, funds of one can come in at $50 million or above. They also benefit from having fund-of-funds style governance, including boards of directors and Cayman Islands Monetary Authority (CIMA).

"Everyone thought managed accounts would be the next big thing," explains Peter Hill, Global Head of Fund of Hedge Fund Services at Citi

Transaction Services. "But, what limits managed accounts is that they are very expensive and they require an entire infrastructure." Separate managed account platforms can involve monitoring tens of managers and the necessary due diligence for each of those managers.

Through a fund-of-one structure, investors have consultation and due diligence baked in. Rather than building that infrastructure in house, investors can access it as they would with a more traditional fund of funds structure while still retaining control through customization.

"Essentially this creates a stickier client. We've seen sovereign wealth funds for example, look at this structure over creating their own hedge fund program. Large institutions are looking, too—Aberdeen runs a $10 billion fund of one program," Hill says.

"We've been able to do this without a change to our flagship product," Mackin adds.

### Working with a Consultant

Often a punch line, hedge fund consultants—like consultants in virtually all other industries—promise expert views and access. When it comes to hedge funds, investors will be able to sort the legitimate consultants from the less than awesome pretty quickly. Unlike the vagaries of corporate mission statements or visioning sessions, consulting on hedge fund allocations requires fairly technical expertise. If a consultant recommends hedge funds that fail to pass a due diligence questionnaire, that consultant is going to find him or herself out of a job. Hedge funds, and the universe of people who can invest in them, are still a pretty small group.

### VETERAN HEDGE FUND CONSULTANT STILL BELIEVES IN VALUE OF ALTERNATIVES

***Beverly Chandler***

Veteran hedge fund consultant Anthony Hodges set out his shingle again in the UK in 2013, offering his services to hedge funds and their investors. Hodges has spent some 30-plus years in the industry, having started working as a commodity trading advisor developing what were then revolutionary mechanical trading systems back in 1978. He has most recently spent seven years in Dubai, as the Executive Director in charge of the Ruler's $1.5 billion hedge fund portfolio. In the 1980s and 1990s he was Managing Director of Rudolf Wolff Fund

Management, a multi-manager hedge fund, and subsequently he was at Sabre Fund Management in charge of their fund of funds.

Hodges pinpoints technology as providing the biggest developments in the hedge fund industry since he joined it. "Technology has added to liquidity which is good for the markets but also has adverse consequences when things like a flash crash happen, but people learn from that. Hedge fund managers are nimble at figuring out what things work and what don't work," he says.

Looking back to the hedge fund industry's early days in the UK, Hodges believes it used to be more of a club, with not many participants. "Now it's more institutional and widely accepted by the pension fund industry," he says. The managed futures sector, where Hodges started out, is now dominated by the big 20 managed futures funds, which haven't had a very good run over the past three to four years, in terms of performance. "The biggest single factor affecting their performance are zero interest rates, which give them no 'wriggle room' as they hold so much money in cash," Hodges says. "Now that has to come out of performance, which is more challenging."

"There are new institutions in the market like central banks which dominate the markets and take action in the markets with announcements and pronouncements which dictate market direction to the exclusion of normal supply and demand fundamentals," Hodges says. Where managers have built models on traditional fundamentals they are over-ridden by Ben Bernanke, former chairman of the Federal Reserve, announcing he is bringing in another round of quantitative easing. "Managers will have to adapt if it's a permanent factor."

Hodges believes that markets have been distorted and it's a question of how long this is going to last. "How long will central banks feel they have to intervene in the markets?" he asks.

During his time running the private investment portfolio of the King of Dubai, which was effectively a family office rather than a sovereign wealth role, Hodges saw similar funds suffering badly through the credit crunch. "A lot of those types of funds were over-leveraged so when the music stopped they were left with a lot of debt on assets that were declining in value—it was a common story across the board," he says. The multi-manager fund of hedge fund style portfolio that he built up in Dubai was well diversified. "It was across as many strategies as I could find and understand but it did suffer from the cash machine phenomenon as it was relatively liquid," Hodges says, as he had to cash in investments to pay out and cover other areas that were struggling.

During the crisis, he was disappointed at the performance of some of the bigger and better managers he was invested with such as Citadel and SAC, which had too many portfolio managers doing their own thing in areas that weren't related to the broader fund. Despite this, he says he would likely invest in the same big names again.

"The managers have learned quite a lot from this and rebuilt their businesses. They are nimble on their feet and react more quickly than a fund of fund business would, as they are dealing on day-to-day business in the market, so they are the quickest to adapt. They are there to make money."

Now back in the UK, Hodges is looking to apply his experience with hedge fund managers who want to outsource some of their due diligence or special research into peer group analysis. He is also working with managers that want someone to review their business processes and non-executive directorships.

He is also interested in working with institutions that want advice on alternatives, how to approach them, and build a business from them. With his 30-odd years of experience of the hedge fund industry, he still believes in it. "I think it's a much cleverer way of managing money than in traditional investments," he says.

"Veteran Hedge Fund Consultant Still Believes in Value of Alternatives," *Opalesque Alternative Market Briefing*, www.opalesque.com/645132/Veteran_hedge_fund_consultant_still_believes_in_value513.html.

## SHOULD EMERGING MANAGERS GO TO INVESTMENT CONSULTANTS?

### *Benedicte Gravrand*

As long as there is a need for expertise in any industry, there will be expert consultants offering their knowledge and services. The hedge fund industry is no different. Hedge fund consultants service hedge funds with their know-how and network—be it in investment strategy, research, or marketing.

Investment consultants help investors, particularly institutional investors, with their hedge fund allocations. Those consultants are gaining more cachet in the industry and are often directly competing with funds of hedge funds.

According a Citi Prime Finance survey[6] published in June 2012 titled "Institutional Investment in Hedge Funds: Evolving Investor Portfolio Construction Drives Product Convergence," global assets invested with hedge fund firms could rise from today's $2.1 trillion to more than $5 trillion as a result of two emerging trends. Firstly, institutional investors may add $1 trillion to protect against risks and get more diversification; secondly, as there may be a *convergence zone* between hedge funds and traditional assets, an additional $2 trillion could come into the hedge fund industry in the form of regulated alternatives and long-only products.

The Citi survey also observes a trend among intermediaries, such as consultants and funds of funds, in which there is also convergence. The number of hedge funds grew by 66 percent from 2003 to 2007 (4,598 to 7,637), and the number of "fund of fund intermediaries" (funds of hedge funds or FoHFs), grew by 251 percent in this period—from 781 to 2,462. During those years, FoHFs were the primary conduit through which many institutional investors channeled their money into hedge funds.

Eventually, both FoHFs and investors were caught off guard by the asset-liability mismatch they had created. After 2008, investors started to invest more directly into single-manager hedge funds and less in FoHFs—to avoid another liquidity problem and the double layer of fees, and because they had more experience navigating through the hedge fund industry. According to eVestment, in 2002, assets invested in FoHFs accounted for almost 53 percent of the hedge fund industry's total AUM; that declined to 48 percent in 2007, and by an additional 12 percent by the end of 2011, to account for 36 percent.

Between 2003 and 2007, some of the institutional investors who wanted to change the 60 percent equities/40 percent bonds approach typically worked with industry consultants to come up with a new allocation into alternatives. After 2008, investors started investing directly into single-manager hedge funds through their newly built alternatives investment teams and through relationships with "an emerging set of alternatives-focused industry consultants to support their portfolio construction and due diligence efforts."

"Before 2008, consultants were almost exclusively focused on providing advice to institutional investors, and though some offered operational due diligence services, this was a little utilized capability," the Citi report notes. The post-2008 shift in the way investors allocated their money "resulted in a substantial realignment of the intermediary space."

Institutional investors became increasingly reliant on consultants, according to Citi. So much so that consultants now often act as an extension of the institutional allocators' team: "Not only have consultants maintained their traditional advice-giving role; they are now seen as a critical 'seal of approval' in terms of operational due diligence, and the 'lists' they maintain of approved funds have become an industry norm in terms of access. . . ."

"There is still room for growth in the aggregate demand for hedge funds. The highest allocation of our clients is at 20 percent, but we have lots of clients that are only at 1 to 3 percent and they could grow to 10 percent. That's a multibillion opportunity per client," an alternatives-focused consultant told Citi.

FoHFs are adapting. They started offering platforms for funds of one (a separate share class for a single investor, to avoid the proximity risk) or of separately managed accounts (SMAs). "Funds of funds could be in real trouble," an outsourced CIO told Citi. "They're not dying. They're just consolidating into consultants."

FoHF managers are also competing with consultants in the advisory space now. Their extensive investment team differentiates them from consultants who do "not have any financial stake in the success or failure of their recommended managers."

A $10 billion + hedge fund told Citi: "More and more, we're seeing people use funds of funds as an advisor and more and more pensions are going direct. We saw a $30 million ticket from a client of one of our former funds of funds. Having old legacy fund of fund relationships has been very beneficial for us. We've raised several million dollars from this channel."

Many FoHFs now also have a series of investor-aligned portfolios where they decide upon allocations jointly with their clients. So from their origins as access vehicles to hedge funds, they are moving on to bringing many other services to investors.

Another intermediary that has emerged of late, especially in the United States, is the outsourced CIO. They may have been FoHFs managers or direct allocators in the past and then set up firms that "work directly with institutional investors to structure their overall portfolios and manage that capital on their behalf."

Traditionally, for manager searches, consultants would provide a shortlist of managers for the client to select from, says Jenny Morton, head of Global Consultant Relations at Man Group, a $52.7 billion hedge fund firm. If the funds did not perform well enough, clients would criticize consultants and challenge them to "put their skin in the game," making the selections themselves.

"With the increased complexity of the asset classes being put in front of Trustees, the amount of resources required to make considered informed decisions had increased significantly over time," she explains. After 2008, pension plans required more diversification and alternatives—therefore the amount of resource required increased still.

To choose managers on behalf of clients, consultants started to either launch their own funds or to charge higher fees. A number of large consulting firms have done well in this area in the last few years, and are now in direct competition with the FoFs business. This comes as funds of funds have started to offer more bespoke solutions to adapt to the changing business environment.

"A good example would be some of the work that we have done recently with a scheme that wanted to specifically add diversifying hedge fund strategies with low Beta to equity markets to its portfolio," she notes. "We built something that only included strategies like Managed Futures and Macro Funds to blend in well with their other assets."

So, what is Man's stance on competing consultants?

"Just as we would hope to be chosen by the client in a traditional search, we would hope to be chosen as a preferred manager in each consultant's implemented line-up. Consultants offering implemented consulting still look for investment manager fund of hedge fund solutions, although I think it would be fair to say that this has decreased in the last few years as they have developed their own offerings," Morton says.

"It is a free marketplace and each client has different needs and can choose the solution and firm that best fits their needs," she concludes. She adds that if she were a client looking at the market place for a third party provider to assist around funds of funds, she would look at research resources, experience in manager selection, performance, and, especially when looking at alternative investments, operational due diligence capabilities.

### Consultants with practical experience are the best bet

Allenbridge, Aksia, Mercer, Albourne are the top investment consultants to investors in hedge funds. Ian Morley, head of alternatives at Allenbridge, is an example of a veteran consultant. Founding chairman of the Alternative Investment Management Association (AIMA),

Morley started his own alternative assets consultancy, Wentworth Hall Consultancy Ltd., in London in 2006. He is also a senior hedge funds consultant for Allenbridge Investment Consultants. He consults on alternatives for institutional investors and family offices through both channels.

"Consultants, historically, used to be involved with asset allocation and these days it has got a lot broader," Morley says. "So, sometimes we might put an independent trustee on a board, sometimes we might help them look at corporate governance."

In 2008, he says, the tide went out and we saw who had been swimming naked. So funds of funds, which had not diversified their portfolios efficiently and invested poorly disappointed investors. Add to that the expensive double layer of fees (underlying hedge funds' as well as the funds of funds' fees) and the fact that consultants were then cheaper than funds of funds, to find the environment became very difficult for FoFs.

Morley notes that the FoFs business grew spectacularly between 2001 and 2008 because pension funds that were badly damaged by the dot-com crash of 2001 took a serious interest in alternatives for the first time and they went to funds of funds. "Because they [consultants] knew little about it, they mostly forced the clients into long/short equity," Morley explains.

"Now, if you are in long/short equity, it is going to be 60 to 70 percent correlated to long equity. It proved quite difficult in those days to push clients into CTAs and global macro, because it all sounded very strange and peculiar, and the consultants basically did not understand it. If the consultants did not understand it, the clients were not going to understand it." Although FoHFs had a bad time in 2008, he adds, most of them have a knowledge of the industry that is practical rather than theoretical.

Consultants are not just used for advising and stock picking; they are becoming a useful element of protection in an increasingly litigious world. "Trustees . . . have personal fiduciary responsibility," he explains. "So, if they are going into a complex area, which they do not know very well, legally it gives them an element of protection to say 'we hired the consultant, the consultant recommended Mr. Madoff' or 'the consultant recommended this fund of funds of Mr. Madoff, it is their fault not ours'."

Morley recommends emerging managers to wait to see consultants when they are up and running as professional firms; "they will only give you a certain amount of time and—it is the old adage—you will not get a second chance to make a first impression." Emerging managers indeed may find it more difficult to get through to consultants who work for institutions. They often require a minimum AUM before allocating, which can be difficult for managers who are still raising foundational assets.

This turf war between FoHFs and consultants is becoming very interesting, Morley says. It will be probably quite good for clients, who will see their fees come down as a consequence. He recommends clients to stick to consultants who have had practical experience in the industry. "You would not get on an airplane with someone who has only done a simulation course," he explains. "You want someone who is a real pilot."

Kevin Cook, founding partner of Autumn Capital, believes that funds of funds may continue to see their assets dwindle. Autumn Capital Partners LLP is an investment consultancy firm, working with managers and allocators to identify and develop businesses and investment strategies. "The larger funds were a little bit cleverer, a little ahead of the curve in terms of understanding that their business model was broken and that they needed to adapt in order to survive," he says.

Consultants have continued to pick up business with the institutionalization of the hedge fund industry, he says. Institutional investors' teams are often small and require more due diligence than before, creating opportunities for consultants. Cook also cites the very useful liability issue also mentioned by Morley.

Consultants are still providing an extra level of due diligence and an extra level of protection for the institutional investment teams.

"In my opinion, funds of funds will always exist and there will always be a place for multi-manager products, particularly at the emerging end of the market, which the consultants do not yet have the breadth to cover particularly well," he notes.

While this conversation highlights some of the benefits of working with a consultant, significant evolution in financial structures like we have seen with the Undertakings for Collective Investment in Transferrable Securities (UCITS) vehicles can also highlight some of the inherent weaknesses of a consultancy relationship. Unlike portfolio managers, lawyers, and fund administrators who are deeply involved in the granular operations of a fund, consultants can face some lag time when big changes happen.

A 2013 survey from Alix Capital[7] shows that 38 percent of respondents believe that investment consultants are behind the curve when it comes to advising their clients on UCITS. The survey showed that 69 percent of respondents planned to increase their allocations to UCITS over the next year even though they are having a hard time finding expert advice. Private banks are expected to be the main buyers of alternative UCITS products, followed closely by pension funds.

"While the majority of institutional investors understand the advantages that UCITS hedge funds can offer them, especially in regards to liquidity, transparency, and regulation, there are still many improvements that need to be made to improve the perception of UCITS as a competitive framework. Providers need to enhance communications with the investment consultant community to improve their understanding and awareness of the UCITS alternative space," said Louis Zanolin, CEO of Alix Capital.

### Third-Party Marketers

Similar to consultants are third-party marketers. Third-party marketers actually work for hedge fund managers or brokers, and may behave similarly to hedge fund consultants, although their underlying agenda will be for the managers they work for, not necessarily investors.

Third-party marketers are a more high touch view of hedge fund distribution. Typically, third-party marketers will use seasoned investment sales professionals to market products to both investors and platforms, thus increasing overall distribution of a fund beyond simple asset raising. Third-party marketers maintain relationship with a universe of financial services professionals that include broker-dealers, investment advisors, investment platform gatekeepers, institutions, family offices, and high net worth individuals.

Unlike consultants who typically serve a single constituency when they work, marketers are often paid a percentage of assets raised. As such, it behooves them to work across as many different relationships as they can to raise assets directly and indirectly by increasing distribution of a fund.

Third-party marketers can work independently or through an established marketing company. Companies or individuals that are able to show a proven track record are generally well known in the industry. Individuals or smaller independent shops have had a harder time in the post-crisis environment as managers are loathe to give away information about how they operate especially while the overall asset raising environment is highly competitive. Still, a manager whose real skill is running money and not marketing will likely reach out to one of these companies or individuals to represent their fund. Investors then may come across one or more marketers during their manager-selection phase.

### Separately Managed Accounts

In the wake of 2008, when many investors found their capital trapped in lock ups, gates, or just illiquid positions, separately managed accounts found new life. The structure itself really came into its own during the 1990s, and has often found favor with investors who prefer to test drive a manager before they allocate.

As the name would suggest, a separately managed account is an investment account that is operated alongside a hedge fund rather than as part of it. In most cases, the separately managed account is run exactly the same way as the hedge fund, but investors in those accounts face fewer restrictions and get a greater amount of transparency. However, with that power comes great responsibility. Investors who opt for separately managed accounts will need to have an operational infrastructure that rivals that of the hedge funds they invest in.

Administration, due diligence, trade evaluation—essentially all of the activities that the hedge fund does—the investor in a separately managed account will also need to do. These accounts often require a greater initial investment, to boot. Still, for an investor that needs or wants the freedom to enter or exit a fund at will, the structure has promise.

Separately managed accounts also mitigate the risk of fraud and style drift, because there are two eyes looking at the trading decisions. Since 2004, the number of investors choosing managed accounts has nearly tripled according to Sungard,[8] a financial services provider.

Initially, fund managers balked at the idea of providing managed accounts given how much heavy lifting is required for their set up. Now, driven by institutional demand, managed accounts are becoming part of the normal offering a manager will have. Sovereign wealth funds have also expressed a clear preference for the structure.

Beyond individual managers offering managed accounts, platforms have emerged that give investors access to managers on the platform through the managed account structure. Sciens Alternative Investments, part of the Sciens Capital Management Group, provides a managed accounts platform. Sciens has a number of managers on the platform, including U.S.-based Revolution Capital Management LLC and Japan's Stats Investment Management Company Limited. Both trading advisors are replicating their existing benchmark strategies in cells recently launched on the Sciens Managed Account Platform.[9]

As of June 2013, the number of institutional users on the Sciens MAP had increased by more than 200 percent year on year end.

Revolution Capital Management has launched a cell on the platform that replicates its Alpha program, which follows a commodity trading advisor (CTA) strategy that develops quantitative systematic trading systems that seeks to have low correlations to existing managed futures offerings.

The Alpha program is designed to be diversified with short- and medium-term pattern recognition and targets 12 percent annual volatility based on daily returns.

The Ginga Service Sector Fund, managed by Stats Investment Management Company, is also replicated in a cell on the Sciens MAP. The benchmark fund is a Japanese Equity Long/Short fund, which focuses on the high-tech (software service, Internet, media telecom) and service sectors (business and consumer services). The manager seeks to take advantage of the low analyst coverage for the service sector, the sector's dynamic business environment, and the frequent valuation gaps as sources of substantial alpha.

The two funds show how diverse offerings on a managed accounts platform can be. Investors are drawn to the platform because the platform provider also offers much of the infrastructure and administrative support needed for managed accounts. Sciens MAP furnishes client users with in-depth access to its proprietary, integrated risk analytics technology, made available to investors via S.M.A.R.T. Sciens' interactive look through application allows investors to perform in-depth analysis of their exposures at both the single strategy and the aggregated portfolio level. Data feeds are based upon T+2 reporting on a by position basis.

By investing through a separate account, the client retains ownership of the assets and sees what's going on in the account. The manager trades in the account, typically following the strategy of a benchmark fund. A third-party administrator performs functions such as accounting and collateral management.

Nathanaël Benzaken, a managing director at Lyxor Asset Management, which oversees a big managed account platform, says managed account providers are not all equal and investors need to do due diligence on the platform before doing due diligence on the hedge fund.[10]

For individual investors, there is a danger is that the manager may not be able to reproduce the benchmark fund's performance because an account has too little money. Other challenges for the manager with a separately managed account include lower fees, the effort to ensure trades are in line with the guidelines, and the risk of disclosing the "secret sauce" by allowing the customer to see the trading in the account.

## SUMMARY

There are a variety of structures accredited investors can use when investing in hedge funds. Those structures range from the single individual allocation to managed accounts. In working with these structures, consultants and third-party marketers also fill the thought leadership gap with expert views and access to funds. Consultants and marketers are newer to the field than funds of funds, which have long been hedge fund kingmakers, but they are giving fund of funds teams a run for their money.

## NOTES

1. BarclayHedge, www.barclayhedge.com.
2. "Swiss Fund of Funds Gottex's AUM Down 5.7 Percent from Last Quarter (to $5.27b)," www.opalesque.com/fullarticle/647988/Swiss_fund_of_funds_AUM_down798.html.
3. "CLOs, Structured Products, Japan Attract the Eye of Fund of Funds," www.opalesque.com/646495/CLOs_structured_products_Japan_attract_the_eye_of649.html.
4. "Boutique Absolute Return Fund of Funds Searches for Compatible Partners Globally," www.opalesque.com/646116/Boutique_absolute_return_fund_of_funds_searches_for611.html.
5. "Citi Transaction Services Responds to Struggling Fund of Funds Model with Fund of One," *Opalesque Alternative Market Briefing*, www.Opalesque.com/644800/Citi_Transaction_Services_Responds_to_Struggling_Fund_of480.html.
6 "Citi Prime Finance Survey: Institutional Investment Increases Competition," *Opalesque Alternative Market Briefing*, www.opalesque.com/industry-updates/2623/citi-prime-finance-survey-institutional-investment-increase-competition.html.
7. "Alix Capital Survey Finds Consultants behind the Curve on UCITS Hedge Funds," www.opalesque.com/industry-updates/3183/alix-capital-survey-finds-consultants-behind-the-curve.html.
8. "Focus: A Look at Managed Accounts," *Opalesque New Managers,* www.opalesque.com/new-managers/58/look-at-managed-accounts.html.
9. "Sciens Managed Account Platform Adds New Managers and Sees 35 Percent Annual Asset Growth," *Opalesque*, www.opalesque.com/industry-updates/3483/sciens-managed-account-platform-adds-new-managers-and.html.
10. "Practitioner Viewpoint: Executives from Lyxor, Lighthouse Partners and Other Firms Discussed Managed Accounts at An Event. We Bring You the Highlights," *Opalesque Futures Intelligence*, www.opalesque.com/OFI1105/Practitioner_Viewpoint_Executives_from_Lyxor_Lighthouse_Partners_and105.html.

CHAPTER 4

# How to Approach Investing in Hedge Funds: Service Providers and Due Diligence

Now that we have outlined the various structures by which an investor can allocate to hedge funds, we'll unpack who supports this process on both sides and why.

## MEET THE SERVICE PROVIDERS

Just like every other established industry, hedge funds have service providers or vendors that perform specific, often bulky, and mundane tasks. Hedge fund service providers can range from the expected—lawyers and accountants, to the less well known—hedge fund administrators, technology providers, prime brokers, and auditors that ensure all the trains keep running on time.

### Hedge Fund Administrators

Hedge fund administrators can be independent entities like Maples Fund Services that only provide valuations and other strictly administrative support. Or, administrative services can be offered as part of a custodial banking relationship—think Northern Trust or BNY Mellon. Custodial banks typically have control of assets and also engage in tax support functions and other bank-type transactions, whereas an independent entity is going to be solely focused on fund services.

So, what are *fund services*? Hedge funds require the use of administrators to help them out with several critical functions like providing valuations of the fund itself, or individual assets. Hedge fund administrators are also record keepers providing a record of fund transaction activity to both the manager and the investor. A special relationship exists between hedge fund managers and their administrators, because it behooves a manager to be transparent to an administrator given this set of duties. In order for an administrator to be able to appropriately value funds or assets, they need to have complete information.

This relationship also makes administrators go-to companies for investors, lawyers, consultants, or researchers looking for information on the hedge fund industry as a whole. In some cases, administrators will provide anonymous, high-level trend data based on the pool of funds that report to them.

Historically, administrators would provide what's known as a NAV, or net asset value. "Striking a NAV," is a common phrase for establishing the value of a fund after expenses. On the surface, this may seem like a straightforward task, but accounting standards break out assets and establish guidelines for how best to evaluate their real market value. For stocks and bonds this is pretty easy. For illiquid or exotic investments, finding the real value can be much more difficult.

Examples of hard to value assets can be tranches of debt a hedge fund invests in or derivatives. Values for these types of investments can often change rapidly (positively and negatively), or they may be hard to assign fair market value to at all, if the instrument is tangled up with some other underlying asset. Hedge fund administrators then, typically have prior experience working directly with these types of assets, or can tap an expert to help assign a realistic value. On a financial statement, types of assets, and their values are broken out as shown in Table 4.1.

Like with almost every corner of the hedge fund industry, administrators have also had to make changes to their business since 2008. The asset breakdown above is one of those changes. Level 1 and Level 2 are pretty straightforward. It's hard to argue on a financial statement that the value of a public company is something other than what its already existing share price and financial disclosures would have you believe (thus, marked to market). Similarly, options pricing models exist and are used in every day transactions, so using these models as guideposts in a Level 2 valuation makes sense (i.e., marked to model). The real sticky wicket, however, is Level 3.

During the crisis, mortgage-backed securities (MBS) saw their value stay the same even when things started to go south. Eventually, like every other asset, they crashed, but for sellers of those securities at the time, and investors who were trying to assess what they had, and what they lost, the fact that their stated value was higher than the reality of the market created significant issues. Some financial markets participants argue that the mark to market rule for Level 1 assets also made the crisis worse.[1] Illiquid and esoteric markets included commonly in Level 3 trade infrequently, and the

**TABLE 4.1** Types of Assets According to Financial Accounting Standards Board (FASB) Topic 820 (Formerly Known as FAS 157)

| Classification | Types of Assets | Valuation Qualities |
|---|---|---|
| Level 1 | Stocks<br>Bonds<br>Anything "marked to market" | Readily observable prices<br>Clear price moves, obvious value |
| Level 2 | Interest rate swaps<br>Non-active bonds<br>Anything "marked to model" | • Values can be easily modeled<br>• Pricing moves are observable/exist<br>• Overall value still mostly certain |
| Level 3 | Mortgage backed securities | Infrequent trading volume on these assets makes valuation difficult to observe |
| | Private equity investments | Price ranges may remain the same even if problems arise |
| | Long dated or complex derivatives | Overall value unclear, can be manipulated |

"Fair Value Measurement (Topic 820)," Financial Accounting Standards Board, www.fasb.org/cs/BlobServer?blobcol=urldata&blobtable=MungoBlobs&blobkey=id&blobwhere=1175822486936&blobheader=application/pdf.

participants in those markets have, in the past, created mutually agreeable values and traded on them, which raises the ire of regulators and can create big problems for investors.[2]

In 2010, the Financial Accounting Standards Board (FASB) started working on making Level 3 better. That's when they changed the asset breakdown to "Topic 820," and sought to require those providing valuations to show their work. This effort is designed to make pricing clearer to both the market and investors. Some market participants argue that the concept of fair value is hopelessly flawed, but for administrators, accountants, auditors, and investors, this is what we have.

Changes like those required by the FASB, and others driven by institutions wanting more disclosures and more active risk management, have significantly impacted hedge fund administrators. Now, they offer more services—often reluctantly—and have really moved into their own within the broader hedge fund business hierarchy. Before, they were almost shadow accountants corroborating the values of equities.

Administrators not only support the fund, but they can also be beneficial to investors—providing independent audit reviews and safeguarding against fraud or inflated values. New regulations requiring hedge funds to provide greater disclosures of their position and transaction activities also brought administrators into the spotlight. Administrators have ready and organized access to much of the information required by regulators, and have taken on greater compliance responsibility by providing that data in regulatory filings. As such, they've also ramped up their use of technology, data warehousing, and risk reporting.

Administrators may be doing more, for less, in an effort to stay competitive, but the amount of assets under administration (AUA) is growing steadily. According to eVestment's 2013 administrators survey, hedge fund AUA grew by 13.31 percent in the first half of 2013, significantly improving from the 5.56 percent AUA increase during the second half of 2012. Total alternative investment assets under administration reached $5.904 trillion. Hedge fund AUA ballooned to $3.411 trillion, while funds of hedge funds' AUA rose modestly to $812.5 billion. The survey compiled data from 33 participating administration firms and 4,036 funds.[3]

"Administrators have grown to become an integral part of the alternatives industry. The rise of regulations globally, and subsequent reporting requirements, have forced hedge funds to lean on their administrative partners more and more each survey period," wrote Peter Laurelli, Vice President and Head of Industry Research, eVestment in the report.

Administrators can also be forces for change in the industry. In August 2011, the Open Protocol Enabling Risk Aggregation (OPERA) standard was launched as a means to align transparency reporting formats and methodologies to benefit investors. OPERA covers all areas relating to performance and risk reporting for hedge funds. It defines common principles, metrics, and language to facilitate better understanding and aggregation of risk information. According to the working group,[4] the Open Protocol guidelines provide a vehicle for managers to provide consistent transparency reporting in the current climate of increased investor demand for transparency. Since the project got underway, administrators and risk management service providers have been actively involved in efforts to standardize data and disclosures.

According to Oliver Scully, Managing Director at Citco Fund Services the largest hedge fund administrator, the fundamental relationship between the administrator and the funds has not necessarily changed over the past few years. However, those funds that were traditionally self-administered had to appoint a third-party independent administrator after the financial collapses of 2008 and the Madoff scandal. A lot of them start by asking the minimum that one can ask of an administrator: the production of an independent NAV. But many are now starting to see that administrators can add value and are thinking about moving "from internal operations to a third party outsourced relationship."[5]

"A lot of managers come to the likes of Citco and look at what additional aspects of their daily operation they can outsource to a third party," he explains. "In other words, to make use of our scalability; and the benefits of scale are to essentially retain the same level of control by outsourcing some of the functions to reduce cost."

Investors now expect new funds to include some high-pedigree managers, but also back office and support staff. And administrators, according to Scully, also look for "first class experienced COOs, CFOs, and operational staff in the funds as well."

## Risk Management

Alongside hedge fund administrators, risk departments and risk management data providers, have come into the post-crisis spotlight. Before 2008, many investors were content to get a thin risk report once a year, put it in the circular file, and enjoy their double digit returns. However, with the crisis and its assorted scandals, risk departments were suddenly catapulted from the back office and into the pitch meeting.

There are a variety of companies that provide hedge funds with the technology they need to create financial models in order to evaluate risk. Others work through administrators and provide risk data based on the transactional information sent to administrators. Maples Fund Services, for example, provides a risk dashboard as part of its administrative technology.[6]

Now, regulators are getting into the mix, requiring detailed risk information and modeling that goes beyond traditional value-at-risk (VaR) models. For providers of such software, this is a welcome change and not just for business. Risk managers have been beating the drum about the ineffectiveness of overreliance on VaR, and the need for more active conversations around risk overall.

As hedge funds look for ways to meet increasing regulatory and investor demand for more information, many are going to firms offering data analytics solutions. More than traditional risk reporting, analytics firms offer multi-model risk and portfolio testing—an approach that is beneficial to both investors and managers looking to understand performance, tail-risk, and overall portfolio risk.

FinAnalytica, a risk data provider, led the way in creating multi-asset class predictive performance analytics for financial services. Zari Rachev, the firm's chief scientist spent more than 10 years on the math powering their products—research which is still being awarded patents. In essence, the process moves away from reliance on historical correlations and provides a framework for modeling asset returns by incorporating a flexible copula function based on a mixture between two copula functions that look at both parametric and empirical factors to provide data that reflects historical correlation and tail-risk.

"Correlations are not constant, they become more pronounced in the tails and are sharply higher in the left tail," explains David Merrill, CEO, FinAnalytica.[7] The process is a core part of their risk management and portfolio construction platform. According to Merrill, the multi-faceted approach is necessary for understanding the true risk of a complex portfolio—an understanding that is missing from coming onslaught of regulations.

"Historical models are not adequate if you have derivatives in your portfolio. Look at what happened with JPMorgan,[8] and in all of the questioning of those trades no one asked about the failure of those risk models," he says.

The same is also true for new requirements like Form PF. "Funds are telling the regulator which risk model they are using, and that's fine but you can't then put all those different models and portfolios together and see the risk—they could be completely different."

Understanding the differences between those models and avoiding the urge to rely on the most simplistic ones is critical. More and more managers and investors are taking this more seriously and having honest conversations around risk, but it's still a work in progress.

"Models aren't perfect, but they should be able to give you relevant results," Merrill explains.[9] Often, managers rely on simplistic models that they know well and are comfortable with, but this can often leave them vulnerable to fat tails, volatility clustering, skewness, and correlation asymmetry. Standard measures like VaR and their traditional modifications often fail to account for fat tails or market correlations, which can increase overall portfolio risk or lead to losses if missed.

According to Merrill, "the lack of evolution from commercial vendors is holding back the industry," in this area. Commercial-grade solutions for models that take into account fat tails, correlation, or volatility are often hard to find. This creates a disparity where managers who are more quantitatively focused build models to track fat tails on their own, and those that aren't comfortable with it don't. Simple models often predict that major events are very unlikely to happen, or at least will not happen on a time horizon soon enough to affect investment decisions, but in reality they happen much more often.

The multi-model approach brings more individuals into the risk conversation, Merrill notes. "Different people are going to need different information at different times." He explains that managers or investors may want to see historical performance, asset class breakdowns, or individual risk factors as they move through understanding the overall picture of a portfolio. "Simple models just aren't going to provide those facets of information," he says.

According to Merrill, the shift away from simple models is gradual, but the increased power of institutional investors is driving managers to models that take into account these additional factors. Given the capacity of institutional investors, and also their investment responsibilities, institutional investors have the capability to hire risk managers themselves and are beginning to ask granular questions in the due diligence process as well as over the life of the investment. "More risk management talent is moving to institutional investors, and it should be. Institutional investors should be willing to pay for it given their power and their recent losses," Merrill said.

Savvy managers can generate alpha by paying attention to risk models for more than just investor disclosures. "Risk concentrates on the left tail, and we all know that the left tail is asymmetric with the right tail. However, the techniques of analyzing the left tail lend themselves to analyzing the right tail. The result is that firms are now looking at the causal relationships that make the tail fat—and on the flip side examining the causal relationships between the securities that will make the right tail, the gain tail, as fat as it could be," explains Damian Handzy, CEO, Investor Analytics, a risk aggregation firm.[10]

Risk management has a certain amount of folklore attached to it. Investors often choose a risk aggregator based on the number of managers on a platform. They may also think that based on the data reported they are getting 100 percent coverage of all managers. Or third, that if they use a separately managed account structure they can afford to pay less attention to risk, or skip a risk aggregator all together.

The point of risk aggregation is to provide a clearer assessment of the real risks in a given portfolio. This data is important to both managers and investors but may not always be as complete or as specific as investors expect it to be—specifically because of data quality issues.

Data quality management is essentially a two-fold process that should take into account the qualitative—which managers are accounted for, and what they do—and the quantitative—is the data right, what data is it, and where are the holes. Risk aggregators in the past have noted the number of managers on their platform as a means of indicating completeness. However, that number can be misleading; just because a manager is on the platform, it doesn't mean that the data is sharable. Relying on the number of managers is one of the most common myths outlined in the paper. "Managers on the platform is almost an irrelevant number because you aren't getting the data, they aren't going to release positions carte blanche," says Handzy. Instead, quality risk aggregators should be focused on bringing on the most hedge fund administrators, as they will have the most complete data available.

However, if investors rely on the folklore when assessing their data they may miss big holes. "The funds are very actively managed because in the small company space things can change quite rapidly and we are not ashamed to admit if we get something wrong—if something changes we cut the investment," he says.

## THE TRUTH ABOUT HEDGE FUND RISK

*Charles T. Hage*

Mr. Hage is currently Compliance Officer at U.S.-based firm Mohican Financial Management, LLC. During his career he has reviewed financial performance measures in alternative investments and managed financial risk in corporate investment programs.

### Need for truth

The hedge fund industry is seriously short on how it treats the subject of risk. Especially in times when challenging economic and financial conditions call for high standards of professionalism to achieve success, the industry should be fine-tuning all of its mechanisms. Instead, in the core subject of portfolio risk, the hedge fund industry clings to misconceptions, is less than honest with itself, and misleads investors. The industry should rethink the role of risk in the hierarchy of investment decisions, embrace universally valid measures of hedge fund performance, and inject responsibility into the system for screening hedge funds.

A full treatment of performance in hedge fund portfolios would incorporate time, without which frequency and correlation analyses related to a history of returns cannot be included. The author has chosen to forego time-dependent analysis of returns because the focus here is on risk, which enters into each investment decision but is not a measure of performance.

### Investor satisfaction

As Peter Drucker said, “To satisfy the customer is the mission and purpose of every business.” He didn’t mean to satisfy merely in the sense of pleasing, but in the sense of retaining clients, because business is clients. When it comes to satisfying clients who invest, George Soros’ cardinal rule is to protect capital in difficult markets, and Benedicte Gravrand’s key to active risk management is to keep negative returns few in number and small in amount. These are various ways of saying that investors want the fat (positive) head and thin (negative) tail distribution of monthly portfolio returns to which all good managers aspire.

That brings us immediately to big surprises, because nothing can ruin a fat head/thin tail faster than the unanticipated occurrence of a major event for which the manager has no effective response. An astute investor should ask the prospective manager "What is it about your investment strategy that insulates the portfolio from negative surprises and accommodates positive ones?" The answer may include a flexible strategy for leverage, an ability to liquidate positions rapidly, and limitations on participation in upside effects. Any talk of tail statistics has no place in the answer. The point is to focus on manager preparedness for surprises early on in the process of investor due diligence. Otherwise detailed discussions of risk analytics and risk management are uneasy and perhaps pointless. Little data may exist on how often surprises are dealt with up-front by investors and managers, but human nature suggests it may be infrequently and inadequately. The lesson should be that unpredictability and lack of quantification do not excuse the manager from the task of dealing in advance with insulation from negative surprises.

Histories of manager performance have received infinitely more numerical attention than strategies for insulation from surprises. Unfortunately, the history of hedge fund performance analytics has produced a plethora of statistics and graphs without standards for validity of application or comparison of portfolios. Industry participants are therefore obligated to find the best content and form to convey performance clearly and meaningfully, with hope that means which excel will be broadly adopted. Here is one proposal for condensing historical data into a set of figures that efficiently characterize the portfolio performance of any hedge fund. Certain statistics commonly displayed in the industry are avoided here, not to simplify, but to avoid invalid and distracting measures.

These figures derive solely from returns and tell the performance story of a hedge fund. Figure 4.1 demonstrates how robustly the fat head/thin tail has been achieved. Figure 4.2, with omega quantifying that robustness as a gain/loss ratio, plots fund performance as a single point against benchmark indices. Figure 4.3 depicts the fund's combination of value added (alpha) and market sensitivity (beta) versus benchmark indices.

The figures inform investors about performance of the fund and frame questions about how results were achieved, such as: What aspects of strategy offer inherently sustainable opportunity? What style and skills give the manager special performance advantages over peers? Under what rules is the portfolio managed to balance pursuit of opportunity and avoidance of risk? How did the manager anticipate and respond to major market events, and which monthly returns are related to those events? Note that risk does not appear in any of

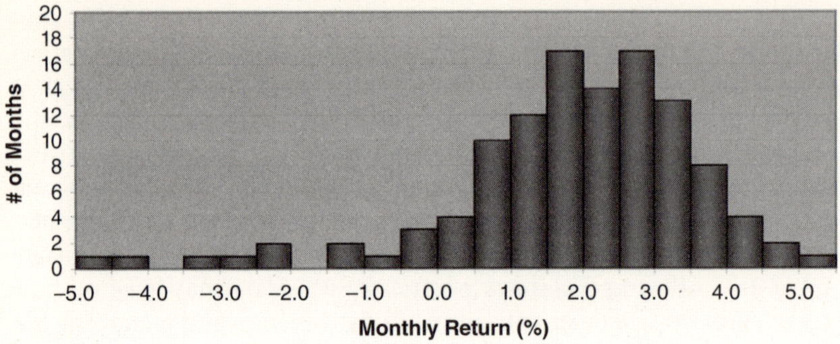


**FIGURE 4.1** Distribution of Returns

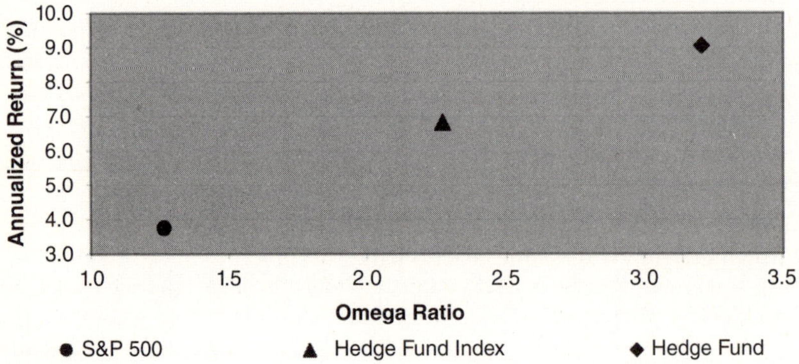


**FIGURE 4.2** Performance versus Indices

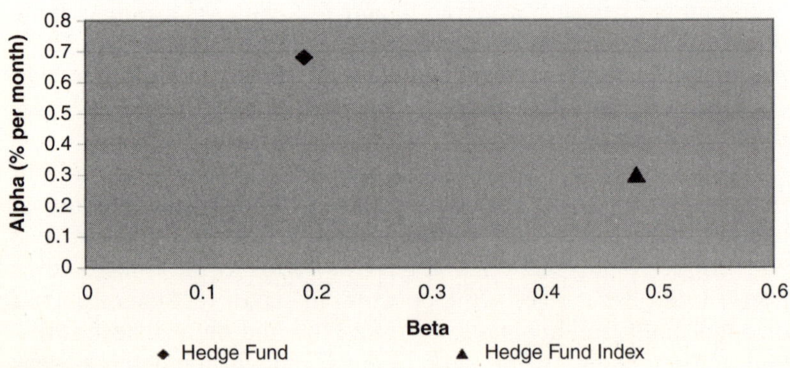


**FIGURE 4.3** Performance versus Market

the return measures displayed in these figures. It is useful to discuss risks along with opportunities in the Q&A about risk management or the source of returns, but post-facto risk tools serve no meaningful purpose, as we will discuss.

Since the figures relate only to the fund objective for return, investor tolerance for loss needs consideration. A simple approach is to quantify it in combinations of how much capital loss, and for how long, the investor will tolerate without redeeming. For example, the investor might tolerate 4 percent loss for seven months but not 6 percent loss for five months. A discussion in such terms can determine whether tolerance for loss on the part of the investor and capital preservation criteria on the part of the manager are compatible. The need for such discussion underscores why capital preservation is not unilaterally quantified in the fund statement of objective.

The technical elements of the foregoing are not new, and the many aspects of investor satisfaction are easy to grasp. What compels exposition is the need for quality in the central exchange between investors and managers. It is challenging enough to convey clear and comparable assessments of a variety of complex investments before further elaborating with statistics to which the parties are partial. Any distortions or distractions are less harmful if introduced, inadvertently or knowingly, only after some central truth.

### Portfolio decisions

A person about to jump toward freedom across a deep rocky fissure understands opportunity and risk, odds and stakes, gain and loss. The act of leaping is elegantly simple, but the decision to do so accounts for all the conditions to be overcome and the consequences of failure. The relevance of such a situation may seem remote from investment decisions, but it's not. It's useful first to proclaim that there is but one reason to incur risk, and that is to pursue opportunity. In other words, without opportunity there is no reason to take risk, and yet portfolio risk has been analyzed ad infinitum and ad nauseam as a thing unto itself and after the fact. When we then ask why the word opportunity barely appears in the vocabulary about risk, we realize that the word decision also receives less than honorable mention. And that starts us thinking about how we've been thinking about risk.

Over two millennia ago, Marcus Cicero insisted that if you wished to communicate with him, you should define your terms, but every generation must overcome sloppy thinking that leads to confusion in the marketplace. Much confusion could be eliminated if we would all agree that opportunity and risk, each with its odds and stakes, are what might happen due to decisions not yet made, while gain and loss are actual outcomes after decisions are made. Every investment decision in the hierarchy of decisions among investors (e.g., manager selection) and managers (e.g., adjust leverage, buy/sell a position) is a dividing point between risk management and performance measurement. In particular, risk analysis to inform a trade decision by the manager helps to pursue portfolio success, but risk analytics applied to portfolio returns are useless because logically (1) they can't figure in any of the decisions made earlier that produced the returns, and (2) returns already booked cannot be at risk. By mixing risk with return for decades, financial theorists and practitioners have contaminated the thinking of managers, investors, and service providers in the hedge fund industry.

This conclusion came from taking an exploratory path with little appreciation for where it would lead. What began several years ago as curiosity about hedge fund performance reporting led first to discovery of newer measures and then to examination of fundamental notions. Others are no doubt approaching the same kind of destination from different directions. For example, starting with the notions of fear (foregoing opportunity to avoid risk) and greed (ignoring risk to pursue opportunity) can lead to the same end point. The conclusion also came with the realization that herds are not exclusive to traditional investors; professionals in alternative investments may be a much smaller herd, but they constitute proportionately as many sheep and possess a level of influence that can do damage as well as good. More generally, deeply ingrained assumptions underlying widespread practice have a hold on minds that is hard to break. But as a friend was fond of saying: "Check your premises." Some may respond to the conclusion only by defending long-standing, widely-accepted scholarly teachings and professional practices, but those who developed or applied tools for risk in the past have earned our respect and we owe them a sincere effort on our part to rethink and improve.

### Performance measures

When his couriers privately reported to him on the news from Waterloo, Nathan Rothschild sold big and high in London, and the herd waiting for the same news eagerly followed his lead. Then, before slower official couriers arrived, he bought big and low. He had sent a false signal to traders that destroyed their wealth in a flash. Today, wealth in hedge funds is being destroyed not in a single dramatic episode but with false measures disseminated by the industry. Before reviewing how, it's helpful to make note of the predictive value of signals by taking a short side trip to the health care industry.

Galen and Gambino* elegantly addressed the predictive value of diagnostic tests by quantifying how prevalence of a condition determines the validity of tests results. It turns out that a test with 90 percent sensitivity (1 in 10 false negatives; i.e., the test fails to identify 10 percent of sick persons) and 90 percent specificity (1 in 10 false negatives; i.e., the test identifies 10 percent of well persons as sick) has high predictive value only when you need it least, like in a full-blown flu epidemic. But if 5 percent of a population has a condition, that test will produce nearly two false positives to match every true one. The prevalence of good hedge fund managers is debatable, but what investor wants to spend any appreciable time on due diligence of managers who are not truly in the top 5 percent and appear to be there only due to false positives? At the same time, investors cannot be expected to search through the chaff of the other 95 percent to separate wheat mislabeled with a false negative. Simply put, false signals in the current system can make Nathan look inconsequential.

Close to the heart of the matter is risk-adjusted return. It deserves mention to reinforce the statement above that "risk analytics applied to portfolio returns are useless." Imagine that you perform final inspection on a manufactured product. You reject 15 percent of units, send them to a rework line, call the rest yield, and send that 85 percent to packing and shipping. The rework department is classifying rejected units by fault, identifying causes of faults, and fixing the faults; that is, managing risk of failure in units yet to be made. Would you as final inspector use any *risk* number to adjust yield numbers in your reports to management? Of course not, for multiple reasons, but particularly because the process of risk management will *adjust* ongoing yield.

Risk has been assigned a vastly bigger role in assessing hedge funds than its companion opportunity. A major reason is its treatment for decades in risk literature, which has repeatedly equated volatility with risk. The familiar advice has been that between two funds with the same return and different volatility, pick the one with lower volatility; that is, higher volatility/risk should command higher return. The argument reduces to suggesting that in flipping a coin to

*Robert S. Galen and S. Raymond Gambino, *Beyond Normality: Predictive Value and Efficiency of Medical Diagnoses* (New York: John Wiley & Sons, 1976).

win or lose identical objects, always choose apples over diamonds as the objects (same odds—zero expected return; different stakes—more volatility/risk in diamonds). This is telling an investor with large resources to play a game of low stakes. The reasoning goes on to add that the choice demonstrates a need to adjust returns with volatility/risk rather than let returns rest on their absolute basis. These ideas have been used to build a body of formulas for risk that leads in wrong directions. To his credit, Bill Sharpe has questioned the validity of his own formula.**

Above all things, the hedge fund industry must apply portfolio performance measures that are beyond reproach. Existing measures have been challenged and better ones have been proposed, but entities that could be influential advocates for change in practice are so far largely silent. Gaussian assumptions*** and all their derivative statistics have lived long and well. It is time for them to go. Bell-shaped curves are not an expression of investor interests. Standard deviation is not a proxy for risk and serves only to waste attention on the higher frequencies and shorter durations of price variations, distracting attention from longer-term ends and means. Ratios incorporating standard deviation are useless for reasons given above.

The Omega function (Keating & Shadwick)**** has emerged (2002) to quantify the robustness (quality) of a distribution of returns. It captures all the data in any shape of distribution and preserves validity by avoiding any and all premises. It has universal appeal as a measure that is intuitive, important, and uncontrived. In its simplest form as a single ratio balanced about a zero-return fulcrum, it is eminently more useful than all the *risk* statistics currently derived from returns. It leverages aggregated monthly gains against aggregated monthly losses, indicating how well opportunity/risk prospects have been managed to satisfy a capital preservation objective. In any quantifiable endeavor, that kind of data analysis appeals directly to the fundamental need for measurable objectives.

**William Sharpe, "The Sharpe Ratio," *The Journal of Portfolio Management*, Fall 1994, www.stanford.edu/~wfsharpe/art/sr/sr.htm.

***E. Forslund and D. Johannson, "What Happens When Gaussian Models Fail?" Chalmers University, www.math.chalmers.se/~rootzen/finrisk/gr15_forslund_johansson_gaussian_cop.pdf.

****C. Keating and W. F. Shadwick, "The Omega Function," The Finance Development Centre, London, https://faculty.fuqua.duke.edu/~charvey/Teaching/BA453_2004/Keating_The_omega_function.pdf.

### Screening hedge funds

Screening can be more important than selecting in the same sense that defining options can be more important than the final choice among them. A selection will be optimal only if the best option is on the table and that will happen only if measures used for option attributes and search criteria are valid and matching. The goal of any screening step is to put an option on the table if and only if it meets the criteria. With that goal met, successive screening steps can reliably arrive at the start of selection through due diligence. The hedge fund industry is not within sight of that utopia. Working toward it will involve commitment and participation from experts, managers, platforms, consultants, databases, associations, and conference organizers as well as demands from investors. Major effort over time will be required to develop a system that directs investors toward better allocation of capital to managers.

How big a payoff can be expected from this kind of effort? A system that tracks visits by accredited investors to leading online hedge fund databases has shown that the number of unique visitors to the top three sites is running at monthly rates of several thousand per site. Visitors who are unique within sites are not all unique between sites, and visitors make multiple visits, only some of which are to perform a screen, so there are ups and downs in any attempt to estimate the magnitude of screening done online. But even if we modestly assume 10,000 screens per year in total and modestly suspect that on average a screen produces one false positive fund or one false negative fund, it is easy to visualize how capital and profits in the billions of dollars could be lost over time as a result of suboptimal selection from among funds that survive flawed screens.

### Industry action

We have considered why the hedge fund industry must rethink risk and have identified elements of correction, but that does not constitute a roadmap for revision. A few years ago Bill Sharpe told Con Keating that Omega Ratio was ahead of Sharpe Ratio in terms of acceptance at a comparable age. That's encouraging in particular, but the general situation calls for leading advocates to step forward and develop a framework for broad-based change. The integrity and practicality of the industry are presently at risk and in need of rescue with the help of some truth.

"Other Voices: The Truth About Hedge Fund Risk," *Opalesque Alternative Market Briefing*, www.opalesque.com/639893/The_truth_about_hedge_fund_risk989.html.

### Prime Brokers

Prime brokers, previously somewhat boring arbiters of trading orders, found themselves front and center in the wake of the Lehman Brothers failure.[11] Regulators and investors wanted to know how these organizations, which were supposed to be bland and stable, were in fact so shaky.

Prime brokers are really central to the success of hedge funds. Consider the number and ticket size of transactions required every day by hedge funds all over the world. In order to support that load, a team of investment bankers needs to be in place building relationships with individual funds. This team is considered the prime brokerage for a fund. Before Lehman collapsed it was common for a hedge fund to only have one of these teams, situated at one of the big banks. Top shelf funds were often with top shelf names like Goldman Sachs. Once Lehman fell apart however, multiple primes became the order of the day.

Using multiple primes is an idea based on safety through decentralization. If one prime folds, the fund can still work across the other firms that it also uses for a prime brokerage relationship instead of having to withstand the full brunt of a single failure. Let's look at how these relationships work.

Prime brokers offer a range of services including order execution, securities lending, margin financing, and assorted other custom services. The prime brokerage works with both hedge funds and other banks willing to provide margin loans, or with institutions willing to lend shares. Custom services can include activities like capital introduction or other fundraising support services, as prime brokers are already licensed and have existing relationships with potential investors. In this role, a prime broker is doing more than just sourcing shares or capital for lending, instead they may serve as a matchmaker between a hedge fund and investor, which they believe to have aligned interests.

Prime brokers also have their own interests at stake in all three of these roles. When a prime broker begins working with a hedge fund, it's essentially a custodial relationship. The prime can make loans to a hedge fund and the collateral for those loans is the existing hedge fund portfolio. Whether the loans are securities or margin capital, primes typically provide more than would be offered by a regular bank. This is because they have direct access to the hedge fund's assets and can transfer them as needed to cover the loan or issue more margin. All the while, primes take a fee for services rendered.

In addition to the fee, the prime gets to set the lending rules. Each prime is going to have its own limits as to how much margin will be extended to a given fund at any point in time. When a hedge fund chooses a prime, they will first look at those limits and determine if that will work for what they need. Hedge funds that are heavy on options trading or futures trading, for example, may need greater margin limits for their strategy to work. It makes them riskier, and so they will have to find a prime that's willing to take on that level of risk, or split those needs among multiple primes. Splitting margin and securities lending demand among more than one prime not only allows the manager and prime to hold less fund-specific risk. It also gives managers a little safety net because their whole portfolio isn't tied up at one firm. This relationship is known as counterparty risk. Counterparty risk is a fancy way of saying each side of a contract needs to size up the other side and think about what happens if either side fails to meet its agreed-to obligations. Counterparty risk is one of the biggest risk factors underlying every single hedge fund-related relationship.

On the investor side, working with prime brokers may mean access to a certain group of managers or a specific manager. Institutions will work with primes if they have shares available to be included in a securities lending transaction or as part of their own custodial relationships. Investors need to be clear however, about who the prime ultimately serves. The prime broker is looking for profitable relationships on both sides, through service fees, lending, and loan resolution. In that vein, hedge fund managers are going to present a more significant upside for a prime broker. On the investor side, if they are introduced to a fund through a prime, they may invest, see lackluster returns, and pull out. On the other hand, even if the fund has a down year, the prime is picking up the fees for brokerage services. So, even a mediocre manager can be a great relationship for a prime—caveat emptor.

A report released by Ernst & Young in October 2013[12] shows how stark this shift has been in the few years following 2008. According to the report, by 2009 hedge funds with assets averaging $3 billion or more had 4.8 prime brokers compared to the single relationship that was common right up to 2008.

The way these relationships work is also going to influence how primes view risk in the broader market and the risk of a given manager, because they are an over-collateralized lender. With the advent of the Dodd-Frank Act in the United States, which ushered in a sweeping overhaul of financial regulations, prime brokers now face new capitalization and risk requirements precisely because of their skewed view of risk and how they did business before the crisis.

Dodd-Frank requires prime brokers to be much more cautious about their business relationships, keep more cash on hand, and clear new types of transactions than they've previously had to. International regulations call for keeping even more cash on hand, forcing ever smaller allowable leverage ratios, and putting additional pressure on prime brokerage units to be more conservative about what they allow.

### Central Clearers

Another way regulation has impacted prime brokerage is through a change requiring that over-the-counter derivatives be cleared through a central clearinghouse. In many cases, prime brokers have taken on the responsibility of setting up approved central clearing mechanisms, as it was a logical follow on to their existing set of services, and in some cases may have already existed internally.

In 2009, the G20 group of nations set forth an agenda to start clearing over-the-counter (OTC) derivatives and securities.[13] Essentially, these are financial instruments and securities that are traded, but aren't traded on an exchange. In that instance, market makers set the rules and traders call around for quotes. After the crisis, regulators wanted to be able to monitor all of the risk in the system in thc hope that they could stem any major downturn like the one the world just lived through. However in practice, this has become far more complicated.

The plan from the G20 was, by 2013, to have OTC derivatives, securities, and swaps all centrally cleared by organizations like prime brokers or other registered clearinghouses who would then report those transactions to the appropriate national regulator. These rules have and will take more time to implement and may not be the harmonized international standard officials were hoping for, but, even so central clearers are rapidly coming into the market as firms work to put themselves in compliance with forthcoming final rules.

The OTC market is approximately $630 trillion in assets as of September 2013, according to figures from the European Central Bank. According to Joshua Sterling and Akshay N. Belani, attorneys for Bingham, the point of central clearing is to reduce systemic risk by eliminating bilateral credit risk to swap counterparties that is inherent in uncleared swaps. The same idea holds for other OTC instruments.[14]

However, setting up central clearinghouses essentially just creates chokepoints for all the risk to go through. As written, the only way around this is for the small group of investors that have enough capital to be able to deal with the clearers themselves.

"Firms are supposed to act within the best interests of their client," Sterling notes. "But it depends on the instrument whether voluntary clearing is in the best interest of the client."

Sterling and Belani note that firms will also need to determine if they meet U.S. person requirements when it comes to complying with the CFTC's version of OTC and swaps rules. This could get tricky if, for example, a firm based outside the United States has a U.S.-based sub-advisor that regulators may consider to have a central function. Even when they've dealt with those considerations, the firm may still fall under the purview of foreign regulators.

Both managers and investors will need to determine where they fit into these rules and who best to clear these transactions with (or find out where the transactions are cleared on the investor side). For people who do business in the United States or for multi-national firms this could be tricky.

In July 2013, the Commodities Futures Trading Commission (CFTC) issued final guidance on swaps compliance issues, and in that guidance the regulator quietly changed the definition of what it means to be a U.S. person. According to new, and final guidance that has already gone into effect, a U.S. person is now amended solely with respect to the Commodity Exchange Act's swap provisions and CFTC swap regulations. Under the new definition, U.S. person can also mean hedge funds and other collective investment vehicles that are either based in the United States or primarily controlled by a U.S. citizen.

These changes mean that managers, investors, and clearers will need to take a close look at all of their counterparties and determine who meets these criteria. Central clearers will have to take into account counterparty risk and reporting requirements, even if most of their clients live abroad. They could find that with the new definition they are still required to make CFTC disclosures in addition to those of an overseas regulator.

## Defining Risk Profiles

On the investor side, hedge funds and service providers fit into a broader portfolio puzzle that is not only based on wealth goals, but a risk profile. Investors who work with financial advisors or who have a dedicated investment officer may begin investing by establishing a risk profile. The risk profile defines the types of investments and potential losses an investor is comfortable with. For example, conservative investors have long preferred bonds, because of the guarantee of at least what was originally paid. Similarly, they tend to prefer bigger, older, dividend-paying equities for their relative safety over new companies or investing fads.

When alternatives started becoming part of the mainstream mix, investors came to realize that there are not only more investing options, but more opportunities for loss. Failure to understand how hedge funds work in a portfolio could mean steeper losses than one might expect. This realization was widespread in 2008, and is part of the overall evolution on risk management education.

Hedged strategies typically require active risk management, as they often contain both long and short bets, and may also contain riskier instruments like derivatives or greater use of leverage. For investors, this means taking a new look at old risk profiles and evaluating the impact of taking on increased risk. As noted earlier, informing providers of risk data how these data are used can have material impact for both investors and managers when they evaluate trades, portfolios, and funds.

## BEST-ADVISED CLIENTS GO ABOVE AND BEYOND BOX TICKING

***Benedicte Gravrand***

Clients, especially institutional ones, have become much more inquisitive and look into risk management procedures in the context of their due diligence, says Giuseppe Ballocchi, a financier based in Geneva and an expert in risk management.

"We also notice that very high net worth individuals tend to use the same type of consultants and follow the practices of institutional investors," he said. "So there is a bit of a convergence between high net worth, ultra high net worth, and institutional clients demanding very tight, very transparent risk management practices. And that is part of the due diligence that clients conduct." But the bigger clients tend to be more demanding and often pay attention to details a lot more, he added.

He expects this trend to continue and intensify. It's not perfect for money managers, though, as often, due diligence turns into box ticking, demanding that all follow the same demands of best practice, of regulators, and of consultants. But some clients realize they cannot apply the same procedures everywhere, and that risk management practices should be adapted to the type of business that is conducted.

"If I am running, for example, an overlay program and I take a position in the billions of dollars, then I have to have super watertight procedures," he explained. "Instead, if I am running some mandate that does not have the same type of operational risk, then my procedures can be a little bit more relaxed. It doesn't mean that I am worse; it just means that in one case I recognize the concentration of risk which requires very strong mitigation, and in the other case I don't see an equal presence of risk, so the risk mitigation doesn't need to be so expensive, and that also saves costs for the clients." It is not easy to convey this concept, he added, because it requires an understanding of where the risk is—and risk is not necessarily everywhere.

### Dynamic hedging strategies, dynamic scrutiny

Daniel Ades, managing partner and founder of Kawa Capital, an asset management firm, explains that investors should not simply ask asset managers about their risk management tools: they should ask for examples of how risk has been managed.

"I can spend an hour telling about all these controls and beautiful things and bells and whistles we have in our fund," he said. "Systematic strategies are different, but in most human-based investment strategies, what really matters is if the person who is taking risk in the portfolio is really making good risk and reward decisions. And that is exactly what people should be able to gauge."

He thinks there are three basic types of risk dimensions, which are:

1. Duration—how long the manager is going to hold the investment
2. Liquidity—how liquid is the investment
3. Credit risk—how likely a permanent loss of capital is.

The problem with risk is that investors do not always understand the levels of risk or the risk management procedures.

### Risk for complex strategies

Hedge funds that make extensive use of derivatives usually apply intensive risk management procedures.

"The types of procedures, models, and practices have to be in line with the actual risk and the actual sophistication of the process and the instruments," Ballocchi noted. "If one doesn't trade derivatives, or if one trades it very rarely, one doesn't need to have a super complex operational procedure for derivatives. There are a lot of things that need to go into fine-tuning the risk management processes."

### An industry or a profession?

Ballocchi does not like the word *industry*, which he thinks is overused: "We have as financial professionals a higher calling than being an industry. A profession is something that is much nobler than an industry; a profession is something that you do for your clients." Although he agrees that risk management is in a sense becoming more and more of an industry, but that is not necessarily a positive.

"Risk management is for the benefit of the clients and for the benefit of, in a sense, society, because we don't want to create undue systemic risk," he continued. "What will happen I fear is rather the opposite, that is, you will have an industry with more and more requirements, but not much in terms of results to be shown in protecting clients' interest or in the ultimate reduction of systemic risk."

### Regulatory concerns and costs

Ballocchi believes that in light of the regulatory developments, more time and money will be spent on risk management. "Headcounts have, to my knowledge, gone up dramatically in the last five, six, seven years in terms of risk control and also compliance," he said. "There will be more and more expenditure, and all of that is not necessarily good, because in the end it creates cost. As for every activity, there needs to be a cost benefit analysis, but regulation seems to be imposing requirements regardless of cost and benefit."

According to a recent Citi Prime Finance survey*, hedge fund managers' expenditures on support personnel and third-party expenses totaled $14.1 billion in 2012, the equivalent of 65 basis points of total industry assets. These expenses include marketing, investor relations, risk and compliance, operations and technology, and business management.

More risk management procedures might be stifling for hedge funds, although let's not forget they are still less regulated than banks or long-only managers, Ballocchi noted. So there is still room for maneuver, and even room for opportunities. "It could even perversely create opportunities," he commented, "because if regulation creates a lot of redundant and sometimes unneeded requirements, everybody would be slowed down. Some hedge funds that don't work under the same constraints may take advantage of marketing inefficiencies that would be created because other people just are slowed down by regulation."

"This is very much in the same way as banks leaving prop trading and thereby creating opportunities for hedge funds that can fill in the gaps. In the end, you can still structure a hedge fund in a nimble way despite the regulation."

"Risk Management: Best Advised Clients Go Above and Beyond Box Ticking," *Opalesque Alternative Market Briefing*, www.opalesque.com/645399/Risk_management_best_advised_clients_go539.html.

*"2012 Hedge Fund Business Expense Survey: Industry Wide Benchmarks for Managing A Hedge Fund Organization," Citi Prime Finance, http://icg.citi.com/transactionservices/home/demo/tutorials8/Hedge_Fund_Dec2012.

### Liquidity

When investors are evaluating their risk tolerance and how closely a given fund or investment aligns with their interests, looking at overall liquidity is also important. Being able to get out of a fund or have access to your invested capital quickly can mean the difference between big losses or capital preservation.

## LIQUIDITY CORRELATION MAY NOT BE ENOUGH

### *Benedicte Gravrand*

Raimond Schuster, CEO of ISP Securities, an independent global financial services firm with CHF1.5 billion in AUM ($1.6 billion) and offices in Zurich and in Israel, believes the current discussion on liquidity is changing the environment for hedge funds. ISP Group has invested in hedge funds since 1994, and has managed its own fund of hedge funds (FoHF) since 1997. The old school approach of managing liquidity in a FoHF portfolio involved spreadsheet listings, which estimated how much of the portfolio was in liquid assets, Schuster stated. But this did not necessarily show the real picture.

According to Schuster,* a traditional hedge fund portfolio consists of liquid and transparent strategies that take directional bets in listed instruments, and of illiquid strategies that employ the liquidity facilities of financial intermediaries. But late 2008 showed that the illiquid strategies were too dependent on the interbank liquidity, as when those dried up, the illiquid strategies suffered from heavy drawdown or became illiquid (or both).

"One can even ask whether a 1:1 liquidity correlation is enough," he noted. After that, investors who needed liquidity redeemed from their funds and found that many of the funds could not return the money.

Furthermore, "the belief in low volatility often encouraged investors to take additional leverage on their side, which led to a toxic outcome." Investors have one of two major motivations for investing in hedge funds, said Schuster. First, Markowitz thinking says the portfolio should be less volatile if there is diversification. In this case, investors only invest a small part of their portfolio in alternatives, and should accept some liquidity constraints for diversification's sake. The second motivation is the search for absolute returns. In this case investors

*"1:1 Liquidity Correlation May Not Be Enough," *Opalesque Alternative Market Briefing*, www.opalesque.com/644611/11_liquidity_correlation_may_not_be_enough461.html.

might invest a greater proportion of their portfolio in absolute return strategies, and retain ready liquidity. "But here is the contradiction," Schuster explained. "Respectable absolute returns require the willingness to take some illiquidity risk. By avoiding these liquidity risks, the investor will end up with average returns. Probably, the investor needs to realize that this is a catch 22."

### Liquidity and performance

As mutual funds are highly regulated and alternative investment funds are becoming highly regulated too (especially in Europe with Undertakings for Collective Investment in Transferable Securities [UCITS] rules and the Alternative Investment Fund Managers Directive [AIMFD]), where is the real difference between fund types, Schuster asks. "You have two kinds of funds, alternative investment funds (hedge funds, private equity . . .), and UCITS funds, which by regulations are forced to have bad diversification and to invest in only certain instruments. Now the whole industry is trying to combine these two kinds. But the questions are: Is a hedge fund in a UCITS really a more liquid hedge fund? Or are UCITS funds just pretending that there is more liquidity in their hedge fund strategies?"

Several strategies have different liquidity terms, and the more illiquid ones are in, or move to, the distressed areas. "In a diversified portfolio, you must expect that you will move into an illiquid situation—even if you feel comfortable being in this grey area—as soon as the market gets distressed."

As for the returns on illiquid investments, you must look at the illiquidity premium. According to ISP, a 2007 study** finds that funds with lockup provisions perform 4 to 7 percent better. These funds often trade in illiquid securities and these strategies suffered during liquidity shocks like the Lehman collapse. Also, investments in illiquid securities do not have market prices and often mark-to-model or rely on broker evaluations. This means that reported hedge fund returns are smoothed, and risk-adjusted figures like Sharpe ratio are inflated. So the performance of hedge funds with illiquid positions could appear better than it truly is.

Another study, by Melvyn Teo at Singapore Management University,*** says that portfolios with liquidity risk exposure

**G. O. Aragon, "Share Restrictions and Asset Pricing: Evidence from the Hedge Fund Industry," *Journal of Financial Economics* 83, no. 1 (2007): 33–58.

***Melvyn Teo, "Research Collection BNP Paribas Hedge Fund Centre," *Journal of Financial Economics*, 2010, http://ink.library.smu.edu.sg/bnp_research/12.

outperform portfolios with low risk exposure by 5.8 percent, according to ISP. The funds that are taking liquidity risk are the smaller funds: "they load up excessively on liquidity risk and generate impressive returns." Furthermore, funds that have gates are encouraged to take on more liquidity risk than they should. Funds with liquid strategies end up being the average performers. "That means that in any FoHF portfolio," Schuster noted, "It's very important to check all underlying investments. Investors should ask for full transparency and check liquidity terms—as liquid investments in liquid vehicles can become illiquid later on."

### New realities

"Fund managers tend to have a survivor mentality. Managers want to gate funds or to suspend funds when they get into trouble." The issue with gates, he said, is that fund managers claim gates protect investors from fire sale, whereas what they really care about is business continuity. Gates do indeed help many funds to prevent further flow-induced deterioration of performance, but they also encourage managers to take more liquidity risks. "Investors should take certain illiquidity risks but they need to be educated." He suggested UCITS funds be licensed under the AIFMD regime, where all the risks are obvious and the investors know what they're buying. "Is a fully liquid fund a hedge fund? I would say no."

## Aligning Interests

Ultimately, the bulk of this conversation comes to learning about all the players and aligning interests. Both managers and investors need to come to the table with realistic ideas about what is possible and what each party hopes to gain. Dr. Sassan Zaker, head of Alternative Investments at the CHF2bn Julius Baer Pension Fund, says the key to investing is simplification. Zaker separates the hedge fund model into three historical versions.[15]

Hedge Fund Version 1 was the version of hedge funds during the 1980s and 1990s; it was meant for mainly private investors. Those investors expected high returns, tolerated high volatility, focused on an individual hedge fund, and had a short-term investment horizon. Most strategies were either global macro or equity long/short.

Hedge Fund Version 2, during the first eight years of this century, saw more institutional investors. "It started almost with Long Term Capital Management, and ended with Madoff," Zacker adds. Those investors had completely different expectations, namely moderate returns and low volatility, with a focus on a hedge fund portfolio and diversification, and long- or short-term investment horizons. This period saw the rise of the relative value arbitrage strategy.

"Investors were part of the problem. The problem was, we investors expected low volatility but weren't worried about the side-effects . . . we got the bill in 2008. If we continue like this, if we have simplified expectations, it will happen again. Right now we are in a similar position as in 2006. . . ." So it is time to think about Hedge Fund Version 3, and investors will have to change their attitudes.

Hedge Fund Version 3 accounts for how hedge funds work after 2008. Zaker suggests investors be separated into two types: private and institutional. Investors expect moderate returns and moderate volatility, their focus is on a portfolio of hedge funds with the same risk budget and their investment horizon is likely to be a rolling three-year period. Strategies are also separated between those that are liquid and those that are not. The key difference between Version 3 and the other versions is that clients now set targets for hedge fund managers. "What we need now is for investors and managers to come to a common understanding about what is possible and how much it will cost," Zaker concluded. "I think that is what Hedge Fund Version 3 is about."

## Due Diligence

Building on the theme of aligning interests, just like managers have to do due diligence on all of their counterparty relationships, so too must investors when it comes to choosing funds and building their own investment infrastructure.

In the hedge fund space, many of the changes in due diligence, investor expectations, and hedge fund business processes, have been driven by institutions. Their ability to offer big ticket allocations and create security for managers means that their unique demands take top priority. As institutions and large family offices have gotten more savvy about what it means to invest in alternatives as part of the core portfolio, managers have seen due diligence questionnaires (DDQ) expand significantly; not only are they longer but they are much more granular.

As we noted in the previous chapter, the growth of separately managed accounts has also been prompted by similar trends. Separately managed accounts can provide investors that have the resources to run them with a deep dive into a fund and how it works. For investors that don't take this route, they rely instead on the due diligence process to try and suss out any red flags before they are committed to a fund.

Due diligence can mean many things. At a basic level it's a background check into the principals of a fund and the funds track record. As DDQs have grown, questions are now asked about operational issues, reputational risk, technology, disaster planning, and succession. Other questions look at what it takes for an investor to get their capital back once they invest in a fund. In many cases the DDQ can be hundreds of questions, and the process can include site visits, lawyer visits, and bringing in independent due diligence companies to get under the hood.

Historically, due diligence on a hedge fund relied heavily on personal relationships, a quick scan by a lawyer, and a good pitch meeting. When returns were high and reports of fraud infrequent, investors were often content to invest on a handshake. As with nearly every other aspect of the industry, that all changed after 2008. Institutions were getting into alternatives pre-crisis and asking more questions, as institutions themselves are often required to invest within certain guidelines. But once scandals from Madoff to Lehman to Bear Stearns captured the public's attention, investors started demanding much more information than they ever had before.

One of the fastest growing areas of the due diligence process is independent due diligence. Unlike lawyers, consultants, or other third parties involved in the investment process, independent due diligence providers come in from the outside and compare what they see from a given fund against indicators of fraud and report back. Typically, these firms only work with investors and avoid making relationships with fund managers or other parties in the investment process in an effort to remain unconflicted.

They argue that due diligence provided by lawyers and auditors who may also work with funds in a fiduciary capacity can overlook or omit indications that a fund may not be the best investment. Investors have relied on independent audits for a number of years, and independent due diligence providers take this to the next level looking at operational and reputational risks beyond the numbers.

Castle Hall is a Canada-based provider of independent operational due diligence. The firm performs due diligence reviews on single strategy hedge funds and managed accounts and has also developed a proprietary process to complete operational due diligence on funds of funds. "We are a pure play operational due diligence firm, so we aren't burning the candle at both ends by working with investors and managers. We only work with investors," says Chris Addy, CEO, Castle Hall.[16] He notes that the driving force of the company is to focus solely on operational due diligence, "I don't think the phrase due diligence and Chinese wall should be in the same sentence."

Addy's philosophy stands out from many firms that rely on the Chinese wall—a structure which some in the industry admit is a myth.

Even some managers, like Christopher Whalen of Tangent Capital Partners, said it bluntly—"there are no Chinese walls, come on, this is Wall Street."[17]

Another firm, Corgentum based in New York, also takes a fully independent approach, providing operational due diligence reviews of fund managers on behalf of investors only. "When you do this type of work alone there is a chance of being overwhelmed," says Corgentum, Managing Partner, Jason Scharfman. "There is a market for institutional level operational review even for smaller allocators. Investors are recognizing that they have to maintain at least a minimum standard of due diligence."

Corgentum takes a multi-disciplinary approach to operational due diligence, with some unique twists. According to Scharfman, the firm will never send out an operational due diligence questionnaire. "If you send out a questionnaire, you're showing your hand and there's no surprise. Many managers already have a standard set of answers ready to go. It doesn't provide a real view of what's going on." The firm also benchmarks managers against their peers to ensure that fund claims fall in line with what's happening in a given strategy or fund type.

Both firms note that independence from investment activities gives them greater ability to protect investors and also provide a realistic picture of what's happening in a fund without any potential for conflict. This is especially important on sticky issues such as direct investment and valuations.

## MOVING BEYOND THE CHECKBOX RISK ASSESSMENT

"More investors are looking to build out a portfolio through a combination of allocations to a fund of funds and direct investment. Investors with the capability to run their own portfolios often need help with the operational component," Addy explains. This combined investment approach is leading to a greater focus on compliance—a boon for both firms. "Investors are more aware of what the risk information means, and are demanding more of managers. A lot of funds didn't have a dedicated compliance officer or a full compliance team and you're seeing them build out that infrastructure," says Scharfman.

The shift to compliance culture is also being driven by significant regulatory changes happening in the United States and abroad. Dodd-Frank, Basel III, FATCA, and a host of other reporting requirements are putting more and more pressure on funds to provide greater transparency about their activities, and investors are asking for the same level of information.

Investors are also seeking independent verification on hard to value assets—sometimes called illiquid or Level 3 assets. According to Addy, there is a growing expectation gap between investors and fund administrators when it comes to Level 3 valuation. Investors are expecting valuations to come from fund administrators but administrators are often hesitant to price the book. This hesitation is adding more to the operational due diligence process as firms like Castle Hall work to verify the information presented about a given portfolio.

"The traditional view in the industry through the 1990s was that administrators were going to price the book. But now there has been a subtle but very significant shift by administrators to say that they are verification agents, this has happened over the last 5 to 10 years driven by concerns over legal liability. Whereas the investor perspective is that if we are paying an administrator we expect that the administrator will price the portfolio," Addy says.

Divisions like this give independent firms an edge—Scharfman explains that independent firms notice this nuance because they aren't working from a particular vantage point such as administration, legal, or accounting. "If you have a legal firm doing the review, they're going to tell you if something is legal, side pockets are legal, thinly sourced valuations are legal, but that doesn't always mean they are advisable from a risk perspective. This is also true for key man risk and business continuity."

## Key Man Risk

Key man risk is a type of risk that is, in some senses, especially unique for hedge funds. In a corporate context, key man risk can mean what happens if the CEO gets hit by the proverbial bus. This is also what it means for hedge funds, however, unlike a corporation where business processes are known and replicable throughout the organization, a hedge fund manager may well be the sole repository of his secret sauce.

Some of the bigger hedge funds have been able to successfully create succession plans that rely on their use of multiple managers and investment teams. For those firms succession planning is, in some ways easier. Hedge fund managers in single manager firms stake their name on their unique view of the capital markets and how to make a trade. The ability and personality of a hedge fund manager is ultimately what makes and grows the firm. So, when a manager wants to retire or does in fact get injured or die, things become especially tenuous for a hedge fund.

After the death of well-known hedge fund manager Barton Biggs, his firm, Traxis Partners, provided a transition plan for investor capital that attempted to absorb investors in the funds Biggs managed himself into the funds managed by others in the firm. However, they also gave investors the opportunity to ask for their money back despite the firm's established track record, a situation that may be an object lesson for fund managers currently examining their own succession plans.

Other managers have taken to closing their funds to new investors as they age. George Soros, who would be well into retirement in most other industries, is still managing money, but his Quantum Fund closed to new investors a few years ago. Julian Robertson closed his Tiger Management Group in 2000 and used some of that money to finance funds run by former Tiger partners. The Tiger Cubs have been successful, but even then investors chose a new place to invest rather than work with an heir apparent. Speculation who will take over for Warren Buffett could be its own sport.

"With hedge funds you have a fairly unique situation where the value of the fund is usually tied up in one person, or a few people, and that is what draws the investor. It makes handing them off to another team in the event that something happens more difficult," explains Kyle Vataha, Vice President, Pluris Valuation Advisors.[18] Pluris works with hedge funds on valuation of illiquid or otherwise hard to value assets.

"What happens in this space is that investment managers tend to be focused on their strategy and bringing in assets. The structure of the firm sort of develops around that out of necessity. So managers don't tend to focus on the business management components as heavily, which is why you might not always see some of these future plans," Vataha says. Investor perception of succession plans and valuation also varies depending on the type and sophistication of the investor involved. Vataha notes that for large, institutional investors considering a manager that evaluation process may last anywhere from several months to a year as institutional investors are more interested in establishing a long-term interest. In these cases, other investment objectives may outweigh the presence of a succession plan as its not just a checkbox on the due diligence questionnaire.

"There is no generic succession plan best practice for hedge funds," he says. "Typically for funds, having half a billion to $1 billion in AUM shows a certain level of stickiness, investors are also going to want to see commitments from more than one institutional investor and the track record. Once managers get over $1 billion investors start to see more staying power there and usually there is a firm in place by that point. That said, I've also seen one man shops running billions of dollars in assets on their own. It's really a question of what everyone is comfortable with."

### Reputational Risk

Reputational risk can also be closely tied into operational and key man risk. Think of the Madoff scandal, many of Madoff's investors were in fact, other hedge funds. While their losses were just as real as any other investor, a manager being unable to see through the Madoff smoke screen is a reputational black eye that can follow him or her around even after they recover. The same is true for institutions who make a poor choice and get tangled up with a freewheeling manager who looks good on paper but is really using pension money to fund a lavish lifestyle. Given the scale of fraud and insider trading uncovered in recent years, reputational risk is an undercurrent rolling through the due diligence process.

### Red Flags

Fraud can be hard to spot. With Madoff, and other Ponzi schemes in the past, regulators have signed off because inevitably the math adds up until it doesn't. Some red flags are easier to see, maybe the IT infrastructure is lacking or a manager has a high headcount for no discernable purpose. Perhaps all the officers in the firm are relatives.

Still others may be what we could call benign red flags. Things that aren't necessarily illegal or malicious, just problematic. Gates can be a red flag for investors at the due diligence process level. Gates have always been part of the hedge fund industry, but they often raise the ire of investors. Managers use them to restrict the amount of investor redemptions at any one time. Unlike mutual funds where investors can get in and out of a fund in the same day, hedge funds typically require advance notice. That could mean 30 days when times are good, it could be much longer if times are bad or the fund is in trouble. If a manager is dealing with a drawdown and is trying to maintain the integrity of a portfolio, gates limit outflows into measurable chunks.

#### BARBARIANS AT THE GATE

***Fraser McKenzie, Managing Partner, 47N Capital Management***

A barbaric trend seems to be emerging among hedge funds; more and more are using investor-level gates. This construct allows managers to restrict investor redemptions (most often to 25 percent per redemption period) based upon their individual investment amount—as opposed to the more common fund-level gate which restricts investor redemptions based on the overall amount of redemptions a fund is experiencing. The fact that Moody's calls investor-level gates a credit positive event for hedge fund asset-liability management should set alarm bells ringing among investors. Any advantage created by lawyers for a hedge fund is likely to have a hairy side.

It's possible that this recent trend toward investor-level gates is part of the five-year hangover from the 2008 financial crisis when managers were trying to find ways of avoiding the massive redemptions that blighted the hedge fund industry. A more cynical observer might suppose that investor-level gates act as a preserver of management fees in the face of increasingly flighty investors. Managers say it's because fund-level gates encourage frivolous defensive redemptions to get ahead of the queue in the event of any stress.

From a board of directors' point of view, what better way to absolve itself of any decision-making responsibility and therefore legal risk? Or perhaps those funds with investor-level gates think that balancing the competing interests of redeeming investors in a sudden wave of redemptions is beyond their capabilities, time, or commitment levels. In that case one wonders just what it is they are being paid for.

Some investors believe that an investor-level gate is a benefit because it stops other investors from placing redemptions that may put remaining investors at a disadvantage. The argument goes that large single redemptions can reduce fund liquidity because the most liquid positions are sold to satisfy departing investors—leaving the rest with a less liquid portfolio. However, this doesn't hold up to scrutiny because one should expect the manager to protect the interests of remaining investors in any event. It should be an extraordinary decision by the board of directors—not a systematic denial of liquidity—to intervene in any problematic redemption.

Another claim is that investor-level gates assure investors of being able to redeem a certain percentage of their holdings is also misleading because this right can be, and most likely will be, overridden by a redemption suspension and the use of side pockets in the stressful event scenario.

The final insult to investors in terms of arguments used to support the use of investor-level gates is that they reduce the so-called ATM effect, where a fund that has good liquidity terms is used by investors to raise cash during tough times. The response to this suggestion from an investor point of view has to be: "take a hike—it's our money and we'll do what we want with it."

Another problem is that investor-level gates make a mockery of redemption terms. For example, what's the value of quarterly redemption with 30-day notice when an investor-level gate limits you to 25 percent of your investment? To make this a default setting is grossly misleading when it comes to the officially stated redemption terms.

Maybe the whole issue of investor-level gates has been allowed to come about because nobody is really paying attention. The investor-level gate concept is still a little fuzzy for a lot of investors. Lawyers writing these terms deep into the offering documents certainly don't have investor interests at the forefront of their minds.

In the final analysis of the investor-level gate debate, investors should simply be aware that acts of barbarism against investors are being committed by the architects of hedge fund governing documents whose main aim is to protect and promote the interests of the manager. In the investment world, systematically stopping investors from getting their money back when they want it is about as uncivilized as it comes.

"47N Series: Barbarians at the Gate," *Opalesque New Managers*, www.opalesque.com/new-managers/193/47n-series-barbarians-at-the-gate.html.

## SUMMARY

A whole range of companies and individuals service the hedge fund industry and its investors. These people are high skilled, but investors and managers alike will need to undergo consistent and thorough due diligence when establishing relationships. For managers, this means evaluating counterparty risk when it comes to brokers and vendors. For investors, this means examining hedge fund strategies as well as hedge fund business operations to assess which managers run a good business along with running a profitable hedge fund strategy.

## NOTES

1. S. P. Avric, M. Djenic, V. Mizdrakovic, and N. Stanisic, "Mark to Market Accounting as a Magnifier of Financial Crises," in *Financial Aspects of Recent Trends in the Global Economy*, ed. R. Mirdala (ASERS Publishing, 2013), vol. II, 110–126, http://papers.ssrn.com/sol3/papers.cfm?abstract_id=2269851.
2. Emma Cusworth, "Investors Continue to Misunderstand Valuation Risk in Level 3 Hedge Fund Assets," Risk.net, www.risk.net/hedge-funds-review/feature/2245907/investors-continue-misunderstand-valuation-risk-level-hedge-fund-assets.

3. "eVestment Hedge Fund Administrator Survey Shows Solid Growth in Assets Under Administration for First Half 2013," *Opalesque Alternative Market Briefing*, www.opalesque.com/fullarticle/648038/eVestment_hedge_fund_administrator_survey_shows_solid_growth803.html.
4. Open Protocol Enabling Risk Aggregation (OPERA) Working Group, www.theopenprotocol.org/top/theproject.
5. "Servicers' Spot Citco: Administrators Can Help Hedge Funds Face Today's Rapid Evolution," *Opalesque New Managers*, www.opalesque.com/new-managers/78/servicers-administrators-can-help-hedge-funds.html.
6. "Maples Fund Services Launches Risk Reporting, Targets Growth," *Opalesque Alternative Market Briefing*, www.opalesque.com/640934/Maples_Fund_Services_launches_intuitive_risk_reporting093.html.
7. "Funds Look to Analytics for Risk Management, Compliance," *Opalesque Alternative Market Briefing*, www.opalesque.com/642474/Funds_look_to_analytics_for_risk_management247.html.
8. "JP Morgan to Admit Wrongdoing, Pay $100 Million to Settle 'London Whale' Inquiry," *New York Times DealBook*, http://dealbook.nytimes.com/2013/10/16/jpmorgan-to-pay-100-million-and-make-admission-of-wrongdoing-in-london-whale-pact/?_r=0.
9. "Simplistic Models Miss Tail Risk," *Opalesque Alternative Market Briefing*, www.opalesque.com/640442/Simplistic_Risk_Models_Miss_Tail_Risk044.html.
10. *Opalesque Connecticut Roundtable*, www.opalesque.com/RT/ConnecticutRoundtable2013.html.
11. Helen Avery, "Prime Brokerage: The Day the Music Stopped," *Euromoney*, November 2008, www.euromoney.com/Article/2037583/Prime-brokerage-The-day-the-music-stopped.html.
12. Ernst & Young, "The Balancing Act: How to Navigate the Evolving Challenges of the Prime Brokerage Industry," 2013, www.ey.com/Publication/vwLUAssets/EY_Fresh_challenges_for_prime_brokerage_industry/$FILE/EY-Prime-brokerage-report.pdf.
13. "OTC Derivatives Market Reforms," Financial Stability Board, www.financialstabilityboard.org/publications/r_130902b.pdf.
14. "Despite Flood of Swaps Rules, Systemic Risk Still Opaque," *Opalesque Alternative Market Briefing*, www.opalesque.com/647984/Despite_flood_of_swaps_rules_systemic_risk_still798.html.
15. Excerpted from "Investors and Managers Must Come to a Common Understanding about What Is Possible," *Opalesque Alternative Market Briefing*, www.opalesque.com/644721/Investors_and_hedge_fund_managers_must_come_to472.html.

16. "Operational Due Diligence Firms Grow as Investors Seek to Manage Risk," *Opalesque Alternative Market Briefing*, www.opalesque.com/641693/Operational_due_diligence_firms_grow_as169.html.
17. "Wall Street's Financial Forecasts," CNBC Squawk Box, http://video.cnbc.com/gallery/?video=3000083992&play=1#eyJ2aWQiOiIzMDAwMDgzOTkyIiwiZW5jVmlkIjoibVpsY0phUkQvWFVhM0JCMDhGNUtPQT09IiwidlRhYiI6InRyYW5zY3JpcHQiLCJ2UGFnZSI6MSwiZ05hdiI6WyLCoExhdGVzdCBWaWRlbyJdLCJnU2VjdCI6IkFMTCIsImdQYWdlIjoiMSIsInN5bSI6IiIsInNlYXJjaCI6IiJ9.
18. "No One-Size-Fits-All Solution for Hedge Fund Succession Planning," *Opalesque Alternative Market Briefing*, www.opalesque.com/643283/No_solution_for_hedge_fund_succession328.html.

## CHAPTER 5

# Regulatory Regime Changes and Impact

Underlying the conversation about service providers, aligned interest, and due diligence is regulation. Since the financial crisis, hedge fund managers have seen a wave of new international regulation aimed at monitoring systemic risk and protecting investors. Here we outline the highest profile of the lot, and how they can impact hedge fund managers specifically. A full resource for further reading is provided for each regulation in its given section.

## DODD-FRANK ACT[1]

In the United States, the response to the 2008 crisis was encapsulated in the Dodd-Frank Act. The law itself is hundreds of pages and contains far reaching regulations for banks, brokers, and all corners of the financial landscape in the United States. Alternative investment firms couldn't escape without also being affected. Title IV[2] of the law deals with hedge funds specifically, and what they must now do to comply with the law.

The crux of Dodd-Frank is aimed at monitoring what regulators call *systemic risk*. Basically, they want to be able to see which financial firms are taking out the biggest positions, and when to either step in or closely monitor them as necessary. Regulators want to avoid, or at least monitor, new bubbles in the economy such that when they burst like mortgages did in 2008, the fallout is contained. Whether this is actually possible under this legislation is an open question, but this is one of its core goals.

We're focusing on systemic risk because this is the part of Dodd-Frank that directly impacts alternative investment firms. Among the umbrella of legislation stemming from the crisis, regulators have sought to isolate what they consider to be "systemically important financial institutions" (SIFIs).[3] The biggest banks are automatically part of this list, but the list is also expanded to include large insurance companies and the biggest hedge funds. Any financial firm with positions large enough that it would take considerable effort to unwind them or would cause tumult if they falter is going to be considered a SIFI.

Title IV explains what hedge funds have to disclose to both the Securities and Exchange Commission (SEC) and the Federal Deposit Insurance Corporation (FDIC), in order to help them monitor systemic risk. Prior to Dodd-Frank, hedge funds operated in the opaque world of private placements, and because they were considered private could avoid registration with regulators like the SEC, which also includes disclosure of their positions. Now, even though hedge funds are still considered private for the most part (they aren't available to retail investors), managers will have to register with the SEC and disclose their holdings.

Hedge funds by their nature take on more risk than you'll see from a bank or mutual fund. In some instances, this puts them at odds with the leverage and risk formulas included in Dodd-Frank initially, although they have had a bit of success in softening the regulations on an ex-post facto basis.[4,5] For example, on the surface it may look very high risk if a fund is levered up two, three, or four times its value, but it may only exist that way for a short period of time, or if it holds a lot of options eventually those margin requirements are going to come due. This is also true for other alternative investment firms like those that focus on real estate. Real estate funds may have an investment that also shows a high leverage ratio, but that ratio will come down as units in a building fill up. Blanket formulas or leverage restrictions may fail to take these realities into account.

While Title IV captures most hedge fund managers in its registration requirement, there are a few exceptions—advisers who solely advise venture capital funds, family offices, or funds managing less than $150,000,000 are exempted from compliance.

Dodd-Frank also knits together regulatory oversight between the SEC, FDIC, and Commodity Futures Trading Commission (CFTC). Under Title IV, the FDIC and CFTC share rulemaking authority involving private funds. In some cases, this means that the three regulators have worked on new rules that will apply across all agencies. In others, this means a doubling effect for funds that must now comply with SEC rules, and very similar but not exactly the same rules authored by the CFTC.

In order to submit the required disclosures, hedge funds are now required to file Form PF,[6] and Form ADV.[7] Form PF includes position level data for a given fund and are meant to create a trailing data set for the FDIC and Financial Stability Oversight Council (FSOC) to use to monitor systemic risk. Form ADV registers a hedge fund manager with the SEC. Data contained in these documents may be reviewed by any of the regulatory bodies mentioned here either for the purpose of monitoring systemic risk or as part of other compliance investigations on the part of a given regulator.

Prior to Dodd-Frank, the SEC for example would have to look for trading anomalies, or rely on investor or whistleblower claims in order to suss out fraud in private placements. Now, through Dodd-Frank, funds must register, pass licensing exams, and submit disclosures that may lead to further inspection if those disclosures are inconsistent or otherwise questionable. This established a new and significant compliance burden for hedge funds and for those that invest in them.

On the investor side, cost of compliance can get passed down as part of hedge fund fees. Hedge fund fees have always included some level of expenses, either those incurred by the manager or the firm, and the number of man hours and technology involved in filing Forms PF and other disclosures has only increased those costs. Dodd-Frank also changed the formula for ensuring investors meet net worth thresholds to invest in hedge funds.

To invest in hedge funds, an investor must beat a threshold of personal wealth that bumps them from retail to accredited. Accredited investors must have $1 million or more, but under the new rules can no longer use the value of their home(s) to meet that threshold. This is a change for many investors who may have used the value of their home or homes in that calculation. Additionally, hedge funds must also verify that any investor they speak with is accredited.

In addition to these changes in registration and disclosure, Dodd-Frank has ushered in a bevy of transaction-specific rules like the OTC clearers we discussed in Chapter 4, capital requirements for banks and brokers have also been increased, and technology expenditure is going up. Headcount is on the rise in compliance departments, and often hedge funds will be faced with compliance requirements from multiple regulators, including those in other countries.

It should also be noted that as of this writing, not all of the Dodd-Frank rules were fully complete and a significant amount of guidance is still expected from regulators. Hedge funds and investors are encouraged to keep in close contact with both regulators and legal counsel in order to monitor these new rules as they develop.

## FATCA

Coming along with the Dodd-Frank Act in the United States is the Foreign Account Tax Compliance Act (FATCA).[8] FATCA amounts to a sweeping change to the U.S. tax code that includes extraterritorial efforts to collect taxes from U.S. persons who may be living or sending money abroad.

FATCA seeks to set up individual tax sharing agreements with the rest of the world, and through these agreements capture information about U.S. taxable income that may be held offshore. In exchange for this information, the United States will also provide reciprocal information about foreign persons.

Final rules for FATCA and its implementation were issued on January 17, 2013. However, full implementation is still underway as many countries have yet to set up tax sharing agreements. For foreign governments who are working with the IRS on FATCA, there are two models of doing this. Under option 1, individuals or entities report their U.S. taxable investments, and the foreign government reports those to the United States on an automated basis. With option 2, the foreign investor or firm sets up a reporting arrangement directly with the IRS and the foreign government will do some measure of IRS reporting on its own.

Foreign governments may also withhold taxes as appropriate to American tax rates. The result of these negotiations, more than the finalized rules, will have a significant impact on hedge funds and alternatives firms, says Michael Laveman, tax partner at EisnerAmper, a U.S.-based accounting firm.[9] Once the agreements are finalized, hedge funds will have to determine which models have been chosen in the countries they do business with abroad. Key hedge funds jurisdictions like the Caymans have chosen option 1, but Switzerland opted for option 2. Monitoring these differences to ensure tax compliance is going to be another addition to the growing regulatory burden faced by hedge funds.

Laveman says that there are "significant differences" between the two compliance models and that those differences have the greatest impact on how alternative investment firms or investors themselves, have to react. The next major hurdles for hedge funds and investors will be registration with the IRS and completing updated documentation of investors and investment interests in order to meet reporting requirements. "One of the most difficult aspects of this is that you have to go back and document existing investors in addition to new ones according to these rules," Laveman explains.

Some American citizens have moved to renounce their American citizenship where they were already living abroad in response to FATCA. The *Wall Street Journal* reported that 1,130 Americans renounced their citizenship in the second quarter of 2013, more than did so in all of 2012.[10]

Foreign jurisdictions are also protesting FATCA, which has delayed implementation since the rules were entered into the Federal Register in January.[11] These countries cite U.S. overreach and compliance overhead with little upside. In some cases, countries have also argued that FATCA violates their domestic rules on accountholder privacy. To get around this issue, the IRS is negotiating intergovernmental agreements (IGAs) in which both governments come to a settlement about privacy and accountholder disclosures. However, many of these are still in process, delaying implementation.

China, for example, has opposed FATCA from the inception of the bill and has yet to make any move toward compliance talks.[12] Foreign financial institutions (FFIs) and their home countries have until December 2013 to be compliant, a deadline which seems likely to pass without anywhere near full compliance. The IRS opened an online portal for FATCA registration in August 2013. Non-compliant entities may face additional tax penalties if they fail to meet the law's requirements, however, for financial firms operating in countries without an IGA or a chosen reporting model, those penalties may be impossible to avoid.

FFIs that find themselves in that situation are supposed to withhold 30 percent on certain payments to payees including salaries, interest, capital gains, dividends, rents, or royalties. This is also true for U.S. entities making payments abroad to individuals or FFIs when they have not been able to verify FATCA compliance. Entities in this position either foreign or domestic must verify each investor's U.S. or non-U.S. status by procuring Form W-8 (for non-U.S. residents) or Form W-9 (for U.S. residents) and then report relevant U.S. account data to the IRS annually. If they fail to do this, the IRS will take 30 percent off the top of their gross receipts.

These requirements mean sweeping changes for U.S. citizens abroad and financial firms operating in countries once perceived to be more tax efficient. They also represent a growing trend among regulators the world over to go to extraterritorial lengths to enforce domestic rules as the world population takes on an increasingly multi-national lifestyle.

## JOBS ACT

More recently in the United States, Congress signed off on the Jumpstart Our Business Startups Act (JOBS Act).[13] The law was officially passed in April 2012, but it took until mid-2013 for parts of the bill relevant to hedge funds to come into force. Specifically, the bill gave legislative relief to private placement funds that want to advertise their offerings.

Prior to the JOBS Act, funds considered part of the private placements universe, that is, hedge funds, private equity, and some real estate funds, were prohibited from advertising publicly. According to the SEC, if hedge funds were allowed to advertise it may lead to increased instances of fraud in already hard to track funds, and potentially confuse retail investors who don't qualify to invest in hedge funds. The CFTC also has its own set of anti-fraud rules[14] that are designed to keep private funds just that. Given that hedge funds are approaching $3 trillion in total assets under management

(AUM), the casual observer may think this prohibition on general solicitation isn't really holding things back for the average hedge fund manager, and they'd be right. However, proponents of the bill would tell you that it is inherently unfair that mutual funds can advertise and hedge funds can't.

The logic underlying that argument is more nuanced than it sounds. If you look at a mutual fund commercial, they too are prohibited from disclosing much of what they do. Hence the sweeping high concept mini-films that make up most financial commercials. The scene opens with a well-dressed middle-aged man considering his desire to own a vineyard in retirement, followed by the logo for Franklin Templeton Investments. To the entirely uneducated viewer, this commercial could make you think Franklin Templeton Investments is actually a provider of grapes, or land, or vineyard accessories, instead of what it really is—a mutual fund company that will help you horde enough cash to move to Tuscany, for a fee. This is by design. Even though Franklin Templeton Investments offers a number of investment vehicles readily available to retail investors with $20,000 nest eggs instead of $1 million, they can't go on TV and outline the high points of those offerings. Instead, what they rely on is that when a retail investor goes in to speak with a financial advisor, they might recognize the logo and a shared desire for vineyard ownership through the twilight years. Hedge funds, historically, have been prohibited from doing this, as apparently just the mere mention of a hedge fund's name might confuse investors into thinking they too can secure a vineyard through Bridgewater Associates with their $20,000 nest egg. Supporters of hedge fund advertising say they too deserve the right to their own information-free logo commercials.

Now, thanks to Congress, they do—almost. The SEC and the CFTC aren't big fans of the JOBS Act,[15] precisely because they still believe that letting hedge funds advertise may lead to investor confusion and increased fraud. Congress gave rulemaking authority to the regulators with the bill, and so in an effort to comply with the law, they've lifted the ban on general solicitation but they haven't made it easy.

Hedge fund managers can now provide, as a matter of course, more public information about their funds, but not much. Think back to our logo commercial example. You may start to see something similar crop up online for hedge funds before you see any commercials. Right now, hedge funds often have a web page that consists of their name and a login form. In many cases, they don't even have that. It's hard to think of a business in 2013 without a website, but some compliance teams read the prohibition on solicitation to mean that anytime a non-accredited investor might run across their fund they could be in trouble for solicitation. So, if you as an investor wanted to see fund offerings you had to know where to go—consultants, platforms, capital introducers, brokers, or other rich people. Going forward, you may well be able to type the name of a hedge fund in Google and at least get a website with a name and a vague description of what it does before being prompted to login.

Is there much upside to this for hedge funds? That remains unclear. The biggest hedge funds, which now resemble asset management firms and have retail offerings, may take to putting out a few logo commercials. For the rest of the industry, the JOBS Act puts a little more breathing room between funds and regulators if they slip up and happen to mention that they run a hedge fund in mixed company. Even if they do start advertising, hedge funds will still have to verify that they are soliciting only accredited investors and they also have to notify the SEC of their intentions and activities.

Indeed, some allocators take a hardline view of the change—"Congress and the SEC didn't do away with accredited investors and that's still a very small niche in the total market; advertising may not be the best way to target those investors," says Charlie Nightingale, of Pacific Alternative Asset Management Company (PAAMCO).[16] "I have yet to hear about any hedge funds planning to advertise. We focus a lot on emerging managers and we'd hope that they are focused on investing and not advertising."

He notes that, at best, advertising could be a tool some of the biggest hedge funds use to brand themselves, similar to advertising done by the Vanguards of the world. "If terms like alpha and absolute returns will enter the marketplace more, people could gain an understanding, but hedge fund strategies and structures are very fundamentally different from mutual funds and so that's going to be a very steep learning curve. All of these advertisements will be probably lead to more consumer confusion."

Norm Champ, director of the Securities and Exchange Commission's Division of Investment Management, has also been up front about the regulator's begrudging lift of the ban. "With general solicitation and general advertising soon to be an option, I want to reiterate the commission's reminder from the adopting release that advisers to private funds are subject to an anti-fraud rule that prohibits fraudulent and misleading conduct with respect to fund investors, including making untrue statements of material fact to those investors. In the adopting release, the commission also noted that investment advisers who have implemented appropriate policies and procedures regarding the nature and content of private-fund-sales literature are less likely to use materially misleading advertising materials or otherwise violate federal securities law. Accordingly, advisers should carefully review their policies and procedures to determine whether they are reasonably designed to prevent the use of fraudulent or misleading advertisements and update those policies where necessary, particularly if the hedge funds intend to engage in general-solicitation activity. Hedge fund sponsors intending to rely on the new rule also should consider whether their current practices for verifying accredited-investor status meet the requirements of the new rule." These comments were part of a panel held for managers and investors on compliance issues.[17]

During the same remarks, Champ also reiterated plans by the regulator to increase scrutiny around firms engaged in broad based solicitation activities. "We are committed to taking steps to pursue additional investor safeguards, if and where such measures become necessary once the ban on general solicitation is lifted," he said. These remarks in of themselves may have a chilling effect on the use of general solicitation by anyone other than the largest firms, which are also equivalently well-resourced on the compliance side.

## CURRENT LEGAL LANDSCAPE FOR FUNDRAISING IN THE UNITED STATES

***Benedicte Gravrand***

Stephen C. Tirrell, Partner at global law firm Bingham McCutchen, New York, talked to me about the existing legal landscape for new investment managers who want to raise private funds in the United States, with a focus on the Investment Advisers Act, the Securities Act, the Investment Company Act, the Exchange Act, and the JOBS Act.

**Gravrand:** Please tell me about the legal landscape that investment managers have to consider when raising any private fund in the United States.

**Stephen Tirrell:** Essentially there are four different regulations that we have to consider; the Investment Advisers Act, the Securities Act, the Investment Company Act, and the Exchange Act.

They act in one or more fashion with respect to either the advisory entity or the fund entity. And in each instance, at least in the Securities Act and the Investment Company Act, there are exemptions from registration that private fund managers typically rely on with respect to the private funds that they sponsor.

The Securities Act is the Act that governs the offering of shares to investors in the market. Typically private funds don't register their shares under the Securities Act with the Securities and Exchange Commission (SEC) but rely on an exemption from registration.

Therefore, no registration filing is required; however fund managers are required to file a Form D, which is a notice filing that is filed electronically with the SEC. There is no registration statement; we just make a private offering to accredited investors under the

Securities Act. And as long as the manager has a reasonable belief that the investors are accredited investors, as defined under the Securities Act, and follow certain other guidelines, they can offer those shares privately to those investors.

As for the Investment Company Act, this is the Act that people generally consider governs registered investment funds or mutual funds here in the United States. Most funds rely on either 3C1 or 3C7, which are exceptions to registration under that Act, such that the private funds aren't considered registered investment companies or public investment companies under the Act.

The Advisers Act actually governs the investment adviser entity, and Dodd-Frank certainly changed the landscape with respect to the rules and regulations governing investment advisers under the Advisers Act. Previously, many private fund managers relied on an exemption from registration under Section 203(b)(3). The Dodd-Frank Act rescinded that exemption. Now under the revised rules, almost all investment advisers located in the United States either have to register with the SEC, or the state in which they operate. There are still exemptions to registration that investment advisers may qualify for but those exemptions are narrower after the passage of Dodd-Frank.

The Exchange Act is a two-fold issue for fund managers. On the one hand, the Act essentially limits the number of investors that a private investment fund relying upon Section 3(c)(7) of the Investment Company Act can admit before they have to register the shares under the Exchange Act. That limit is 499 investors.

The Exchange Act is important for fund managers in another regard; because most private fund managers are continually raising assets, many hire placement agents, finders, or solicitors, and when you are operating in the United States or you are offering to U.S. persons, the solicitor or placement agent needs to be an "associated person" of a registered broker-dealer, which means he or she is required to be affiliated with a registered broker-dealer here in the United States.

Unfortunately, in some instances, these placement agents have not been registered broker-dealers. The SEC has stepped up its enforcement in this area; in fact there are two recent enforcement cases that deal with funds that have used unregistered broker-dealers or persons that are not affiliated with a registered broker-dealer in order to raise assets. The consequences of hiring an unregistered broker-dealer to solicit investors can be severe. Private fund managers really need to consider the registration status of the people they are dealing with when they are contracting with third parties to help them place assets.

**Gravrand:** And for the Securities Act and the Investment Company Act, has anything changed?

**Stephen Tirrell:** In the Investment Company Act, no.

In the Securities Act, there have been minor adjustments to some of the definitions, such as the definition of an accredited investor, which has changed in the last few years, but not in a major fashion. Basically the rules focused on the definition of an accredited investor: it's either a net income test or a net worth test. A net income test is that an individual has made $200,000 and has reasonable belief that they will continue to make $200,000, or with their spouse $300,000 over the next two years.

The net worth test is $1 million, and again, you can count your primary residence, but how the liabilities associated with the primary residence are counted toward that $1 million has changed slightly.

**Gravrand:** What about the JOBS Act?

**Stephen Tirrell:** The JOBS Act, which was signed into law by President Obama in July of last year, mandated the SEC to finalize rules dealing with how companies can sell their shares. Generally under the Securities Act, one of the tenets of making a private offering in the United States is that the issuer must not make a general solicitation, which is generally considered to be some sort of advertising. So what you don't typically see, although not in all cases, is hedge funds or private funds market or advertise their offerings in the United States.

If you are deemed to be making a general solicitation such as on an Internet website, in magazines, whatever goes to the public at large, the issuer may be deemed to have violated the ban on general solicitation and may not be able to make a good private offering under the Securities Act. This means they can't qualify for that exemption we discussed earlier and, absent some other exemption, may be required to register their shares under the Securities Act. The JOBS Act mandated that Congress come up with rules to rescind that ban on general solicitations.

When that Act was first signed into law, hedge fund managers and private advisers said "we can start advertising and marketing our hedge funds in a general solicitation and therefore not have to worry about our status, our private offering status under the Securities Act."

**Gravrand:** Yes. But the JOBS Act will really be more about letting hedge funds publish their results on their website, letting the media talk about their performance openly, whereas now it's difficult.

They are not exactly going to start advertising in the newspapers or billboards.

**Stephen Tirrell:** Don't be so sure of that. There are always people and companies that are going to push the boundaries. I do think you will see more advertising in trade magazines and maybe billboards.

Even when rules go into effect that rescind the ban on general solicitation, what advisers have to consider are the rules and regulations governing advertising and governing the performance advertising in particular. There will be a lot more emphasis on performance advertising, particularly considering it will be out there in the public domain. They really have to pay attention to those rules and what the SEC staff has said historically regarding performance advertising.

**Gravrand:** You talked about five different Acts that new fund managers should take into account. Is there anything else within the legal landscape that they should be wary of?

**Stephen Tirrell:** There have been a lot of changes over the last few years in regards to regulation. Every couple of months, there is a new regulation that's being promulgated, such as pay-to-play rules with respect to how investment advisers interact with government officials. There are filing obligations, such as Form PF. There are new regulations governing how investment advisers trade futures and options, how they trade derivatives under Dodd-Frank. There are different registration statuses under the CFTC with the NFA.

And so there are a panoply of new rules and regulations to consider when an adviser is looking to start a new business and launch new funds, many of which have created higher barriers to entry into the market. Given the change in legal and regulatory landscape, choosing your service providers, whether it be legal, compliance, administrators, and others, is more important now than it ever has been before.

## AIFMD

As we outlined earlier, the Alternative Investment Fund Managers Directive (AIFMD)[18] is the big compliance change for hedge funds that are in Europe or foreign funds that market to Europeans. The AIFMD is essentially the EU-wide version of the Dodd-Frank act, seeking to monitor systemic risk, provide greater investor protections, and require registration and disclosure from previously private funds.

The Directive came into force in July 2013, and implementation should be fully complete by 2015. The Directive outlines registration and reporting requirements for managers (Table 5.1) and also sets up a clear preference for the Undertakings for Collective Investment in Transferable Securities (UCITS) structure. Funds that do not fit within the UCITS wrapper are considered alternative investment funds (AIFs), and face a different set of compliance challenges. Let's unpack what this means.

To review, here's how these funds are structured:

*AIFs*

Traditional private placement hedge fund.

Tailored to the non-retail investor.

Traditional hedge fund strategies.

Onshore firms, onshore structures, and/or a limited group of offshore firms approved by European regulators on a case-by-case basis.

Open and closed-end funds.

Cannot be: holding companies, joint ventures, pension funds, family offices, securitization special purpose entities, and employee participation or savings schemes.

Managers must be licensed to participate in portfolio and risk management; may apply for EU passport to work in all EU countries.

*UCITS*

Regulated alternatives, similar to liquid alternatives (hedged mutual funds) in the United States.

Money Market funds.

Available to both retail and accredited investors.

Public disclosures, highly liquid structure.

Allowable investments limited to: transferable securities, money market instruments, units of collective investment schemes, bank deposits, and FDI.

UCITS funds can also gain exposure to non-eligible assets in certain ways, notably FDI based on financial indices, closed-ended funds, or structured transferable securities.

Managers seeking to run or market UCITS funds must be registered and approved within the EU, or have the approval of a member state to be listed as the member state of reference and have a licensed and registered domestic point of contact serving as the primary European face of an offshore fund.

**TABLE 5.1** Registration Requirements for AIFMs/AIFs

| | |
|---|---|
| Potential managers will need to show | Resume, experience, and background of AIF management team; |
| | Remuneration policies and practices of the fund; |
| | Shareholders with qualifying holdings; |
| | Delegation and sub-delegation arrangements to third parties; |
| | A detailed plan for how the fund will meet passport conditions, transparency requirements, operational procedures, fund structure, and marketing plan. |
| The fund itself will need to show | Fund structure—Master/feeder, domicile, and so on |
| | Fund incorporation documents |
| | Depository arrangements |
| | Typical investor disclosure |
| | Investment strategy |

Once a manager registers they can choose to manage a fund in their own country only, or get what is called a passport license allowing them to manage funds across EU member states. If a manager wants a passport, they will need to provide a full list of the funds they intend to manage and in which countries, along with a full organizational and operational structure for the multi-national company. If a manager already has UCITS funds, some of these disclosure requirements may already be fulfilled. Once a manager is registered, that manger's name and firm will be listed in a public register of all the managers in the EU.

Once passed, the AIFMD effectively up-ended private funds on the continent, as evidenced by the breakdown and registration requirements noted above. Hedge fund managers local to the Eurozone, and those doing business there have had to evaluate how their funds fit into these new structures and what they must do to comply. For multi-national firms, this can mean compliance with parts of Dodd-Frank, FATCA, and the AIFMD.

In other ways, the preference for UCITS outlined by the Directive has bolstered the use of the structure in the EU and abroad. Some non-EU countries are seeing UCITS funds brought to market domestically, as the registration and reporting requirements have set a new standard, readily adopted in more conservative markets like the Middle East.

Keith Hale, executive vice president of client and business development at Multifonds, multi-jurisdictional investment fund software platform provider for administrators, says that the directive may also make AIFs more attractive. "There is a lot of convergence between traditional UCITS structures and alternatives and AIFMD is a catalyst for this convergence," he says.[19]

The AIF is more institutional in its nature than the UCITS vehicle. It may also allow hedge fund managers to overcome the limit on performance that fitting into a UCITS structure inevitably has. "It may enable hedge fund managers to perform better as AIFs have more of the characteristics of an offshore hedge fund than a UCITS structure does," Hale says.

With an AIF-regulated structure, non-European funds will have an increased opportunity to sell and market funds across Europe. "That's where the growth will be," Hale predicts. "We have seen a big growth and convergence between traditional long only funds and hedge funds and we are seeing a growth in the alternative space." The Multifonds platform accounts for $3 trillion in assets, and specifically in their transfer agency and investor servicing business, some $140 billion is accounted for by hedge fund structures.

## MiFID

Along with the AIFMD came the Markets in Financial Instruments Directive (MiFID),[20] which seeks to restructure local exchanges, and how certain instruments are handled from a regulatory standpoint. MiFID hasn't seen as much notoriety as the AIFMD, but will have an impact on hedge fund strategies, and how hedge funds participate in these newly restructured exchanges.

The UCITS directives essentially outline the structure of the UCITS wrapper, how it works, and who can use, market, and manage the funds. MiFID looks at who asset managers can sell to. UCITS compliant funds can be considered complex or non-complex based on what they do. Non-complex UCITS funds also come under the scope of the MiFID directive, which then impacts how asset managers can sell them.

The underlying issue with MiFID is investor protection when funds use riskier instruments like derivatives. Even some long-only managers use derivatives in the management of those portfolios, which can still be UCITS compliant, but the presence of riskier instruments can trigger additional regulations like MiFID. The effects of MiFID are more likely to be felt by hedge fund managers that work with institutions.

For managers running their own money, or high net worth/family office money it may well be perfectly within the scope of those mandates to undertake the use of riskier trades and instruments. For managers working with institutions that have certain investor protection rules embedded into their relationships, MiFID is meant to step in and bolster those protections. MiFID requires organizations that have outsourced parts of their operations to third parties to maintain the same duty of care and internal controls as they would were they running it themselves.

MiFID changes how exchanges are run and orders are executed, mandating that participating firms execute orders using the best available means, and that disclosures are made to support those choices. This means that brokers will have to become neutral by design, eroding some of the value proposition embedded in platforms and technologies driven by access to certain managers. This neutrality then has knock-on effects for hedge fund managers used to seeing client interest based on those relationships. MiFID pushes hedge funds to behave more like sell-side firms or banks. This changes the game for managers in a variety of ways, requiring new technologies, disclosures, and vendor relationships.

MiFID rules are still being finalized, and the EU has already released a second MiFID directive draft to reflect these changes.

## EMIR

The European Market Infrastructure Regulation (EMIR)[21] sets up complex reporting requirements for financial markets participants that are, in some ways, harder to comply with than Dodd-Frank or the AIFMD.

EMIR is an EU regulation for OTC derivatives, central counterparties (CCPs), and trade repositories (TRs), which entered into force in the summer of 2012. EMIR requires certain financial counterparties, including banks, insurers, and investment firms as well as certain non-financial counterparties, including energy and real estate firms to report details of new, modified, or terminated MiFID derivatives contracts to a registered trade repository. These same counterparties may also be required to comply with certain risk mitigation requirements, collateralize and in certain circumstances clear their OTC derivative contracts through central clearers. EMIR and MiFID essentially try to harmonize how OTC instruments are dealt with in both the United States and EU, but the EU put its own unique spin on these rules that can make compliance more complex.

Unlike Dodd-Frank, the reporting requirement under EMIR applies to both counterparties to a trade (dual reporting requirement) and will capture OTC derivative trades as well as exchange traded derivative trades (such as futures).

The pieces of EMIR including central clearers are still coming together and won't be fully operational until 2014, which actually puts the EU behind the U.S. implementation timeline and has already led to a delay of implementation in the United States. In order to maintain its harmonization agreement, the United States has agreed to delay implementation of the OTC rules under Dodd-Frank until December 31, 2013. EMIR will require financial firms to report interest rate derivative and credit derivative use that comes under the scope of MiFID. At a basic level, EMIR and MiFID are working together to create the same type of OTC clearing infrastructure ushered in by the SEC and CFTC, and explained in Chapter 6 in our section on central clearers.

Renaud Huck, Head of UK Institutional Investor Relations at Eurex, an exchange is already seeing changes in the OTC market based on these sets of regulations. "On the OTC side, the big elephant in the room is called EMIR, and the European regulators such as ESMA are quite keen on seeing this regulation going forward in parallel with what is currently taking place in the United States with Dodd-Frank," he says.[22,23] Huck believes that with EMIR and Dodd-Frank, second and third tier buy-side and equally sell-side participants will exit the OTC space as it will become too expensive and structurally challenging for them to continue trading in that space.

"So the opportunity for us as an exchange and a clearinghouse is to list OTC proxy futures instruments, such as swap futures, inflation futures, to name a couple, and I think this is what will help the industry. Those products are the result of the unintended side-effects of the new regulation. The regulators didn't think that by implementing these regulations the way the marketplace was going to operate will change dramatically, but that's going to be the case."

## SUMMARY

Regulations aimed at hedge funds have changed drastically in the years following 2008. Whether it is Dodd-Frank in the United States or AIFMD in the EU, the way these rules are finalized will dominate the industry for the next two years or more. Moves to come after tax cheats like FATCA, or to regulate exotic financial instruments as seen in MiFID provide a glimpse into how far regulators are willing to go.

## NOTES

1. "Dodd-Frank Wall Street Reform and Consumer Protection Act," Securities and Exchange Commission, www.sec.gov/about/laws/wallstreetreform-cpa.pdf.

2. "Title IV: Regulation of Advisors to Hedge Funds and Others," Legal Information Institute, Cornell University, www.law.cornell.edu/wex/dodd-frank_title_iv.
3. "Consultative Document: Application of the Key Attributes of Effective Resolution Regimes to Non-Bank Financial Institutions," Financial Stability Board, www.financialstabilityboard.org/publications/r_130812a.htm.
4. "Whale of a Problem: Regulators Subvert Will of Congress," ProPublica The Trade, www.propublica.org/thetrade/item/whale-of-a-problem-regulators-subvert-will-of-congress.
5. "What the Banks' Three Year War on Dodd-Frank Looks Like," Sunlight Foundation, http://sunlightfoundation.com/feature/dodd-frank-3-year.
6. "Derivatives Lobby Has US Regulators on the Run," Bloomberg, www.bloomberg.com/news/2012-04-17/derivatives-lobby-has-u-s-regulators-on-the-run.html.
7. Form PF, Securities and Exchange Commission, www.sec.gov/rules/final/2011/ia-3308-formpf.pdf.
8. Form ADF, Securities and Exchange Commission, www.sec.gov/answers/formadv.htm.
9. "Foreign Account Tax Compliance Act," Internal Revenue Service, www.irs.gov/Businesses/Corporations/Foreign-Account-Tax-Compliance-Act-(FATCA).
10. "FATCA Regs Finalized, Hedge Funds Still in Limbo," *Opalesque Alternative Market Briefing*, www.opalesque.com/645227/FATCA_regs_finalized_but_hedge_funds_still_in522.html.
11. "US Expats Balk at Tax Law," *Wall Street Journal*, http://online.wsj.com/news/articles/SB10001424127887323585604579007860126146566.
12. "Complying with U.S. Tax Evasion Law Is Vexing Foreign Banks," *New York Times DealBook*, http://dealbook.nytimes.com/2013/09/16/complying-with-u-s-tax-evasion-law-is-vexing-foreign-banks/?_r=0.
13. "Tax Deal with US a Win for China, Lawyers Say," *South China Morning Post*, www.scmp.com/business/china-business/article/1302888/tax-deal-us-win-china-lawyers-say.
14. "Jumpstart Our Business Startups Act," U.S. Government Printing Office, www.gpo.gov/fdsys/pkg/BILLS-112hr3606enr/pdf/BILLS-112hr3606enr.pdf.
15. "Anti-Manipulation Final Rule," Commodity Futures Trading Commission, www.cftc.gov/LawRegulation/DoddFrankAct/Rulemakings/DF_23_DFManipulation/index.htm.
16. "SEC Lifts Hedge Fund Ad Ban Amid Uncertainty," Risk.net, www.risk.net/hedge-funds-review/news/2280810/sec-lifts-hedge-fund-ad-ban-amid-some-uncertainty.

17. "Derivatives Rules, FATCA Delayed, Glass-Steagall Revived," *Opalesque Alternative Market Briefing*, www.opalesque.com/647250/Derivatives_rules_FATCA_delayed_revived725.html.
18. "SEC Director Outlines Hedge Fund Regulatory Scene," *Investment News*, https://home.investmentnews.com/clickshare/authenticateUserSubscription.do?CSProduct=investmentnews&CSAuthReq=1:173506063984164:AID%7CID:5CD85A0B2CE88E2A9559F910DCD68ABF&AID=20130922/REG/309229977&title=SEC%20director%20outlines%20hedge%20fund%20regulatory%20scene&ID=&CSTargetURL=http%3A%2F%2Fwww.investmentnews.com%2Fapps%2Fpbcs.dll%2Flogin%3FAssignSessionID%3D173506063984164%26AID%3D20130922%2FREG%2F309229977.
19. "Alternative Investment Fund Managers Directive," European Commission, http://eur-lex.europa.eu/LexUriServ/LexUriServ.do?uri=OJ:L:2011:174:0001:01:EN:PDF.
20. "Multifonds Finds New AIF Structure Offers Business Opportunities to Alternative Funds," *Opalesque Alternative Market Briefing*, www.opalesque.com/645411/Multifonds_finds_new_AIF_structure_offers_business_opportunities541.html.
21. "Markets in Financial Instruments Directive," European Commission, http://ec.europa.eu/internal_market/securities/isd/mifid/index_en.htm.
22. "European Market Infrastructure Regulation," European Commission, www.esma.europa.eu/page/European-Market-Infrastructure-Regulation-EMIR.
23. "EMIR Reporting More Complex and Extensive than Dodd-Frank," *Opalesque Alternative Market Briefing*, www.opalesque.com/647249/EMIR_reporting_more_complex_and_extensive_than724.html.

CHAPTER 6

# Managed Futures

***Mark Melin***

Opalesque Futures Intelligence

Here we will break down managed futures strategies and learn more about how each of these strategies can bring value to a portfolio. At the end we present our criteria for evaluating CTAs, or Commodity Trading Advisors, the name for managers that use managed futures strategies.

Broadly speaking, managed futures is a term for hedge funds that rely on the use of futures contracts for the core of the trading strategy. Futures are contracts to sell something—metals, crops, or currencies usually—at a future date. Investors in futures do not carry with them any immediate ownership in the asset that is part of the contract. Instead, both sides make good faith deposits on the contract. Both sides must also keep margin accounts in case the price for the contract goes up, requiring a larger deposit. This is known as a margin call.

Managed Futures funds are typically run by a CTA. CTAs registered with organizations like the National Futures Association, which provide audited track records of performance and basic background information. (We will cover how to evaluate a CTA later in the chapter.)

Managed futures contracts can go up or down in price and can be bought or sold at any time before the delivery date, which is the bread and butter of most managed futures strategies. Here is one example:

Two parties agree on a $40,000 pork belly contract on Monday for a contract that comes due in October. The deposit value on this contract is 10 percent or $4,000. Both sides put up $4,000 and have enough cash in their margin accounts to cover increases between now and October. By Friday, pork bellies have gone up in price, so the value of the $40,000 contract is now $40,400. If the CTA sells on Friday, he just made 10 percent profit on his $4,000 deposit.

CTAs trade these contracts using computer algorithms that attempt to capture trends over various timeframes. While *trend following* is the most predominant strategy, other strategies that rely on market volatility or the relative value between two different types of commodities are also worth noting. We'll break out these approaches in the next section. First, let's understand how managed futures responds to market cycles.

Managed futures strategies typically do better in volatile markets. The P(A|B) Method for understanding managed futures portfolios described below, attributes this to the fact that volatility is usually driven by market shock and change in perception, which tends to generate price persistence, relative value dislocations, and volatility opportunities. Most CTAs use computerized algorithms to look for trends in the direction of markets (whether prices will go up or down) and make trades based on those trends. While other CTAs are discretionary, relying on discretionary thought processes and the trading manager's skill. Market trends can be timeframe dependent—that is, prices will go up over short, medium, or long term. Typically, managed futures are uncorrelated to equities, and uncorrelated to the underlying assets of the futures contracts. This means that when equities are going down, managed futures could find strong price trends and generate positive performance. Managed futures funds also tend to appear as though they are long volatility, which affects how they respond to market cycles.

### THE INSTITUTIONAL PERSPECTIVE ON MANAGED FUTURES

Tom O'Donnell has a long memory. While at the Virginia Retirement System in the early 1990s he and his colleagues were tasked with evaluating managed futures. The experience changed the course of his career, as he is now a principal and director of global business development at the Bornhoft Group, a firm that has specialized in multiple CTA portfolios since 1985. Today more than ever Mr. O'Donnell believes that managed futures is something institutional investors should investigate. "Institutional investors need to consider all potential portfolio outcomes. Preparing portfolios for the next 2008, or even for an environment that is only half as bad, should be on the agenda. Seeking out investments that have the potential to limit downside volatility should always be of interest."

"An Institutional Perspective on Managed Futures," *Opalesque Futures Intelligence*, 2012, www.opalesque.com/OFI1333/A_Former_Institutional_Perspective_on_Managed_Futures333.html.

## EXPLORING DIFFERENT WAYS TO TRADE MANAGED FUTURES

Here we will break out the different ways CTAs use managed futures and trade them. Each of these represents its own strategy-type, and each has different goals.

### What Is Trend Following?

In order to follow a trend, CTAs work with sophisticated computer algorithms to find movements in prices that will last for a certain period of time. The trick is to learn when a trend starts and when it ends in order to avoid getting caught in a broad trend reversal in the long term, or get whipsawed in the short term. The most basic way to understand trend following is that CTAs go long markets with recent, consistent positive returns and go short markets with recent, consistent negative returns, based on a chosen period of time.

Once a trend ends, regardless of the time frame, the tendency is for markets to compress or absorb volatility, thereby setting up the next wave of directional movement.[1]

"We tend to see trends come in three-to-five-year rolling waves, or cycles, in the longer duration timeframe," said Cole Wilcox, a CTA, who operates three funds at Longboard Asset Management. "With an ultra-long-term trend follower, for instance, we may have three to five years of above mean performance environments and three to five years of average to below mean performance environments, with some of those years substantially below average."

There are several ways CTAs can break out trend following; we've broken out some of the more common ones below.

**Long Term[2]** As the name would suggest, long-term trend following as a strategy seeks to capture trends within the future market over a long (one year or more) time period. Long-term trend followers typically rely on a combination of historical and current market factors to identify a trend. The trick is to avoid false trend signals. The CTA will then put a stop-loss order either below or above a chosen trend line to ensure if the trend shifts they won't lose too much.

Long-term trend following can be considered the old guard of managed futures. Indeed, the original funds in this space are called the "Original Turtles." One of the original turtles, Jerry Parker of long-term trend follower Chesapeake Capital, explains his approach.

Chesapeake should experience positive market environments during periods when market trends, or *price persistence*, are occurring. "When the markets we trade experience trends, we tend to make money; when the investment is not trending we will not make money," he said, noting that 2012 was the trend follower's worst year, down 17.81 percent, the worst performance in a 30-year history.

Long-term trend followers such as Chesapeake, which have average hold periods of more than one year, buy and sell commodities and financial futures in 100 markets. Investors in such long-term programs might expect volatility to occur during periods of non-directional market environments. "Volatility in a positive trade (upside deviation) is entirely tolerated in this system," noted Parker. CTAs with a long hold period often have a wide berth on the downside, particularly because once a trade becomes profitable investors might expect the CTA to let the trade run. "Once a trade becomes profitable, we let the (upside) volatility run."

Typically long-term trend followers such as Chesapeake Capital can be expected to have a large win size with win percentage not as a statistically significant variable for consideration. "When you have a non-normal distribution with profitable outlier trades that dominate the portfolio, applying normal statistical measurements on top of that is probably incorrect," he said.

### WHEN PRICE PERSISTENCE HITS A MARKET SHOULD ALL TREND FOLLOWERS PARTICIPATE?

As drought ravaged U.S. agricultural regions for the second year, something not seen since the dustbowl that occurred during the great depression, crop supply generally decreased and prices of corn, soybeans, and other agricultural products moved higher. Price persistence gripped these markets as commodity costs consistently moved in a singular direction.

Managed futures investors might assume that price persistence should benefit investments with agricultural exposure, but in fact all managed futures strategies should not be expected to perform positively during periods of price persistence. Corn is up near 60 percent from June to mid-August, while soybeans are up 24 percent over a similar period. The BarclayHedge Agricultural Traders index was up 1.93 percent in July 2012, mirroring similar gains across the complex of managed futures indices. Each CTA has a strategy that should be understood on many levels. The managed futures strategy along with trade time frame and markets traded all need to be considered.

CTAs with grain exposure across the industry spectrum mirrored this thought. "As a manager who benefits from directional movement and trends we have enjoyed steady performance primarily in the soybean complex throughout the year," noted Jeff Roy, senior portfolio manager at Pardo Capital Ltd., an NFA registered Commodity Trading Advisor and trend following program with a mid- to long-term trend following time window. "The abrupt regime change in the price action of the rest of the grain complex in June and July has been just the type of activity that a reactive, systematic strategy like XT99 thrives on."

Industry insiders have noted that some discretionary managers were caught off guard by the rapid price appreciation in the grains and, unlike systematic managers, they might not be accustomed to buying into buying so might not participate in such abrupt moves with the same commitment.

The recent price action in agricultural products is a good point to illustrate the importance of understanding how a CTA's strategy, trade timeframe, and markets traded relates to market environment. Take trade timeframe, for instance. Long-term trend followers such as Longboard Asset Management, which runs a markets traded commodity fund, benefited during July as their algorithm picked up the trend in the grain markets and held on to the trade and continues to hold to this day.

"Our long-term model identifies a trend and stays with the trade until that A to Z movement runs its course," said one long-term trend follower. "We trade very infrequently. Our algorithm identifies assets that are in the top or bottom 5 percent deciles, those markets we believe have potential to significantly outperform in either direction."

This long-term model bought assets in the agricultural complex and held this exposure, some trend-following CTAs with shorter-term time frames didn't fare as well in the 2012 market environment. Neural Capital, for instance, which operates a short-term trend following algorithm, found the intra-day volatility in corn and soybeans to be challenging. Patrick de Villiers, the trading manager for Neural Capital noted that volatility, particularly to close out the weekend on a Friday, triggered sell stops on their long grain positions. "Our average trade time window is 8 to 10 days," Mr. de Villiers, said. The CTA noted their write off positions were impacted by end of the week volatility and position squaring. "We are using a trailing stop loss according to our system, the formula behind our market philosophy. As increases in volatility occur there is a higher probability that the stop is going to get triggered."

While the CTA's time window is important to consider relative to market environment, so too is trade strategy. Jerod Leman is the primary grain trader for Typhon Capital, which operates a spread/arbitrage strategy in the agricultural markets. The strategy works by purchasing one contract and selling a related contract. It is not dependent on the overall move of the underlying market, up or down, as it is between the relationship between the contract bought and sold. In the case of Typhon the CTA typically utilizes calendar spreads, buying and selling different time frames of the same contract. Leman noted that the front months of corn, for instance, had dislocated from historic norms. "Most spread relationships are inverted, with the front months gaining on the back month," he said. Other spread, or *relative value*, strategies might sell related commodities, such as oil and gasoline, while other high-frequency strategies might arbitrage the price difference between the cash and futures contract.

Performance and related market risk in the CTA space can vary based on strategy, risk management regime, trade timeframe, volatility, and market environment. CTAs that benefited from the recent market environments in the agricultural complex tended to be those whose systems identified that volatility lead to price persistence but had stops in place that gave the position a wide berth. This is not to say that any one strategy is better than another; it is to provide understanding that many just work under different market environments. It is to point out that each strategy operates differently depending on the market environment. It is in understanding the CTA's strategy and how it impacts risk and performance expectations that investors can better understand the managed futures investment.

"The Untold Story," *Opalesque Futures Intelligence*, September 2012, www.opalesque.com/OFI1293/The_Untold_of_the_recent_surge_in293.html.

**Short Term** Short-term trend followers basically shrink their time series down to one day or one week, making for a more active trading strategy. Swiss CTA, Amplitude Capital[3] holds its positions for eight days in one program, and only one day in another.

Amplitude Klassik holds for eight days, and trades liquid exchange-traded futures across equities, foreign exchange (FX), fixed income, and commodities, and its strategy is based on a systematic and fully automated directional short-term program. It uses extensive quantitative analysis of real-time price data and sophisticated portfolio methodology to detect ultra-short to short-term market trends and reversion.

Amplitude's flagship fund, the Dynamic Trading fund, holds for one day on a similar program to Klassik, but with an additional set of strategy indicators that makes the program less affected by the sideways market movements, and would help it maintain performance should a large scale event take place. Both funds have been able to mitigate downside risk with the help of high powered quantitative analysis, and adding diversification layers like the strategy indicators added to the Dynamic program.

The year 2009 was a banner year for short-term CTAs,[4] spurred by improvements in electronic trading technology and positive market conditions. The returns from short-term CTAs drew significant investor inflows through the first quarter of 2009. But after 2009, the market changed, making it much more difficult for short-term CTAs and raising questions about the staying power of the approach.

While assets are still coming into short-term CTAs, they are arriving at a decreased rate and the spread between short- and long-term CTAs has widened. As a result, it can be more difficult for smaller short-term CTAs to last and attract assets.

"If you are a large institution, and have decided that all this academic work is compelling, and have made a decision to get involved in the space, then the concern for reputational risk is very important. You need to be sure, before making a large allocation to a manager, that the manager is actually able to handle the allocation. As a result, many large institutional investors have ended up giving their money to firms that trade with a longer time frame, who are well established, who have a recognized reputation and can handle large assets," says Ernest Jaffarian, from Efficient Capital Management, of the trend.

Despite this, there may be some added benefits to short-term traders that can outweigh these business risks. Specifically, short-term CTAs are typically less correlated amongst themselves as well as other CTAs. Whereas larger, long-term CTAs tend to display a higher level of correlation between one another. Because of this, short-term CTAs may also serve as a means of mitigating correlation if added to a portfolio.

"A lot of the money that comes into the CTA space goes to the longer-term traders; people that are allocating longer-term would benefit from also including allocations to the shorter-term traders, because that creates a more balanced CTA portfolio," notes Doug Bry, of Northfield Trading. Another institutional tendency is to allocate only toward a small group of CTAs with the largest assets under management. However, this allocation strategy might end up increasing investment risk because, due to their large market footprint, such CTAs might have difficulty entering or exiting positions quickly and are limited in the markets they can trade.

**Quantitative Trend Following** The quantitative approach to managed futures requires more mathematical and statistical analysis than the types of trend following outlined above. Trends may in part be determined by fundamental valuations of some markets, whereas quantitative strategies rely more heavily on statistical understandings of markets looking both forward and backward in time. One of the oldest examples of a quantitative CTA is Campbell & Company.[5] The firm was founded in 1972 as a trend follower, but has spent the last 30 years putting solid mathematics research behind their quantitative approach. Their quantitative strategy is hypothesis-driven. Think of it like transferring the same scientific method one might use in the lab to the financial markets.

While Campbell has kept a core risk allocation to trend following strategies, the firm has evolved substantially beyond traditional market-based trend following. Campbell's flagship funds have diverse styles of trend following that identify trending markets, sectors, and correlation factors. These styles may have their own explicit time windows or dynamic holding periods that range from a few weeks to a few months. These alternative forms of trend following have been implemented over the course of the last five years or so.

In addition to the core trend-following strategies, Campbell was one of the first managers to develop systematic strategies in currency carry and other forms of non-trend following strategies, starting in the late 1990s. Since then, Campbell has used its sector-specific expertise to develop strategies that exploit the term structure in commodities and fixed income, as well as strategies that use cross-sector information from other markets such as equities and derivatives of futures price information. Most recently, Campbell has focused on developing strategies that fall in the shorter time horizon (less than one week).

Taken together, these approaches allow the research team to look at hypotheses they have about a given market, and model them in order to place their bets.

## QUANTITATIVE STRATEGIES CAN ALSO SERVE AS AN EQUITY RISK HEDGE

Typically, as assets under management grow, CTAs suffer the same problem as their equity hedge counterparts—they become less nimble and lose some of their returns to size; they also become more correlated to each other and broad market trends.

New research from CTA Quest Partners,[6] shows that quantitative trend following, which has primarily been used and sized as a portfolio diversifier, could actually be used and sized as an equity risk hedge, and at a lower cost than some of the tail-risk strategies that have become popular in the wake of 2008.

Splitting classical trend following strategies such as the 10-day to 100-day simple moving average crossover (MA10 × 100) into complimentary components, that are less biased toward fixed income, longer-term trading, and long biases can actually hedge equity risk, and provide portfolio diversification without a negative carry, or drag, on performance during equity market rallies. This is done by establishing a covariance filter on trend-following trades that only accepts trades which have negative covariance to equities.

**Systematic** Systematic strategies seek to capture trends and make trades without overreliance on behavioral biases. In practice, this typically means leaning heavily on computerized trading to avoid human responses to fear, or selection biases that are common to human-only decision making. Systematic traders sometimes have the reputation of being *black box* traders due to their preference for computerized trading, but that's not always the case; often very human decisions are made on stop-losses and other factors as markets move.

iStar Capital, an Amsterdam-based CTA, is a systematic shop that carries with it the distinction of being the only CTA seeded by an institutional investor in 2011. This is notable, as large institutions rarely seed funds at all, given the need for institutions to distribute large sums of money at once, but also because emerging managers often carry a higher risk profile than that tolerated by institutions, precisely because they are new.

"We are not a pure trend-following firm, we have three main focus points: a trend-following strategy, a currency-carry strategy, and discretionary risk management," Shally explains. "We very much believe in having systematic strategies that avoid all of the behavioral issues which everyone is exposed to, however, being traders for two decades we want to utilize that experience so we added a discretionary component."

He notes that by combining trend following with the currency-carry strategy the fund can be an absolute return fund by offering currency carry in the market cycles where trend following doesn't perform as well. The small percentage of discretionary risk management also allows iStar to be marginally reactive to changes in the market. "We don't want to be 100 percent black box," Shally says.

This combination drew the attention of institutional investors early on. Dutch seeder IMQubator chose iStar for an allocation, and the principals moved to Amsterdam to live and work. The fund is now part of the Holland Financial Hub, the building that holds IMQubator along with several other startup funds.

**Discretionary**[7] Managed futures is typically an investment often perceptually correlated to mathematical probability and quantitative-based strategies. But there is a strong breed of manager, often taking a more traditional discretionary hedge-fund style approach to human-based trade logic, who can provide interesting correlation benefits in a portfolio.

Discretionary managed futures strategies are those defined as using human-driven decision models or combining more than one strategy. Proprietary performance studies benchmark discretionary strategies as having the second lowest drawdown average, at 20.61 percent, compared to average trend-following drawdown of 24.92 percent. Perhaps most interesting is the category's downside deviation, the sophisticated risk manager's look at how well a risk program operates during a relative crisis situation.

Discretionary traders in a study had a downside deviation of 2.41 percent, on average, compared with a 3.08 percent downside volatility with trend following. (The strategy study referenced in this report is not designed to be definitive, but rather used as a guidepost for relative value analysis.

Based on its variety in approach, discretionary trading lacks a direct correlation to any single market environment. Price persistence, volatility, and mean reversion do not always correlate directly to a discretionary or tactical approach to the markets, making it difficult to identify beta market exposure.

Discretionary traders produced interesting relative downside volatility numbers and as a general category measured in this limited study, they have controlled loss size to a greater degree in the past. Based on the study, average loss size in this category was 2.85 percent, while 3.63 percent was the average in the trend-following category. While such studies of performance are not empirically definitive, they do provide insight into risk management protocols one might consider when evaluating and managing the investment going forward.

One example of a discretionary fund, Witherspoon Asset Management, comes from a group of former Commodity Corporation executives who launched a managed futures mutual fund targeted to provide a multi-strategy portfolio of managers averaging 75 percent discretionary and tactical specialists and 25 percent systematic/trend following.

"Discretionary sources of alpha are underrepresented in the current managed futures funds," said Lee Gladden, who has more than 30 years' experience in managed futures, beginning with Commodities Corporation (now Goldman Sachs Hedge Fund Strategies Group) in 1981.

"The biggest limitation facing a portfolio composed primarily of trend following managers is that most such managers tend to exhibit high degrees of correlation with one another," Gladden adds.

Gladden explains the difference. "Witherspoon usually allocates approximately 75 percent of the capital in its portfolio to managers who are not trend followers and who have a low correlation with each other. As a result, we believe our portfolio is designed to have less volatility and to be more consistent. Currently we have two trend-followers and seven discretionary traders/tactical specialists in our CTA portfolio."

**Multi-Strategy** Multi-strategy funds, just as their name implies, can take a number of these different approaches and overlays and include them in one fund. Some funds also include multiple managers, each with their own specialty contributing to a larger organization. Kevin McDonald, the co-founder of Taylor Investment Advisors runs a single manager, multi-strategy CTA and explains his approach.[8]

"The Taylor Xplor Managed Futures Strategy Fund utilizes a single CTA that implements a multi-strategy approach, as opposed to a fund of funds with multiple CTAs. Our single manager currently trades five distinct disciplines or strategies, including medium-term trend following, fundamental, countertrend, momentum, and short-term pattern recognition," he said.

"In our world, momentum is a sub-set of trend following. Trend following typically captures the move from point A to point B over the medium term, while momentum is shorter term and captures the point in time where the velocity of a trend is increasing. Pattern recognition is a much shorter time frame, ranging from intra-day to several days. The pattern-recognition strategy is important because it can help to dampen or offset volatility of longer-term trend following strategies that can struggle in sideways markets or during trend reversals."

For him, having a single manager taking multiple approaches allows for dynamic, and in some cases, real-time portfolio rebalancing in response to market conditions. The more traditional structure for multi-strategy is a fund of funds with several underlying managers, each executing their own specialty. Fund of funds typically rebalance on a slower basis and take a more traditionalist, institutional view of the market. Both are effective at achieving returns, and will draw from a mix of strategies like those listed above. Investing in one way or the other depends on risk tolerance and due diligence factors outlined in our section on evaluating CTAs.

**Volatility** Volatility strategies can take on a number of stripes. Some investors look at volatility traders as a means of hedging tail-risk (we have a discussion of this in Chapter 7), others consider it in their managed futures investments. Within a portfolio, volatility funds can often underperform when the rest of the portfolio is doing well because they rely on more volatile markets, which often hurt equities performance.

Volatility trading uses the Chicago Board Options Exchange Market Volatility Index (VIX), a popular measure of the implied volatility of S&P 500 index options. The VIX is also called the fear index, in relation to the overall comfort level market participants have with current market conditions.

Volatility trading is a fairly sophisticated arena that tends to be the domain of fund of funds that have their own investment teams managing investments on top of what underlying managers are doing. However, it is worth discussing at a high level what these types of funds do.

T2 Associates[9] is a volatility specialist Commodity Trading Advisor founded by James Tann, who has been privately trading since 1967. The primary strategy is to engage in countertrend trading during periods of high market volatility. The emerging CTA primarily trades the mini S&P 500 futures contracts. T2 operates by counter trend trading during moments of market volatility spikes. Typically during periods of volatility, the theory holds that price trends are exaggerated in the direction of the trend and ultimately revert back to the mean.

In the case of T2, they are looking for mean reversion on a short-term basis. The counter trend trader, with a quantitative knowledge of the point at which a price trend might be overextended, establishes a position in the opposite direction, in this case holding trades for an average of three days but sometimes up to three weeks. It can be a highly risky play on a number of fronts, particularly if the portfolio isn't properly diversified even with the long volatility sub category.

From one portfolio management standpoint, the concept with such a niche long volatility program is to pair it along other long volatility components in the sub category of a portfolio. The long volatility might not find profitable market environments as the short volatility programs, but when the right market conditions exist is when this and other programs might be expected to benefit. From a portfolio standpoint, combining long volatility exposure to the market environment of price persistence, short volatility, and divergence/convergence to a mean is an example of using volatility combinations with the goal to manage downside deviation. This is a sophisticated risk management technique operated by certain hedge fund professionals.

It should be noted that different, and more common, methods of trading volatility takes in VIX futures/options across time horizons and in option put spreads across major stock indices.

**Spread Arbitrage**[10] Managed futures is largely dominated by the trend-following variants outlined above, however, spread arbitrage, or relative value, is also gaining traction as a new choice for investors and CTAs in the space. Spread arbitrage generally operates based on price relationships between related products, as outlined in the book *The Complete Guide to Spread Trading* by Keith Schap and *The Encyclopedia of Commodity and Financial Spreads* by Jerry Toepke and Nick Colley.

*Strategy Tactical Operation:* Spread arbitrage programs are those in which a trader buys one commodity and sells another contract of a related commodity or time frame to capitalize on a discrepancy in prices.[1] For instance, a spread arbitrage program may sell (short) the September oil contract and purchase (long) the December RROB gasoline contract. In this case, the goal is that the short September oil contract falls in price and/or the long December gasoline contract rises in price, which may or may not occur.

*Macro Market Environment Influencer:* Spread arbitrage programs are typically influenced by market environments that feature price dislocation and related convergence back to a mean. Spread programs may benefit when they properly identify the price dislocation and then the market ultimately reverts back to its mean. "The mean reverting property is true in spreads," noted former Chicago Board of Trade economic writer Keith Schap in his book *The Complete Guide to Spread Trading*. One strategy risk is that prices dislocate and then do not revert back to the mean, which is where risk management comes into play.

**The Math Behind Spread Arbitrage** In order to understand how a strategy can be uncorrelated to the performance of equity markets and properly assess risk in an investment, professional investors might consider the strategic drivers of each investment.

Spread arbitrage programs often determine trade execution through the use of mathematical probability tables that consider relationships between related products, time frames, and pricing and may benefit when prices of related products temporarily dislocate but then revert back to the mean. "Spreads can trade higher or lower than a mean, but, in the normal course of events, they work back to a mean," Schap wrote in his book, highlighting the core strategic driver of the strategy.

**Spread Prices Can Widen and Contract in Trend Trading Behavior** Spread price variance, like outright markets, have been known to trend in price, dislocating from a price mean and potentially reverting to that mean. "One (contract price) can be trending in one direction, while another trends in the other direction," noted Schap in his book. In effect, spread trading can be subject to price momentum and persistence, just not in outright markets but rather in price relationships between contract months or related commodities. Spread arbitrage programs "have a basis in the economics of the markets involved," Schap notes. For instance, if the value of the front month oil contract is below that of the back month, this might indicate markets are expecting oil prices in the future to rise in price through increased anticipated demand or reduced supply. This *contango* occurs when a futures contract is higher in price the further it is from expiration. It is sometimes used by economists to determine the strength of economic activity, as spread prices often exhibit movement from contango to backwardation on each leg of the trade. Backwardation is the opposite, when the near futures price close to expiration trades higher than the back month away from expiration.

It is important to note that the spread trade might rely on one leg of the trade to revert back to the mean of its normal price relationship while the other leg remains relatively consistent in price, which is sometimes utilized by program managers with the goal to provide protection against exposure to the overall market moves. For example, the spread program outlined in this example is only a play on the relationship between oil and gasoline, not in the overall direction of the energy market either higher or lower. Thus, if an outside market force influenced the overall price of the energy market, taking the price of both oil and gasoline dramatically higher, the spread strategy typically does not desire exposure to the overall market move, but rather only the relationship in price between related products. This is not to say a spread strategy is less risky than an outright long or short position often taken by a trend following program, it is to say that the risks and market environments that influence performance can be different.

"What matters is that both trends responding to the same set of economic drivers," Schap said, highlighting the importance of strategic performance drivers when evaluating strategies. "They (spreads) exhibit a structure that responds to economic drivers."

## STRATEGY RISK CONSIDERATIONS

It is important to note in any mathematical algorithm there are points at which the strategy changes and historically consistent price relationships no longer work. One risk in the strategy is when prices dislocate based on historical probability tables they do not revert back to the mean. This is where the phrase "past performance is not indicative of future results" is given meaning.

Many economists have indicated that markets are so efficient that such opportunity for spread arbitrage may be limited, while other economic voices, such as MIT's Andrew Lo, note that while market places may be efficient, decisions of market participants can be irrational—resulting in irrational market price movement. Indications are the market environments are constantly changing and risk management is tested when the formula and probability tables no longer apply to a given market environment. When considering risk, it is also important to note that macro strategy risk is different from more complicated factors not outlined in this document involved with individual manager risk, to which investors should be aware.

## HOW TO EVALUATE A CTA

In addition to considering consultants and independent due diligence providers when approaching any investment, investors that are looking at managed futures will have to add some unique questions to their due diligence checks. Fortunately, the CTA space has some quality controls already in place. Individual CTAs, in many cases, can be checked against a profile with the National Futures Association.

As an investor, it is always best to have your interests, and risk tolerance clearly established before approaching any fund in order to ensure that a given manager aligns well with your goals. In this section, we're going to start with baseline considerations and move into more technical evaluations of CTAs in the broader portfolio.

### 10 Due Diligence Considerations for CTAs

Mark Shore, who has experience both in due diligence and managed futures and is now a consultant, offers 10 starting points for evaluating a CTA. He was vice president and chief operating officer at Morgan Stanley's VK Capital Inc., a commodity trading advisor.

Mr. Shore says managers should:[11]

1. Be open to providing information.

   It is not helpful to tell people who are doing due diligence, "You don't need to know this, it does not matter," even if the request for information is about a minor issue.
2. Understand the markets they trade in.

   The experience can be longer or shorter, at different places or just one place. But there has to be a demonstrable appreciation of how the markets work.
3. Explain what caused the drawdowns.

   Everybody has drawdowns, but they should learn from the experience and help us understand what caused it. "It was bad luck" is not a good explanation. There is always an element of luck but managers have to be aware of what makes their investment program vulnerable.

4. Have a well-organized research process, undertaken by confidence-inspiring people. The manager needs to discuss how they do the research and what kind of process they have in place.
5. Generate the type of volatility that diversifies the investor's portfolio.

   Like cholesterol, there is good and bad volatility. Good volatility fits the portfolio. I don't like using the Sharpe ratio to assess performance because it makes no distinction between the good and the bad—this is due to the assumption of a normal distribution.
6. Take care of business issues.

   If the manager's time is taken up by investment and trading-related work, then there should be other senior people at the firm who have the ability to run the business.
7. Create an organizational structure that covers necessary tasks.

   It should be clear that all functions are taken care of.
8. Make sure the back office is staffed with capable people.

   The back office can be internal or outsourced to a third party, like a large prime broker or administrator, as long as they have the necessary capabilities.
9. Have a reasonably stable investor base.

   There should be long-term clients and not a lot of turnover in the investor base over the history of the fund.
10. Be prepared for key personnel risk.

    There needs to be qualified people at the firm who can take over if something happens to the managing partner.

### CTA Evaluation and Portfolio Correlation Considerations[12]

How might one best go about this early-stage due diligence task? Walk through the analysis of Quantica Capital's Managed Futures Program to see how one might consider different variables in a managed futures selection process.

**Categorize Based on Strategy, Markets Traded, and Trade Timeframe** To effectively organize the due diligence task, it is best to determine strategy based on what drives trade decisions. It is important to differentiate between strategy and markets traded or trade timeframe, as you will see.

We will consider the case of Quantica managed futures fund, a Schaffhausen, Switzerland-based trend following program. Their beta performance driver is price persistence. When categorizing a portfolio, and modeling it through various market environments, it is helpful consider the mix of beta performance drivers in the portfolio as well as markets traded and trade time frame, key factors in trend following.

**Markets Traded Considerations** Some managed futures funds may narrowly focus their markets traded on various niches while others may be exceedingly broad. As an investor, understand the logic behind the market traded choice, and benchmark, on a going forward basis. For instance, Monsoon Capital is a CTA who trades only Asian equity markets due to the fund manager's belief that they are driven more by the emotion of retail investors than U.S. or European equity markets. The manager's logic explains this by believing trends are more prevalent and pronounced. With this understanding, he sets expectations but also understands correlation considerations.

When considering markets traded in an investment, also recognize the depth and related liquidity of the market relative to the size of the trading program. Certain trading programs in highly niche markets—Asian rubber markets, for instance—are generally only available to smaller funds. Larger funds may be limited only to trade larger markets, which impacts performance expectations. In a due diligence report, one might also want to consider volatility (speculators v. hedges) relative to markets traded.

**Trade Timeframe** In managed futures it is always interesting to consider the timeframe of a trade as it relates to downside risk management. For instance, with an understanding of trade timeframe the investor might ask questions relative to risk management in certain long duration programs. Some long-term managers may ignore short-term drawdown if the longer-term trade signal remains positive. Thus, in such a program the investor might be expected to tolerate drawdowns in order to remain in the longer-term trend. In a due diligence report, outline the trade timeframe and implications relative to risk management and drawdown tolerance.

**Evaluation by the Numbers** Different strategies have different average performance numbers that might be used as a guidepost (but not definitive) measurement. (The following is based on studies conducted in 2008[13] and then again in 2011.)

**Use Loss Size, not Win Percentage** In a trend-following program, win percentage can be among the lowest of all primary strategy types at 57 percent. Compare this with the options (volatility) category that has the highest win percentage at 74.25 percent. With an understanding of the premise of each strategy this is logical. However, in trend following the measurement one might want to better consider is control of loss size. In trend following average loss size was 3.63 percent compared to the options category with 5.38 percent. This can be explained because fundamental to many trend strategies is to let upside deviation run while managing downside deviation. Conversely, many of the option strategies are focused on small but consistent wins and can experience difficulty during periods of rapidly rising volatility. In the case of Quantica, their average monthly loss size was 2.08 percent and their downside deviation was 2.01 percent, two key performance numbers the investor may wish to benchmark.

**Margin to Equity** After the investment has been categorized at a high level, then start to consider different performance variables. One interesting consideration is their margin to equity ratio, which can differ based on strategy. Studies of average margin to equity levels can vary, but a benchmark study conducted in 2010, averaged systematic trend following at 15.56 percent. In Quantica's case, margin to equity was reported at 12 percent. This is an interesting number to keep an eye on going forward, particularly if a trading program experiences volatility, as the risk manager may wish to watch margin to equity for signs of strategy shift. With a margin to equity ratio of 12, Quantica has an attractive leveraged returns ratio but a more impressive leveraged volatility ratio.

These are a few considerations to help narrow choices in the managed futures investment selection process.

## THE P(A|B) METHOD TO ANALYZE AND SUPERVISE A MANAGED FUTURES INVESTMENT[14]

This section introduces you to the P(A|B) Method of managed futures investment evaluation and ongoing risk management. The P(A|B) Method has heretofore been a private method for managed futures evaluation. The P(A|B) Method takes its name from Baye's Theorem, which is an algebraic formula to assist probability factoring.

This system walks professional asset managers through a series of queries based on the risk exposure of each managed futures program. At its core, managed futures is a derivatives-based investment and as such often has unique sets of performance measures relative to time horizon, related product structure and contract type.

The P(A|B) Method starts by considering the beta performance factors in the investment, then moves into alpha considerations.

## Background

The P(A|B) Method is based on several academic studies, but the majority of its foundation resulted from statistical modeling in the CTA Sustainability Study and separate study of the statistical averages of CTAs broken down by beta market environment exposure. Both these studies were revealed in the book *High Performance Managed Futures* (John Wiley & Sons 2010). The studies were used to develop a statistical model of *unsustainable* and *sustainable* CTAs that is used in investment rankings, risk analysis, and diversified portfolio building, as outlined at the end of this section.

**CTA Sustainability Study** This study was an examination of the BarclayHedge CTA Graveyard database, which contained the performance records of all CTAs who de-listed, a large percentage doing so after reporting negative performance. The objective of the study was to develop a statistical model of failing CTAs so as to reverse engineer a method to assist investors with the goal to avoid significant loss. The four-year study considered performance of all CTAs who reported performance from 1975 to 2010. The combined performance of the CTAs was analyzed through logistic regression modeling (sometimes referred to as the *logistic model* or *logit model*). In statistics these models are used for prediction of the probability of occurrence of an event by fitting data to a logistic curve, a linear model for binomial regression. Like many forms of regression analysis, it makes use of several predictor variables that may be either numerical or categorical. Here is a practical example of how such probability analysis works in health and then in managed futures.

In the case of determining the cause of heart attacks, logistic regression modeling first identifies all people who had a heart attack and then considers their statistical profile such as age, body mass index, gender, and dietary habits. From this a statistical model is developed of a *heart healthy* model and an *at risk* statistical model. This information has significant value. For instance, health insurance companies use statistical modeling to determine premium costs.

In the case of managed futures it's more complex. At first, the modeling of the CTA Graveyard was confusing, as many of the failed CTA headline statistics such as Sharpe Ratio, win percentage, and even compounded annual return appearing positive relative to live CTAs with a sustainable ongoing track record. It wasn't until the data was dissected based on market environment exposure and performance was modeled relative to the CTA's last year did key relationships between statistics become clear and point to sustainable and unsustainable behavior. From this, a model was developed that ultimately led to 19 primary indicators of CTA sustainability and with many sub-indicators used in rankings and risk analysis.

One of several key findings in the study related to beta market exposure. Sustainable CTAs effectively captured the beta market opportunity in front of them without overreaching to chase returns or exhibit abnormal performance during negative market environments. In fact it could be said that the alpha that matters is not to significantly overperform the beta. Other study findings determined the importance of different performance relationships relative to strategy, including the relationship between win and loss size, downside volatility, and leverage usage, while another set of findings spoke to the importance of business viability as much as returns performance.

**CTA Strategies/Beta Market Environment/Statistical Benchmarks** In conjunction with the CTA Sustainability Study, a study of statistical averages of strategies based on beta market environment exposure took place on three different occasions. These studies averaged performance numbers to develop consistent benchmarks.

Distinguishing between strategies in managed futures has always been less than uniform. Some CTA database categorization is based on *agricultural traders*, which is a market-traded variable, while other CTAs are categorized as *short-term* traders, which is a timeframe. These are important, but the P(A|B) Method categorizes managed futures strategies based first on beta market environmental exposure and then provides sub-categorization based on variables such as markets traded, trade timeframe, and more.

While there are a variety of beta market environments, some of the primary categories include price persistence (when prices trend higher or lower on a consistent basis); volatility (where prices rapidly fluctuate over a short period of time); or divergence/convergence of price relationships (where the value of two related products diverges from their statistical averages and then converges back to their normal price relationships).

When strategies are categorized based on beta market exposure first, certain statistical modeling truths appear, as do portfolio development opportunities. For instance, trend-following strategies, which rely on the market environment of price persistence, statistically have the lowest win percentage but the highest win size. A relative value strategy, on the other hand, has the lowest ratio between average drawdown and worst drawdown while volatility strategies have the highest win percentage but the highest downside deviation numbers.

This is the basis upon which the P(A|B) Method operates. Next we will outline the steps to use this method in analysis and then provide concrete examples of how this is used in the generation of CTA rankings and diversified managed futures portfolios.

**Step One: Understanding System Analytical Structure** The P(A|B) Method considers risk factors at the start of the process, applying a top-down approach. It examines managed futures investments in different category slices, prioritizing based on factors that influence performance. For instance, the system's first priority are beta performance drivers affecting the investment. In this respect, the system is similar to the analysis structure a hedge fund investor might view a private equity IPO. In the aftermath of the Facebook IPO occurred, for instance, many private equity managers accurately noted that the "market environment for IPOs has changed." Market environments tend to be viewed as cyclical, and the attitude among those seeking to bring IPOs to market would return after market forces played their statistically validated game of asset rotation favoritism.

In the case of this example, the P(A|B) Method will examine the volatility managed futures investment category.

**Step Two: Understand Strategy Categorization** Building reasonable credible performance expectations for the professional asset manager is an important point of the confidence building process. For this reason, the P(A|B) Method places a priority of beta performance. As a strategy replication quant will attest, understanding the strategy's beta is an interesting point of analysis. Some call it key to setting performance expectations in a fashion that a private equity fund manager may say the "market environment" is not right

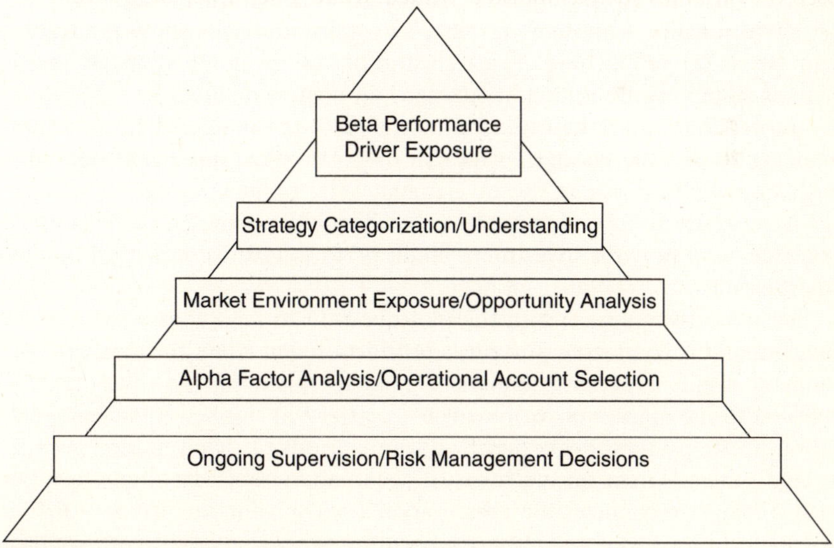


**FIGURE 6.1** The P(A|B) Method Educational Hierarchy

for IPOs or a financial advisor might say to their client, when explaining a string of negative performance, the "market environment" doesn't favor tech stocks at this point.

With an understanding of the beta performance drivers, asset managers can communicate with a degree of intelligence and confidence when discussing an investment. For instance, this issue is considering the volatility strategy, which is based on statistical probability of market outcomes. The strategy typically engages in the purchase or sale of options contracts. Like an insurance company considering probability tables to determine the rates for insurance in a given market, for instance, the managed futures volatility category often bases investment decisions on statistical probability of price movement and price duration in a given market. Trading managers might base their decisions on probability tables, but the key to success might be found in how risk is managed and positions are sized.

This strategy categorization and understanding is used as a beta overlay on top of the alpha factor analysis and ongoing risk management.

### Step Three: Market Environment Risk Exposure

**Start with Beta Market Environment Considerations** With an understanding of strategy categorization, look to the individual exposure of the managed futures program and pay particular attention to their forthright nature and respect for the intelligence of the professional asset manager. No credible investment should be entirely black box and the expectation should never be that an investment will always generate return through all market environments. Although certain *all weather* strategies show interesting promise, as David Harding's research staff of 100 might attest, market environmental factors are known to change and possess nuance.

Professional asset managers should expect the managed futures fund manager to provide enough insight so they can make intelligent decisions regarding the true risk in the investment. Start by identifying if the strategy is generally short or long volatile. This includes providing a reasonable expectation of how the investment might perform given a variety of market environments.

In a volatility investment, the first question to answer is what market environment is conducive to returns production and when the market environment might experience enhanced risk. In this case, the investment is exposed to the market environment of volatility, as implied by its categorization. Certain investments benefit during periods of rising market volatility and others benefit during times of declining market volatility. Once the asset manager recognizes the beta market environment performance driver to which they are exposed they can begin to establish a set of performance expectations.

Examination of historical price patterns indicates that volatility is a market environment that has been reasonably cyclical to various degrees and implications. As we can see from the stock market crashes from 1900 to today, on a past performance basis, volatility has been reasonably unpredictable but it has entered the market with increasing frequency, particularly in the equity markets. While past performance and probability tables don't dictate the future, planning for a variety of scenarios and recognizing how standard deviation plays into risk management decisions is considered.

**Volatility at Its Core Is Defined by Surprise** Volatility is often, by definition, a result of a market surprise. If an event is known to the market, volatility can often be reduced through the lack of an implosion of chaos. For instance with the U.S. debt crisis, if an event were to surprise the market it could have a much more dramatic impact than if an event were known, expected to a certain degree. This highlights one of the key points relative to a volatility investment.

While by definition volatility cannot be predicted, because of its surprise nature, the volatility investor must understand their risk/returns exposure to this market environment, which has always occurred on a cyclical basis as evidenced by considering the stock market crisis listed above or pretty much looking at the ebb and flow of market volatility in any commodity market.

**Long Volatility** Long volatility and short volatility programs, as their descriptions suggest, have very different risk exposures and returns profiles. Both investments are involved in buying (long) and selling (short) options. It is assumed that an advanced audience understands the core asset traded is an option with premium being a primary influence in the value of the investment (assuming a delta neutral stance that does not take positional risk).

If the long volatility investment were to have a delta neutral stance, without a positional bias in the market, the returns profile this investment might exhibit skinny tails in the returns profile due to the fact the numeric distribution of positive returns might be slight, only existing during a volatility explosion. Such volatility implosions have been statistically rare, thus the market environment exposure of a long volatility investment is toward those rare moment of the market environment of volatility entering the market. A long volatility managed futures CTA exhibits such market environment exposure.

Due to its returns profile of low win percentage, a long volatility investment is not as popular as a short volatility investment. Some long volatility investments that come to mind include Shield Plus, which was a long volatility play along the energy complex. The CTA also structures custom hedge accounts as a play against rising energy prices. While understanding the benefits of long volatility during crisis is interesting to a professional asset manager, the more popular strategy is the short volatility program due to its more consistent return pattern, but there is a hidden risk.

**Short Volatility** While the true long volatility program may exhibit a different returns pattern than a short volatility program, the market environment of volatility is nonetheless the beta performance driver.

The short volatility program engages in selling volatility as opposed to buying volatility. While a pure delta neutral long volatility program, the returns profile would be expected to exhibit significantly large win size but low win percentage. Conversely, the pure delta neutral short volatility managed futures investment would be expected to incur a moderate win size but a high win percentage. This is statistically confirmed, as the average win size in the volatility category is benchmarked at 3.75 percent compared to 4.22 percent for all CTAs, while win percentage benchmark for the volatility category is 74.25 percent compared to 59.99 percent for all CTAs.

With an understanding of the individual strategy underneath the volatility, investment asset managers recognize that the returns skew is almost reversed, long volatility is expected to exhibit high win size and low win percentage, while short volatility is expected to exhibit low win size and high win percentage.

**Market Environment Risk Exposure of Short Volatility Investment** The first step in considering a managed futures investment in the P(A|B) Method is analysis of the beta market environment. In the case of LJM, the managed futures program as one example, we know they are a short volatility-based investment and we can expect returns patterns and risk exposure relative to the market environment of price volatility in the markets in which the program trades.

At the end of the first phase of analysis, the asset manager should be able to determine the overall beta risk exposure of an investment. In this case, that exposure is to the market environment of volatility. The short volatility investment might exhibit enhanced risk during periods of rapidly rising market volatility while the long volatility investment might find this environment rewarding, and vice-versa.

**Questions to Consider** What does the returns distribution of a short volatility strategy often look like and why? What is the typical win percentage of a short volatility strategy relative to win size? In what market environment can a short volatility be expected to find opportunity and conversely find enhanced risk?

**Step Four: Alpha Factor Analysis** Once strategy categorization and market environment exposure has been determined, we move from beta to alpha considerations. With a short volatility investment, the P(A|B) Method starts by considering risk management tactics and then reviews key statistics in past performance relative to the unique features of a volatility investment. Note that with each beta exposure strategically significant performance measures are favored during both analysis and ongoing management.

**Risk Management Strategies** With a volatility strategy, the professional asset manager may wish to consider how the trading program has planned for the worst-case market environment. Trading programs that have not considered the worst case are those one might want to view with suspicion, and in fact this system eliminates managers who have not thoroughly considered probability tables and a variety of potential outcomes.

The primary point to consider in a short volatility risk management discussion is the point at which volatility may rise significantly. The key question is: What is the trading manager's strategy to manage such an environment?

In the volatility segment, sophisticated consultants might recognize various volatility hedging tactics, including corresponding long volatility purchases across different time horizons and different price event levels. Still others with familiarity of this strategy might consider a time horizon roll into the forward month and still others might prefer an indirect hedge through a spread relationship with a related futures contract. Each of these risk management strategies has different risk implications. The consultant should document these tactics and use it as a benchmark for ongoing risk management phase, for it can be key toward making the tough decision to cut ties with a particular manager.

While even sophisticated asset managers might not need to understand the implications of each of these factors, an industry consultant should be aware of how risk management strategy can impact downside deviation and consistency of worst drawdown performance, which is used for performance analysis given to the asset manager.

**Past Performance Analysis of Risk Management Acumen** It can be said with a degree of certainty that every successful trading manager/quantitative program has experienced a negative returns environment and will likely experience unfavorable market environments in the future. The interesting point is the understanding achieved during this period of time and how statistical knowledge learned translates into risk management techniques going forward. While this can be true in the trend following or relative value strategy more so than the volatility strategy, these are important points to consider and often a good point at which to engage the managed futures asset manager in a conversation. The reason volatility investments are different in terms of risk management from trend following, for instance, is in part due to the very unpredictable nature of volatility. In fact, the sophisticated asset manager may wish to employ early in their interaction with a volatility investment play is to ask the manager how adapt their system is at predicting volatility? This can bring up an interesting discussion, because volatility by definition is unpredictable. Volatility is often based off crisis, which, we can logically determine, is driven by surprise. If something can be predicted it is not a surprise. The issue isn't predicting volatility but rather having a realistic grasp of risk management during the inevitable unpredictable period.

With a short volatility program, past performance can point to logical questions for the asset manager to further explore. One topic of discussion could with the worst drawdown. If a short volatility program has any track record duration of note, they have likely experienced a rapidly rising volatility regime. The professional asset manager should first focus on these periods of time, asking the short volatility manager to explain their risk exposure and tactics along with lessons learned. Specifically ask regarding margin usage and volatility spikes intra-month. All of this will yield valuable information for analysis.

**The Importance of Standard Deviation from the Market When Considering Risk Exposure** Risk in a short volatility program can be in part measured by the standard deviation the trading manager often places between the market price and strike price time horizon they have selected. For instance, a short volatility manager may sell options closer to the money, which indicates the distance from the current market, and thus the cushion in time decay of the option. He might experience a higher downside deviation level, but with a higher returns profile than compared to a short volatility program that places trades further from the money. As an example, a volatility program may be short a $133 oil call when the market price for oil is at $100. As measured by standard deviation of prices, this might be considered a far out of the money short volatility strategy. However, if the volatility trader sold an option closer to the market, say at $116, for instance, this impacts the expected risk/return profile of that investment.

In the short volatility strategy, the distance from the money is often measured by standard deviations of variance—this indicates the expected risk profile. A managed futures volatility program close to the money might be expected to exhibit a higher degree of expected volatility but also a higher level of expected returns (an option premium collected closer to the money, is higher than that which is out of the money. The gamma of that option position might exhibit a higher variance).

**Importance of Markets Traded and Time Horizon** When considering a volatility investment, P(A|B) Method disciples should recognize the implications of markets traded and time horizon on a short volatility program. Many short volatility programs operate on a 45-to-90-day time horizon, collecting option premiums during the period of greatest theta/time decay. When evaluating a short volatility strategy, the asset manager should recognize the time horizon and its implications on a projected returns profile. Further, this time horizon target should be benchmarked, and utilized as a method to identify strategy drift in the investment supervision stage.

Also of consideration are markets traded. The short volatility strategy is known to have its origins in the S&P options pits. Today, certain programs trade primarily equity options, finding the greatest premium collection opportunity in puts. Other programs trade diverse markets, finding variable opportunities in income collection. When evaluating various short volatility programs, the asset manager should heavily weigh markets traded when considering correlation among other volatility programs. For example, a well-diversified portfolio might include a variety of beta market environment exposures, and four volatility programs, two of these being short volatility. If the asset manager selected two short volatility programs with similar markets traded profiles, the short volatility aspect of the portfolio might be highly correlated during times of crisis. Thus, the goal when building a volatility program is to include a variety of markets traded, not just correlation to equity markets. Additionally, asset managers must carefully risk model the program during times of stock market crisis.

**Consideration of Leverage Usage** When considering a short volatility program, asset managers might want to consider issues of using leverage relative to volatility, and separately, relative to returns. Asset managers may also want to consider a number of performance measures, including the leveraged returns ratio, and the leveraged volatility ratio that are encompassed in the program.

With the P(A|B) Method a professional asset manager will consider whether a volatility investment has margin usage relative to the standard deviation. In particular, this consideration recognizes the implications of margin on performance during times of crisis. The investor might expect a degree of enhanced leverage usage during times of rising volatility, and reduced leverage during periods of declining volatility.

Leverage is an interesting risk measure to consider from several standpoints. An interesting risk management tactic is to look at leverage usage after a drawdown. Asset managers may want to examine whether after a volatility spike, certain managers may wish to increase margin to equity ratios to benefit from a declining volatility regime. Assuming that markets revert to the historical mean, this strategy may prove opportunistic under conditions of shrinking theta, or time decay factor in the option.

Asset managers and consultants should know the patterns and have realistic expectations for performance and risk management when an inevitable volatility spike occurs. These benchmark performance assumptions are built during the first four steps of the P(A|B) Method and used in the final step: managing the investing on a going forward basis.

#### Questions to Consider

- How does standard deviation and "distance from the market" impact the risk profile of a short volatility investment?
- What is the typical win percentage and win size of a short volatility strategy relative to the managed futures benchmark?
- When analyzing a managed futures program are the benchmarks used for ongoing risk management?

#### Step Five: Operational Due Diligence and Account Type Selection Determines Risk Controls

**Operational Considerations** There are a wide variety of operational checkpoints the asset manager should consider when investing in a managed futures program. In this section, we will review a few top issues.

The decision process for managing risk is important. Is a committee structure involved? Can the trading manager override decisions of the committee? If the trading manager utilizes a systematic approach with a discretionary overlay, at what point does discretion enter the picture? How often are decisions overridden?

In managed futures, each program is audited by the National Futures Association, which includes a business process audit in addition to a performance audit. It can be instructional to ask the trading manager for a copy of this report, if they are open to sharing.

**Account Decisions Drive Risk Management Technique** In managed futures, the type of investor account drives risk management options to a significant degree. Professional investors should be aware of the liabilities and fee structures of each of the account types.

Of consideration to the professional asset manager should be: transparency into leverage usage; position risk exposure and fees; ease of access; defined loss liability; liquidity, and the restrictions and hidden tax benefits in a CFC corporate structure.

**Step Six: Managing the Investment Going Forward** Many times, setting up the supervision of an investment occurs in the initial investigation stage of the process. This can be particularly true with a number of performance measures as they relate to real time risk measurement.

With a volatility CTA, investors might want to initially benchmark the manager's stated margin use during a variety of market regimes, and compare it to actual performance. After a volatility spike, an asset manager might expect the CTA to capture high option premiums (during a potential period of time of heightened margin requirements). As volatility reverts to statistical norms, an asset manager might expect this investment to exhibit decreased levels of option premiums collected, with a declining theta profile.

During the analysis process, an asset manager should benchmark seven primary points for consideration, and twelve secondary points. A scoring algorithm is used as a benchmark to highlight potential areas of concern which may require additional investigation or individual due diligence. This includes a flagging system for both initial evaluation, and ongoing risk management decisions. These risk management decisions can actually be more significant than the initial allocation decision.

## USES OF THE P(A|B) METHOD IN CTA RANKINGS/RISK ANALYSIS

The P(A|B) Method has several practical uses in managed futures investment management.

*CTA Rankings:* The CTA Sustainability Study is the basis of statistical analysis that provides insight into the profile of what a CTA looks like as it enters the final years, as well as clues to potential unsustainable CTA behavior. The algorithmic formula considers both CTA performance, and business sustainability issues that can be seen through reported performance. From this, rankings and real time warnings are generated to provide investors guidance.

*Red, Yellow, and Green Flags:* As a CTA starts to exhibit behavior consistent with the modeling of unsustainable graveyard CTAs, a warning note is delivered in the form of a yellow caution flag, which means the strategy should be investigated, and a red flag, which indicates that immediate attention to an identified issue might be required. A green flag indicates the investor should proceed with caution.

Red and yellow flags can relate to a wide variety of issues, including performance during periods of beta market strength or weakness, abnormal asset flows indicating potential business sustainability issues, or items as diverse as professional investor commitment relative to assets under management. The list below shows items listed on a sample report.

*AA/Top 25 Percent*
*Strategy Considerations Flags*

Strategy Consideration Note: Performance Recovery Time

Strategy Consideration Note: Beta Performance Capture

Strategy Consideration Note: Performance Driver Explained by Relative Performance of Newedge CTA Index

Strategy Consideration Note: Relationship between Win Size, Loss Size and Strategy

Strategy Consideration Note: Past Performance/Maximum Risk Exposure

Strategy Consideration Note: Statistical Relationship between Win Size, Loss Size, and Strategy

Strategy Consideration Note: Performance Driver Explained by Relative Performance of Newedge CTA Index

Strategy Consideration Note: CTA Performance When General Managed Futures Indices Generate Positive Returns

Strategy Consideration Note: Correlation to S&P 500

Yellow Caution Flag: Relationship between Track Record and Assets Under Management

Yellow Caution Flag: Returns Recency Ratios

Green Flag: Audited Performance Duration

Green Flag: Professional Investor Commitment/Assets Under Management

Green Flag: Leverage Reporting

## Beta Market Environment

**Price Persistence** In our example, the (CTA Name) program appears to favor the beta market environment of price persistence. This market environment is considered sound, in that past evidence suggests price persistence, or price trends, have appeared throughout a variety of economic environments. Strategies reliant on price persistence are typically not dependent on economic strength and thus correlations with the equity markets can remain low. However, due to the popular nature of the strategy, correlation among managers who base success on price persistence can be high. This strategy may not provide a normalized returns distribution.

## HOW TO ANALYZE THIS STRATEGY

When analyzing a managed futures strategy, first understand the beta market exposure of the strategy, then drill down to alpha considerations It is the individual manager skill/strength of the algorithmic formula that can make a significant difference in how the manager effectively captures the beta market opportunity. Expecting a CTA to consistently outperform the beta market opportunity—and CTAs who make such claims—might be considered unsustainable.

### Key Statistics with This Strategy

CTAs have generally sustainable statistical modeling and each strategy has a reasonably unique statistical profile, some more nuanced than others. Trend following strategies, correlated to the market environment of price persistence, have statistical performance commonalities and certain indicators have more importance. A long price persistence strategy typically has a statistical profile correlated to relationships between win size, loss size, win percentage, and leverage usage—particularly with mid- to longer-term time horizon traders. Concentrate on the Leverage Risk Rewards Numerator on a going forward basis, along with beta market capture, and correlation to the major CTA indices. Items that might not be the best to consider with this strategy are: worst drawdown, Sharpe ratio, and compounded annual return.

### Considerations Regarding This Strategy

With this strategy, focus on the extent to which the CTA effectively captures the beta market environment, and manages risk. First, consider the trade time frame and markets traded. Depending on the assets under management and trade footprint, this can be either limited or expansive. Next, determine the trade entry methodology. Answering these questions should provide clues as to the expected worst drawdown. Determine if the CTA utilizes one of the following: a portfolio position scaling method; an all-in stop methodology; volatility-based risk management, or another identifiable risk management technique.

### CTA Benchmarks/CTA Uncorrelated Parings

Generally this strategy might be compared to the following CTAs in the style category: LJM. On a strategic basis, this CTA would be expected to exhibit low correlation with the following CTAs and thus might be good for potential portfolio inclusion: Dominice & Co (Cassiopeia USD), Crow Trading, Emil van Essen, Doherty (Relative Value Volatility 1x), Cranwood Capital (Fixed Income Arb-C), and LJM Partners.

## P(A|B) Method Use in Portfolio Development

In addition to providing CTA rankings and real time risk analysis, the P(A|B) Method is also used in portfolio development.

The method essentially creates strategy sleeves based on beta market environmental exposure and then fills each sleeve based on the rankings for each program. A key component in the system is the investment minimum, which can limit choices and the number of investments made.

## $5 Million Portfolio Development Example

In this example, the first consideration is allocation size. With a $5 million portfolio we are going to be limited to investing in approximately 10 CTAs with an average investment minimum of $500,000. While we can consider a $1 million allocation to one CTA, this exposes the investor to a higher degree of individual manager risk and such concentration is not ideal.

Our first step is to allocate assets to the major beta market exposure categories, then allocate to sub categorizations. For this exercise, we'll take a look at one of the most popular categories—trend following. Trend following strategies are correlated to the beta market environment of price persistence, as are breakout, momentum, and other strategies that rely on the price to move in one consistent direction over time.

*Allocation Percentage and Timing:* The first step is to determine the ideal allocation to each of the primary portfolio category sleeves. For trend following, a strategic allocation percentage of $2.5 million (50 percent) has been selected. This is a large relative allocation, but is done because the strategy has experienced a difficult market environment up to 2013. Investing in a strategy after an extended period of difficulty can actually work to an investor's advantage in certain circumstances. For managed futures, markets tend to have a mean reversion aspect—meaning, the best time to invest is after prolonged periods of difficulty. Given this, we will overweight the exposure to price persistence, for this example.

*Sub-Criteria:* With an allocation of $2.5 million to the trend following space, we're going to want to allocate to approximately 6 to 10 strategies that cover several sub categories. Given this, we are going to be limited to CTAs with investment minimums near $500,000.

The next step is to determine sub-category allocations. To accomplish this, we will look for solo counter-trend strategies, as well as trend following strategies that have a dedicated exposure to counter trend strategies. We will fill out our other needs based on: markets traded, trade timeframe, subtle strategy wrinkles, NFA membership criteria (such as an audited performance record), and whether the CTA is open to direct investment with daily transparent access to the account balance and exact position details. The goal is to capture both alpha and beta market opportunities, and effectively monitor the investment on an ongoing basis.

*CTA Selections:* Once the allocation sleeves have been determined, use CTA rankings reports to fill each category. It should be noted here that, algorithmic rankings have inherent limitations. A more helpful way to use rankings might be to list all top rated CTAs in each category first. Then use the rankings as a guide to more detailed, qualitative due diligence, with a human decision being the ultimate deciding factor.

## WHAT ABOUT MANAGED ACCOUNTS?

Managed accounts may be another option to consider if you'd like to test out your relationship with a manager. Below, we've broken out the considerations around managed accounts, which have grown in popularity since 2008.

### Understanding Managed Accounts—By Chidem Kurdas[15]

It is useful to distinguish three main types of accounts. One, the investor might open a dedicated separate direct account with a hedge fund manager. Two, the investor can get access to selected funds via a commingled pool on a managed account platform. Three, the investor may have a separate account on a platform. Table 6.1 summarizes the features of these three structures.

Commodity trading advisors are the largest group on managed account platforms, accounting for 30 percent of platform assets according to Moody's. Global macro accounts for another 15 percent. As such, close to half of the assets on managed account platforms today, are in these two trading strategies.

Investors have to decide whether an account offers sufficient advantages over a pooled fund, then identify the right type of account and level of customized reporting. Fund managers vary in their willingness to take on the added complexity of a separate portfolio and to provide potentially sensitive information. Managed account platforms also offer different levels of reporting.

**TABLE 6.1** Three Structures

| | Separate Account with Fund Manager | Managed Account Platform | Separate Account on Platform |
|---|---|---|---|
| Control of assets | Investor | Platform | Investor or platform |
| Subject to gates or suspensions? | No | Yes | No |
| What does the investor own? | Underlying securities | Share of account | Entire account |
| Responsibility for risk management | Investor | Platform | Entire account |
| Transparency | | Customized reporting | |

*Source:* "Hedge Funds Investing through Managed Accounts," Moody's, May 2010.

The list below shows some of the components of a CTA report. The administrator can independently confirm pricing sources, position reconciliations, fund assets and liabilities, counterparty risk concentration, portfolio liquidity and where the assets are held in custody.

**Sample Operational Risk Disclosure Report: Selected Services and Information**[16]

Confirm: cash, collateral balance, over-the-counter position, pricing, investment position

Fund Asset/Liability Confirmation: NAV, percent of NAV confirmed by administrator

Pricing Analysis: percent confirmed by administrator

Third Party Exposures: Each third party as percent of NAV

FAS 157 Classification (from manager)

Management and performance fee calculation

## Managers' Objections

Some managers simply will not do separate accounts because of various complications caused by accounts compared to commingled funds. Credit fund manager Claren Road Asset Management is in this group. Suzanne Murphy, head of strategic development at Claren Road, says they want to treat all investors equally, and a client with a separate account can fire the manager at a moment's notice—hence the account holder would have a different level of liquidity from investors in the pooled fund, creating inequality.

John Phinney Jr., chief operating officer of Apollo Capital Markets, says managed accounts have unintended consequences. Well-intended investors create inconsistencies, for instance imposing restrictions that cause the account to drift from the fund's strategy. Hence returns in a separate account can diverge from the returns the manager makes in the fund.

Another concern managers have is about divulging trade information via separate accounts that allow investors to watch the trading. A question for the manager is whether the investor can be relied on to protect confidential trade data and making sure it does not fall into the wrong hands. Managed account platforms offer a solution; only the platform operator sees the trades.

In any case, to benefit from trade-level information an investor needs to have the capability to monitor trading and take action if there is a problem. A managed accounts platform will do this for investors. Managerial concerns about investor equality are also generally self-serving and investors will need to be wary of the agenda behind these objections.

In addition to negotiating the level of transparency and frequency of reporting, investors have to consider the question of minimum investment. Larger CTAs typically require a large investment, while CTAs with a track record less than five years typically offer a direct account with a $50,000 minimum. CTAs may agree to trade an account for less than a million dollars but established hedge fund managers often will not consider a separate account for less. There are reports of large managers that will not do a separate account unless the client commits at least $1 billion.

By contrast, commingled accounts on a platform typically have low minimum investment requirements. Another consideration is that a separate account may be easier to negotiate via a platform rather than directly from the manager, especially if the manager already has a relationship with that platform and is comfortable with the platform's monitoring.

### Food for Thought: Consider Managed Futures Investing in a Fashion Similar to Growth Stock Investing

In a proprietary study released in *Opalesque Futures Intelligence*, one of the largest managed futures fund managers in Europe and Asia reveals insight: investing in a managed futures CTA as one might consider growth equity investing strategy. This touches on the third rail issue of emerging manager selection and evaluation, always a lively topic inside the industry when one looks to mitigate survivorship bias when drawing conclusions. The founder of Sweden's Risk and Portfolio Management takes the conversation in a new direction.

In managed futures the Pareto Principle, commonly known as the 80/20 rule, is alive and well, and clearly visible in the distribution of assets under management. Twenty percent of CTAs command anywhere from 80 to 90 percent of assets under management, depending on the reporting database one subscribes.

But is investing only in the top decile CTAs based on assets, as is commonly the case, the best investment strategy? Emerging manager investing has been a hot topic of discussion in managed futures on several levels. On one hand, once a CTA obtains a lethargic asset management footprint, nimbly executing trades on thinly traded markets can be problematic. Counter to this argument, is the experience and organizational gravitas that comes from the more established managers. It is these larger managers who make up mainstream indexes such as the Barclay BTOP 50, NewEdge CTA Index, or the Altegris 40, which is the most credible from a study bias standpoint, exactly due to their history.

A proprietary study from Sweden's Risk and Portfolio Management (RPM), a $5 billion manager of multi-CTA managed futures portfolios, reveals data that supports the concept of investing in smaller managers after they have moved from the startup phase to the growth, or "evolving," stage.

"Our study shows a performance bias based on CTA maturity," observed Mikael Stenbom, RPM's founder and CIO. "Consider a managed futures program as one might analyze a stock. There is the start-up phase, the growth phase, the maturity phase and the decline/rejuvenation phase."

In studying the BarclayHedge CTA database, RPM tracked the age of CTA alongside net asset flows and performance. The majority of investment in these CTAs occurred during the maturity phase, just as performance might be declining, according to the study.

The study drew sharp analytical distinctions, noting that increased age and assets under management have negative influences but at the same time offered opportunity. "The CTA universe holds largely untapped resource of competitive CTAs not (yet) hindered by the negative aspects of success."

## SUMMARY

Managed futures can be a way to add diversification to a portfolio, and mitigate losses when equity markets go down. However, understanding these strategies and the managers running them is important because of their critical difference from equities strategies. Futures by their nature behave differently, and investors in these strategies will want to understand those performance nuances before investing.

## NOTES


1. "Is Long-Term Trend Following Broken?" *Opalesque Futures Intelligence*, 2012, www.opalesque.com/OFI1326/Is_Trend_Following326.html.
2. "Original Turtle, Jerry Parker Discusses Managed Futures" *Opalesque Futures Intelligence*, 2012, www.opalesque.com/OFI1322/Original_Turtle_Jerry_Parker_Futures_Name_and322.html?utm_source=twitterfeed&utm_medium=twitter.
3. Benedicte Gravrand, "Another Good Year for Swiss Short-Term Trading Shop Amplitude," *Opalesque Alternative Market Briefing*, www.opalesque.com/645225/Another_good_year_for_Swiss_trading_shop522.html.
4. Bailey McCann, "Can Short-Term CTAs Survive Investor's Preference Toward Long-Term Strategies?" *Opalesque Alternative Market Briefing*, www.opalesque.com/644284/Can_CTAs_survive_preference_toward428.html.
5. "Original Trend Follower Campbell & Company Passes Reigns to New Generation as Founder Receives Pinnacle Achievement Award," *Opalesque Futures Intelligence*, www.opalesque.com/OFI1339/Original_Trend_Follower_Campbell_Company_Passes_Reigns339.html.
6. Bailey McCann, "New Research Examines Quantitative Trend Following As an Equity Risk Hedge," *Opalesque Alternative Market Briefing*, www.opalesque.com/646534/New_research_examines_quantitative_trend_following_as_an653.html.
7. "Discretionary Strategies in the Spotlight," *Opalesque Futures Intelligence*,www.opalesque.com/OFI1331/Discretionary_Strategies_In_The_Spotlight331.html.
8. "Kevin McDonald Discusses Single-Manager, Multi-Strategy Funds," *Opalesque Futures Intelligence*, www.opalesque.com/OFI1329/Kevin_McDonald_Discusses_Manager_Funds329.html.
9. "Highly Volatile CTA That Trades Volatility," *Opalesque Futures Intelligence*, www.opalesque.com/OFI1340/Highly_Volatile_CTA_That_Trades_Volatility340.html. (Full analysis of the fund is offered in the article.)
10. "Futures Lab: Spread Arbitrage Is a Little Understood Managed Futures Strategy When Compared to the Predominate Trend Following Strategy, but Offers Interesting Diversification Possibilities," *Opalesque Futures Intelligence*, www.opalesque.com/OFI1237/Futures_Arbitrage_is_a_little_futures237.html.
11. "Manager Profile: What Do Investors Look for When They Approach a Manager? Consultant Mark Shore Distils His Experience in Ten Tips," *Opalesque Futures Intelligence*, www.opalesque.com/

OFI1221/Manager_Profile_What_do_investors_look_for_when221.html.

12. "CTA Evaluation and Portfolio Considerations," *Opalesque Futures Intelligence*, www.opalesque.com/OFI1330/CTA_Evaluation_and_Portfolio330.html.
13. HPMF Strategy Benchmark Performance Study, 2010 (John Wiley & Sons). The study on page 239 was conducted by averaging the performance of all managed futures programs with a 36-month track record or longer reporting to the BarclayHedge CTA database at the time of the reporting period. Spot-checking of the study has occurred since 2010 but no inclusive study of the topic has taken place since that point.
14. "The P(A|B) Method to Analyze and Supervise a Managed Futures Investment," *Opalesque Futures Intelligence*, www.uncorrelated investments.com/OFS4.
15. Chidem Kurdas, "Futures Lab: Three Types of Managed Accounts," *Opalesque Futures Intelligence*, www.opalesque.com/OFI1218/Futures_Lab_Three_types_of_managed_accounts_What218.html.
16. SS&C GlobeOp.

# CHAPTER 7

# Investment Mechanics

In this chapter we look at how certain strategies can fit into a portfolio. This chapter serves as a further exploration of hedge fund strategies, to offer a deeper understanding of how an investor or financial advisor might structure a portfolio of hedge funds that is well diversified.

## DIVERSIFICATION: REAL AND IMAGINED

We spoke a little bit about diversification in Chapter 1, and about how investors got burned in 2008 by allocating to multiple types of funds that essentially held the same positions. To review: Allocating to the largest blue chip equities mutual fund and the largest blue chip equity long short hedge fund or liquid alternative in many cases means doubling your equities exposure in the exact same positions with a little aid from the short book of the hedged side. This works out when markets are heading up, but when markets correct, and they always do, the downside of your portfolio will double.

Being diversified doesn't mean just allocating to more than one fund or holding more than one company in a given sector. As an investor or portfolio manager, those that truly understand diversification will be able to discern that if IBM goes down, there is also only so much upside one can gain from holding Microsoft and often they both go down together. In this instance, you might also see a drop in Lockheed Martin, which is a defense contractor and not necessarily a tech company, until you realize that the biggest employer of all three of these companies is the government, and it's cutting the budget. Missing out on these connections or on connections between funds (there are only so many large cap dividend payers for example, even if they all have different businesses) is how you get caught in the trap of thinking you're diversified, but instead you just bought 10 of the same shirt in different colors.

In a pure play hedge fund portfolio, managers can rely on different hedges—shorts, CDS, overlays, or pair trades—to avoid the 10-shirt problem.

At a foundational level, these portfolios have more than just stocks, bonds, and cash. They may have stocks, bonds, cash, and managed futures batting clean up. Or they may have stocks, bonds, cash, and an out of the money put option tail-risk strategy acting as a safety net. Again, the skill lies in understanding how each part of the market is connected.

Research from Nigol Koulajian, founder and CIO, and Paul Czkwianianc, head of research at Quest Partners,[1] a New York-based systematic fund, looks at how quantitative trend following could be used as an equity risk hedge. Trend following, which has primarily been used and sized as a portfolio diversifier, could actually be used and sized as an equity risk hedge, and at a lower cost than some of the tail-risk strategies that have become popular in the wake of 2008. The research also shows significant style drift in the BTOP50[2] and large trend following shops.

Historically, trend following has helped bolster portfolios during a correction in the equity market, but that function has become weaker over the years, limiting the value added to a portfolio. According to Koulajian and Czkwianianc, trend following managers have reduced their core style exposures and increased risk-on trades, which have a greater correlation to equities. Risk-on trades include being long equity beta, long hedge fund beta, and long foreign exchange (FX) carry. These managers have also increased the time frames of their models as well as increasing their long biased trading overall.

"The biggest CTAs [commodity trade advisors] have a diminished ability to hedge equities, many of them use a longer time frame which isn't as good at hedging equities," Nigel Koulajian, paper co-author, founder, and CIO, Quest Partners explains. Longer time frames, risk-on trades, and long-biased trades have been helpful in maintaining positive performance in a post-2008 market, but they represent a material shift from the fundamentals of trend following.

"Shorter time frames can let you capture market reversals but there is also the risk of getting whipsawed. CTAs that have optimized and lengthened their time frames have benefitted from the risk on trade and haven't felt the pain of those longer time frames yet, but they did in 2008. There is a risk for correction again, and we expect large CTAs to underperform again," Koulajian says.

Figure 7.1 illustrates what he means; trend followers who go for the risk-on trade reduce their volatility, but they also lose the ability to hedge an equity drawdown. While this choice helps with fundraising, the overall contribution to a hedge fund portfolio is lacking.

Market forces are driving more than just style drift, "most investors and CTAs are allocating more to the factors in the market that have been doing well in recent years. One of these factors has been fixed income, and larger CTAs have benefitted the most from that," Koulajian says.

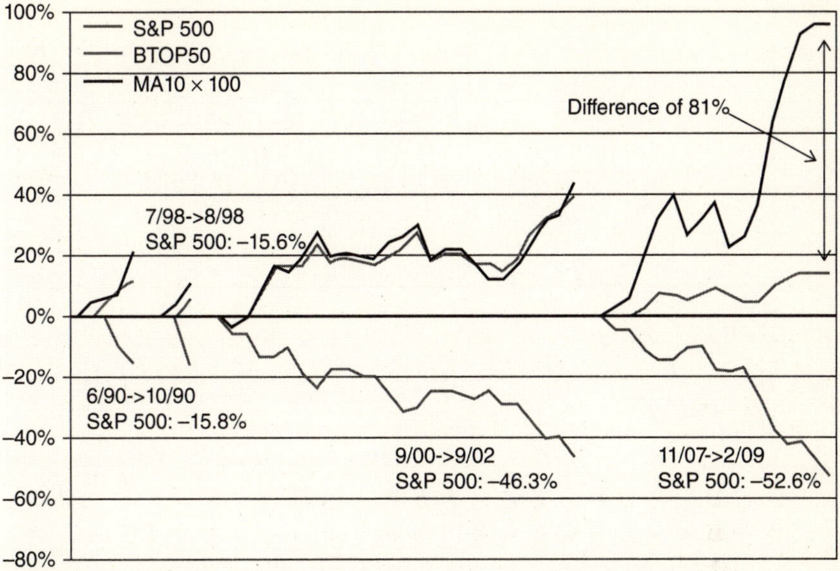


**FIGURE 7.1** BTOP50 and MA10 × 100 returns during S&P 500 drawdowns
*Source:* Quest Partners Legend: MA10 × 100 = 10 day to 100 day simple moving average crossover.

The research shows that fixed income has been effective for trend followers as a means of cheap equity hedging. Price trends over the last 30 years have been a boon for trend followers, "since 1987, the established uptrends in Fixed Income further accelerated during equity corrections, which provided CTAs with outsized returns," the authors explain. "These returns during equity corrections came without the typical delay and losses experienced by TF [trend following] models as trends reverse at such a critical time in a portfolio." The authors further note that outperformance of long-only trading strategies also supported larger exposure to the uptrend in fixed income.

However, this may not be the case indefinitely. If changes in the fixed income market make it less cooperative, large CTAs could feel the pain. "This is highly likely as yields have come down about 90 percent in the past 30 years and have relatively little room to come down further," the authors note. According to Koulajian the risk for a change like that is real. "The market environment is primed for a major change to happen because volatility is compressed and the skew is very negative." Intermediate-term timeframe and short market duration trades can work for trend followers

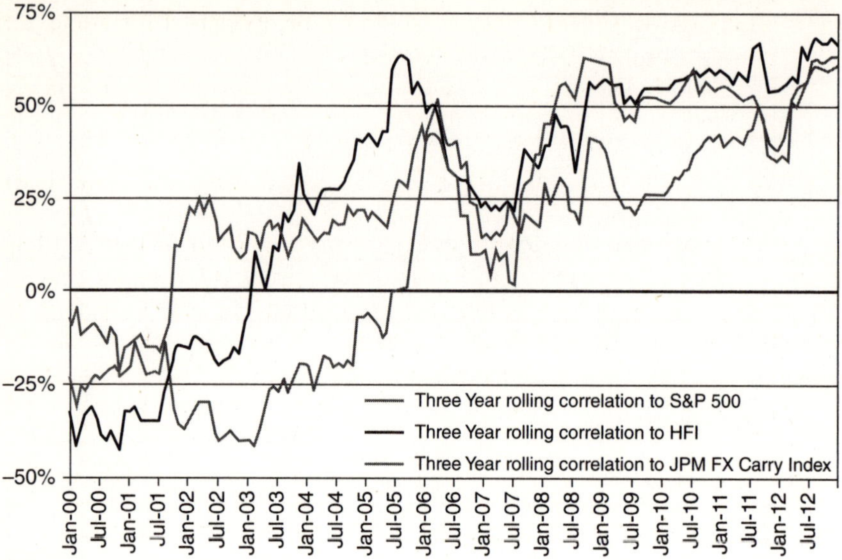


**FIGURE 7.2** BTOP50 - (0.37 × MA10 × 100) Three Year Rolling Correlation to Risk-on Factors
*Source:* Quest Partners.

without fixed income, but they are more cost sensitive. Large CTAs can have a hard time with these options as they are less agile.

For investors who don't fully understand how their returns breakout, this type of exposure risk could come with a little déjà vu. Part of that is due to a lack of investor education and part of that is due to how investors react when CTAs act like CTAs. During risk-off periods, CTAs can provide positive returns, but during risk-on periods they tend to have higher volatility than investors would like. In an effort to respond to this, big CTAs have made these style shifts at the expense of some of their value to a portfolio.

Koulajian notes that some investors are starting to catch on, but few are asking hard questions while returns are still relatively good. "Investors are understanding more and more about how the market but haven't changed their allocations yet. CTAs have been able to post returns that don't require much skill, and without a lot of questions from investors because the performance has been good so far."

In the research, authors suggest that for investors looking for a better equity hedge, they consider working within classical trend following strategies such as the 10-day to 100-day simple moving average crossover (MA10 × 100), splitting the strategy into "complimentary components."

This strategy is less biased toward fixed income, longer-term trading, and long biases. "We propose a covariance filter on TF[trend following] trades to accept only trades that have negative covariance to equities," the authors write. By doing this, investors can realize the equity hedge they hope for from CTAs, while realizing alpha. This approach also sets the strategy apart from tail-risk strategies, which are typically negative carry until a significant correction.

"It is counter to portfolio theory and behaviorally inefficient that both investors and TF managers have drifted away from these trades over the recent years," the authors write. Our exploration of portfolio testing for managed futures in the previous chapter also points to some of the themes uncovered in this research. Taken together, investors can use these guideposts to evaluate their own potential CTA investments and overall diversification.

## Evaluation of Risk

In our exploration of risk data providers in Chapter 4, we discussed how those metrics can be used by both investors and managers to look at diversification and game out fat tails. Often, managers rely on simplistic models that they know well and are comfortable with, but this can often leave them vulnerable to fat tails, volatility clustering, skewness, and correlation asymmetry. Standard measures like value-at-risk (VaR) and their traditional modifications often fail to account for fat tails or market correlations, which can increase overall portfolio risk or lead to losses if missed.

Instead a multi-model approach that is less reliant on historical data can point to weaknesses in an investment thesis. When used by investors, a multi-model approach can help investment committees go beyond the pitch book and better discern the true capabilities of a manager or given strategy.

### WHERE'S THE BEEF?

#### *Fraser McKenzie*

McKenzie, a veteran of the fund of funds business, explores how diversification woes impact funds of funds, but this can also be a lesson for individual investors who allocate to multiple managers.

Almost 30 years ago, during the U.S. presidential primaries in the Spring of 1984, the Democratic Party presidential candidate, Walter Mondale, famously retorted to Republican Senator Gary Hart during a televised debate, "When I hear your new ideas, I'm reminded of that ad, 'Where's the beef?'."

Mondale was referring to an advertising campaign run by the Wendy's fast-food chain earlier that same year, designed to denigrate a competitor's hamburger. The slogan went on to become a famous catchphrase, although it didn't win Mondale the election against Ronald Reagan—who had a few good lines of his own. It became the rhetorical question posed to anyone or anything that appeared to lack substance.

In financial market terms, investors in hedge funds and, in particular, funds of funds are also entitled to ask, "Where's the beef?" Among the wreckage that litters the fund of hedge fund business landscape, it's an increasingly difficult question to answer.

Long gone are the days when a selection of 16 hedge managers across several different hedge fund strategies created the optimal diversification and decent returns. Promises of operational due diligence, thrown into the fund of fund proposition to make investors feel safe, began to ring hollow after Bernie Madoff was exposed in December 2008. Less than stellar results have compounded industry woes.

Hedge fund industry returns have diminished along with interest rates. When Libor was at 5 percent, hedge fund strategies that ran large cash balances effectively had an automatic return of 5 percent—without doing anything other than placing the money on deposit. Of course this makes historical returns look optically much better than today's with deposit rates effectively at zero. Who can get excited about low single-digit returns even while acknowledging the fact that interest rates are zero? Investors at least need the hope of outlandish returns if all the stars align.

One of the main reasons is that the core attribute of the classic fund of funds approach—diversification across managers, strategies, and geographies—does not necessarily help you avoid a market meltdown when correlations between previously uncorrelated assets rises to extreme levels.

Indeed, this was the painful lesson of 2008. Even the most astute risk manager would have been hard pressed to anticipate how, during periods where liquidity is very low, a forced liquidation by one manager might possibly affect assets held by another manager—with a supposedly unrelated strategy. A high correlation between a Japanese convertible bond strategy and a U.S. merger arbitrageur was difficult to understand in 2008 until after it happened.

In fact, the diversification of strategies often means that the best ideas are being mixed with the not-so-good ideas, resulting in a mishmash of conflicting underlying positions without any clear thinking behind them. In a market where the weight of money is eroding profit margins and the velocity rendering investment themes increasingly transient, finding sustainable alpha generating trades has become more and more difficult. The promise of high returns via the classic fund of funds investment model has become unrealistic.

Enter the smaller assets under management (AUM) emerging manager as part of the solution. It serves little purpose here to re-hash familiar arguments in favor of emerging managers relating to flexibility, transparency and better investment terms. At this stage of the debate, if you've been paying attention, you either like them or you don't.

The crucial point here is that it's the emerging managers who are the most willing to provide the transparency and commit the time to communicate such valuable ideas. They are not burdened by a lot of investors clamoring for their time, and are hungry to develop their business. The advantage of developing these ideas at the fund of funds level is that they can be understood in a wider context by comparing them to other competing investment opportunities, spotting trends across asset classes and identifying dangerously crowded trades. In general, taking a broader view of the risks and rewards has its benefits. In contrast, hedge fund managers usually operate in a silo, unable to see the wider implications of the trade idea or theme.

## THE HEDGE IS THE EDGE—TYPES OF HEDGES

### Short Trade

One of the ways that hedge fund managers generate their big returns is by being able to identify overpriced stocks. With the ability to both buy and short stocks, hedge funds have roughly double the opportunity set of long only investors, a critical competitive advantage. Shorting stocks isn't easy however, markets tend to go up more often than they go down. If more than one manager gets in on the short side, it can also significantly increase the volatility of a stock, which can have implications for the risk profile of a fund as well as the viability of the trade. Sometimes heavily shorted stocks see a big run up before they go down, creating losses that can be hard to recover.

A recent example of how this can play out is with the controversial company Tesla Motors. Tesla makes electric cars, and has enjoyed growing consumer interest because unlike some electric vehicles, the Tesla looks and drives like a traditional car. Tesla's CEO Elon Musk also has a storied history as an entrepreneur including being the principal of well-known companies like Space X and Paypal. Musk wanted to prove that an electric car could compete on style and quality with other top tier automotive brands but it hasn't been easy.

Then in May 2013, the stock price started taking off. At that time, short traders had a 41 percent position in stock but Tesla posted its first ever profit, causing the stock price to tick up. Conventional wisdom around Tesla was that the company would falter like other electric car makers who were over reliant on government subsidies, in addition to the persistent weakness of the carmaker group in general.

Other electric vehicles (EVs) backed by big names like the Chevy Volt or the Nissan Leaf had only seen limited adoption. The company also had a hard time getting state lawmakers on board with direct sales in states like Texas and North Carolina,[3] which both passed bans. The shorts said that the company was surviving on selling its lucrative EV tax credits back to automakers, not on sales.

When all this started, Tesla was around $30. Over the span of a few weeks, the stock price increased, closing at +76.76 percent on May 10.[4] Analysts said that Tesla's share price was gaining on the news of its newfound profits, and shorts rushing to cover their positions. Over the rest of the year stock price increased pretty steadily, creating pressure on short positions—by October 2013 Tesla's share price was hovering at around $170.

In other cases, short selling can be and has been directly banned[5] for a time as a result of actions by regulators. This happened during the 2008 crisis as regulators worked to stop the bleeding. The effect of those bans often doesn't do much, except ding short traders. Lower interest rate environments, like those that have persisted since the crisis—also as the result of government intervention—lessen the short rebate, limiting the upside for those trades.

Regulators are also looking for more disclosure so they can better monitor short trades and avoid naked shorting, which reduces the opportunity set. Andrew D. Beer, the CEO of Beechhead Capital Management explains how this works in practice. "When a hedge fund borrows a stock and sells it short, the hedge fund provides the cash proceeds (plus a little extra) as collateral to the lender. The lender typically invests this cash and generates a return, a portion of which is shared with the hedge fund. This short rebate is typically tied to the Fed Funds rate."[6] The problem with this is that the Fed Funds rate is at historically low levels and isn't slated to rise anytime soon.

"The decline in interest rates has a material impact on the economics of shorting. To use a simple example, when short-term rates are 4 percent, the hedge fund might expect a short rebate of, say, 3 percent. If the hedge fund runs an average gross short exposure of 70 percent, it can expect to earn around 2 percent from the short rebate (assuming that the dividend yield on the stock is zero, a reasonable assumption for companies with deteriorating business models). This 2 percent gross return offsets the higher fee structure of hedge funds relative to long only managers. Conversely, when short-term rates are close to zero, the short rebate essentially is zero," he says.

In October 2008 the SEC issued temporary Rule 204T to curb naked short selling by shortening the delivery window and expanding the rule to cover all equity securities. This amounts to direct regulatory intervention designed to make shorting more difficult. Brokers now have less time to obtain shares, which impacts shorts that have to be closed on the settlement date. Brokers are also less willing to lend shares because of these developments, which means hedge funds in general are shorting less than they have historically.

Even though they are shorting less aggressively than they once were, equity long/short strategies still account for the biggest group of hedge funds and readily post new launches. For investors then, the trick is finding a manager that is actually skilled at running a short book and isn't just relying on trading with the herd or using ETFs. These managers have always been hard to find, and get harder still as the industry grows. However, they will be the most consistent performers of the lot.

According to Beer, "the most important factor in the profitability of a short book will be the ability of a given manager to identify securities that materially underperform the market, and hence add alpha." Based on his research,[7] "the most heavily shorted U.S. equity securities outperformed (hence short sellers underperformed) the S&P 500 in both 2010 and 2011, in sharp contrast to the several hundred basis points of annual underperformance during the mid-2000s. We later saw some evidence that this trend abated in 2012, when heavily shorted equities performed in line with the S&P."

**Tail-Risk Hedges** Tail-risk strategies are another big arrow hedge funds have in their quiver. Some hedge funds focus solely on tail-risk strategies, seeking to be one part of a broader portfolio. Others bake it in as part of their hedge overlay.

Tail-risk strategies are essentially designed to perform well in the worst of market conditions. They act as insurance policies, requiring investors to pay in to a losing strategy until something bad happens. Tail-risk hedges are said to be most effective in environments where market participants see declines of at least 20 percent, providing much needed liquidity while the rest of their portfolio is spiraling toward the bottom. These declines are commonly known as fat-tails or black swan events. The individual strategies themselves are derived from calculating the probability of such events.

Tail-risk hedges are gaining more attention from institutional investors like public pension funds, which have a mandate to provide a certain level of return and have been on more or less shaky ground since 2008. Tail-risk hedges can however, act like a double edged sword for this type of investor as they lose money until a fat-tail event happens, thereby making it seem as though the fund just allocated into a strategy doing the exact thing it seeks to avoid.

Tail-risk hedging can take a variety of forms most of which require fairly technical understanding of investing, but, in essence an investor or fund will take a contrarian macro position. One of the more popular forms of this is buying long-term put options. Put options give a fund the right to sell an underlying stock or security on the expectation of a drop in price. Long-term put options are typically available in smaller quantities and become more expensive as volatility increases. Other variations on this theme include variance swaps a derivative that bets on the magnitude of volatility.

The CBOE Volatility Index (VIX), also known as the fear index, is a measure of the implied volatility of S&P 500 index options. The VIX, as an index, also serves as the basis for several Exchange Traded Products (ETPs), which track its performance. As a result, many products which track the VIX often get lumped into tail-risk hedges, this is where things get murky for investors and some managers trying to understand tail-risk.

## The Paradox

"Tail-risk funds are going to be popular until the markets improve again," says Damian Handzy, CEO of Investor Analytics, a U.S.-based risk management firm. Tail risk is often simplified as an insurance policy against adverse market events, akin to a homeowner's policy. On the surface this looks like an easy sell, however, the same people that can readily imagine various levels of home destruction often have a difficult time imagining portfolio destruction. This is especially true at the top of a market—the precise point when investors should have a tail-risk plan in place. "Tail-risk protection is needed the most at the top of the market, but people start panic buying at the correction, when it's too late and too expensive," he says.

Part of the problem is that tail-risk strategies in of themselves aren't especially cheap at any point. It is less expensive overall to take an out-of-the-money position at the top of a given market, but it's not free. According to Richard (Jerry) Haworth, Co-Founder and CIO of UK-based investment firm 36 South Capital Advisors, investors need to examine the cost relative to the return.

"A tail event is a rare event so you should get paid multiples. If it's likely to occur once every 10 years and it'll pay 10 times, then the payoff equals the probability and that makes sense. But, if it looks to happen every 10 years and only pays 3 times, that's very expensive, then it becomes tail insurance not a tail fund opportunity. It comes down to what the investor is willing to pay for both of those."

## What Color Is Your Swan?

In order to understand the probability of these events and their potential effect, investors and managers alike have to understand what tail events are and if they can be adequately predicted. "People have a hard time defining tail-risk, (we say a move greater than three standard deviations), but they don't know what volatility to apply to get to that number, or how to implement an effective hedge. I've seen some ridiculous strategies. Hedging for a 10 percent move is not a tail event," Haworth explains.

"There are two types of tail events—grey swans and black swans. Black swans are unknowable. Grey swans are knowable. What we see going back to 1987 is that about every five years you see a tail event, so 1987, 1994, 1997, 1998, 2000, 2001, and 2008. So we try to be realistic in making those predictions. To Paulson, 2008 was not a black swan event. It was a grey swan event." He defines a grey swan as having medium probability with medium impact. Whereas, black swans have a low probability and high impact when they occur. According to Haworth, a key realization that people need to make about portfolio management overall is that volatility and correlation are not constant. Once investors and mangers shift their perspective, they can begin to understand risk and tail-risk hedges more appropriately.

These distinctions are what separate tail-risk hedges from plays on volatility. "Some people interpret tail-risk as extreme volatility but they are fundamentally different. Volatility players use a combination of options and aren't always focused on extreme events," Handzy says. "Tail-risk hedges are focused solely on extreme price movements." Understanding the nuances around tail-risk is important to constructing a strategy that will be an effective hedge without simply transferring risk or moving money to the sidelines.

## Cash Is Not Always King

"You need a bespoke tail-risk solution that looks at targeted securities. The idea of a generic tail-risk fund is tricky to me. Tail-risk hedges are typically buying deep out of the money puts, buying a lot of put options is a really expensive proposition, if you're just doing it without a plan as a big hedge," Handzy says.

According to Haworth, if a tail-risk strategy is going to be effective, it should be at least a five-year plan that buys convexity when it's cheap and has the full backing of the investment committee. Poorly constructed tail-risk hedges without a long-term plan can simply transfer the risk. "Writing calls to buy puts is a bad tail-risk hedge, all you are doing is swapping the risk of one tail for another, if say, there was a significant increase in inflation," Haworth says. Both men agree that investors cannot simply diversify their way out of tail-risk. Handzy notes that during the 2008 crisis all correlations went to one, making diversification irrelevant.

Some investors and managers argue that a significant cash position is another way to approach tail-risk. However, both men note that while going to cash does effectively remove the risk, it can create its own set of complications. Cash makes investors heavily dependent on timing in terms of when to get back into the market, it can also expand the length of time it takes for them to recover losses. While having an effective tail-risk hedge in place would have paid out when the rest of the portfolio was going down. "Just going to cash is not really a viable hedge against a tail event. You're just taking all the risk off the table, and you're saying deflation is on the horizon. If it goes to inflation there's not a light at the end of the tunnel there, you're looking at an oncoming train," Haworth says.

## Evolution

Traditional portfolio construction typically had large clients at a 60/40 split between stocks and bonds. For institutional investors, this split also gave itself to being long-only, and operating on a buy and hold approach. With the rise of alternative investments, portfolio construction evolved to offer investors more options for their allocations including strategies that go both long and short, and offer access to a broader asset class mix.

Over this course of this evolution, the risk profile of a given portfolio has also changed often to reflect increased risk as a result of pursuing higher returns. In response to this, investors have seen the rise of a variety of risk mitigation measures, with some notable failures. Leland and Rubinstein's portfolio insurance,[8] which was designed to replicate the performance of a put option systematically, was one approach, and is now generally acknowledged to have exacerbated the 1987 crash.

Other synthetic instruments, originally created for one purpose and then broadly utilized by people who handle them poorly, can have similar consequences. Take for example, the multi-billion dollar write-downs[9] during the credit crisis resulting from collateralized debt obligations (CDOs) that were poorly constructed, underwritten and rated, yet used writ large by banks and hedge funds alike. CDOs are a type of asset-backed security (ABS) that have multiple tranches and are collateralized by debt obligations including loans. The poor use and misuse of these types of instruments can help precipitate tail events when used as broadly as these were, even though they are typically used because of their reputation to have low risk or act as a risk mitigator to the broader portfolio.

As such, left tail-risk hedges have become more popular recently, as a means of protecting the portfolio from an event several standard deviations outside of its normal risk profile. Some of the most well-known research on left tail-risk hedges has been done by Dr. Nassim Taleb, who has authored several books explaining in detail the underpinnings of tail events and their impact. He is also a principal at Universa Investments LP an investment management firm that specializes in convex tail-hedging and tail-investing, ranging from hedging stock market crashes and inflation to macro and equity options strategies. Universa runs tail-hedging and tail-investing strategies for institutional investors, and manages the world's first tail-protected ETFs launched in May 2012 and traded on the TSX via Horizons ETFs.

"Nassim Taleb is really the grandfather of the tail-hedging field. What he is doing in terms of work on tail-risk and its influence on the financial industry is not unlike Markowitz's impact on portfolio management back in the 1950's, and in fact counterbalances the mistakes of Markowitz's followers that created flawed models like Value at Risk," explains Claude Bovet, Founder and Managing Director of Lionscrest Capital, which acts as the conduit for institutional investors seeking to invest in Universa's tail-hedging and tail-investing strategies through its own TailPro series of commingled funds.

Universa is the dominant player in the tail-risk space, managing approximately $6 billion in assets and providing much of the research basis for understanding how to hedge these events. According to Bovet, following Lehman's collapse in September 2008 (a black swan event) until the end of the year, the S&P 500 lost –30 percent whereas a tail-protected S&P 500 using Universa's tail-hedging strategy would have been up +15 percent. The Universa strategy's stand-alone gain notionally was more than 130 percent for that period and on a cash basis using a typical funding rate of 5 percent was over +2,600 percent. The key driver of these returns is how the hedge is structured.

## Structure

"If your objectives are to keep beta near zero, mute volatility, and catch the upside of your trades, you have to have a tail hedge plan in place to meet all three of those conditions," says Warren Wright, CIO of Diversified Global Asset Management (DGAM), a Canadian fund of hedge funds. DGAM implemented a proprietary, direct tail-risk hedging strategy in 2007. According to the firm, when the 2008 crisis hit, their approach to left tail-risk generated 600–800bps of positive return across all portfolios.

Left tail-risk hedges are dependent on size and capturing convexivity. "Sizing a hedge in a portfolio is a function of the perceived level of market risk, the amount of risk embedded in the portfolio, the cost of hedges, and an investor's utility or objective function," explains David Hay, Managing Director, DGAM. A significant tail event, is usually a minimum of two or three standard deviations outside of the normal risk profile, or a loss of 20 percent or more. Investors considering left tail-risk hedges will then determine what they are willing to pay in premium now to keep the portfolio flat or cover that 20 percent.

Once the size is clear, buying convexity when it is cheap in order to achieve that size, is a way to keep costs low when putting on a tail-risk hedge. Convexity is a measure of how sensitive the duration of a bond is to changes in interest rates. If the convexity and duration of a trading book is too high, so is the risk—effective hedges bring this down. This is especially important for institutional portfolios, like pension funds, which are mandated to generate low-risk returns.

The most common structure for a left tail-risk hedge is to buy out-of-the-money put options, essentially taking a position contrary to the current upside. DGAM has also used synthetic credit instruments including equity market calls, super senior tranches, single name credit protection, and CMBX—a group of indexes made up of 25 tranches of commercial mortgage-backed securities (CMBS). "We use a range of instruments across all asset classes. We consider the cost of a hedge versus its potential upside while remaining cognizant of the basis risk between that instrument and our underlying portfolio," Hay says.

"At times we have held entirely credit based hedges, while at other times we have held exchange traded equity options. The relative cheapness of equity options, a reduction in counterparty risk and enhanced liquidity were key drivers of the decision to exit credit hedges in favor of equity hedges in the spring of 2008, as one example. The point of DGAM's tail hedge is to capture the asymmetry between a well-diversified portfolio of high Sharpe ratio assets and lower Sharpe ratio market factors."

According to Wright, tail-risk hedges should be discretionary, and cannot be market timed, "acting on an ex-ante basis is critical." Both men note that making tail-risk hedges discretionary is also tied to the need for dynamic hedge sizing, in order to remain ahead of changes in the market. Hay offers two examples of how this works for investors, "in August 2011, underlying fund managers were cutting back on risk so we pulled back on our hedges, generating material gains during that time. We also often look at the steepness of the volatility curve, monitoring the shape of that curve and the price of VIX options against the shape of the curve, in some instances we have been paid to put on hedges."

Bovet notes that liquidity is also an important structural component, "tail-hedging strategies (particularly pooled funds) that require long lock-ups have extreme liquidity risks and cannot be relied upon when mitigating tail-risk."

Left tail-risk is often discussed in terms of an equities focused portfolio, however, the potential for a tail event exists across investments—equities, credit, commodities, and fixed income. Individual investors may opt to examine or "hedge out" those risks ahead of investment in a given fund or within their existing portfolio in order to effectively size a tail-risk hedge. Dynamic sizing is an important structural component of this type of hedge in order to realize maximum protection during a tail event and control cost before an event strikes.

Funds of hedge funds do this on a bigger scale by constructing portfolios made up of different funds and different risk profiles toward a broader set of investment objectives. In this case, they look at tail-risk at both the macro and micro level. "We have an integrated risk management program, on one hand its independent from the investment committee and on the other hand it's integrated into how we pick managers and their approach," explains Oleg Movchan, Director of Risk Management, at Attalus Capital. Attalus Capital is a Philadelphia-based investment and trading firm specializing in fund of hedge funds and active core equity and bond strategies.

When it comes to choosing managers, the firm will carefully examine the risk of a given fund at first on a standalone basis as part of the due diligence process and then more broadly against the other managers already in a given portfolio and its objectives. "For us, tail-risk hedging is a component of portfolio construction, we look at the entire probability distribution, we aren't looking at just downside equity risk. Our portfolios are exposed to different kinds of risk: equity, credit, commodities, fixed income," he says.

Managing the risk of individual managers against the broader portfolio is also important in order to avoid an unintended concentration of a given strategy, according to Movchan, a bias toward a certain strategy or style can create tail-risk and potentially undermine the performance of a portfolio. He cites the quant crisis of 2007, as an example of micro-level tail-risk. Avoiding unintended concentrations also ensures a better understanding of broader financial markets activity, which can, in turn, give portfolio managers greater ability to take advantage of conditions such as the mispricing of risk.

## Are Puts the Only Option?

Movchan notes that he has seen an increase in the types of instruments available to hedge against tail-risk including—vanilla derivatives, credit swaptions, inflation protection, and volatility products, in addition to the more standard choice of buying out of the money puts. Indeed, the market for tail-risk products continues to grow as markets remain choppy; this growth has also ignited a debate among investors and managers about what really constitutes a tail-risk hedge. For Movchan, each of these instruments can have a place in tail-risk hedging depending on the type of risk an investor is trying to hedge against.

"We think there are products that deal with inflation protection for example, that have a place. If a portfolio is heavily weighted in fixed income, then out of the money puts on the S&P 500 are not necessarily going to help if there is a re-pricing of inflation expectations. You also have to decide if you're going handle this issue directly, or outsource it to a manager. Volatility instruments, vanilla derivatives have a place as tail-risk hedges."

Cost is also a factor, "we seek to identify the assets that are likely to move the most and give the best return on the price of the insurance in a risk off scenario, be it in equity markets, currencies, or bonds. Our preference is to use out of the money put options, which give us large notional exposures at low cost. Of course price is very important and when the price of the insurance (the option premium) becomes expensive, we will construct the positions differently, perhaps by using option spreads, or trading in the money put options with stop losses," says Greg McEntyre, Director, Symphony Financial Partners, a Tokyo-based firm.

Symphony manages an Asian-macro fund, Sinfonietta, that focuses on tail-risk. The fund was established in June 2008 to invest Symphony principal capital outside the scope of its existing funds with tail-risk in mind. Symphony opened the fund to outside investors at the end of 2011. The fund seeks to generate alpha through investments in equities, equity indices, derivatives, fixed income, and currencies. According to McEntyre, Symphony's approach is designed to manage the exposure of long positions and take profits during market corrections.

As an Asia-based and Asia-focused firm, McEntyre also outlines regional considerations that can come into play in terms of how they approach tail-risk. "Asian markets tend to be very liquidity driven, so one needs to be focused on liquidity flows. For example, foreign investor flows, or domestic retail flows, can be a very large part of the markets in Hong Kong, Korea, and India. Central Bank flows are currently having a large impact on the Australian dollar and Australian bond markets," these factors, in addition to cost can impact what instruments the firm uses when constructing a tail-risk hedge.

This variable approach raises some flags for other managers. "Using OTC derivatives is a completely nonsensical tail-hedge—when a real black swan hits, like in the fourth quarter of 2008, you need to be sure that your counterparty will be able to pay, a rather unlikely and irrational expectation as financial firms that are the counterparties are most at risk of failing," says Claude Bovet, Founder and Managing Director of Lionscrest Capital. He adds that taking on basis risk is not a wise trade-off to protect against tail-risk.

## Volatility

The use of VIX-based instruments is often also included in tail-risk discussions. The VIX is a measure of the implied volatility of the prices of S&P 500 futures. When the 2008 crisis hit, the CBOE Volatility Index (the VIX) soared—up 126 percent over the S&P 500. Since then, the VIX has been getting the attention of investors looking for protection from tail events. VIX futures were first offered in 2004, but investing in the VIX didn't really take off until 2009 when the first VIX exchange-traded products were added. Since then, average 30-day trading volume in VIX futures has increased significantly, making it a multi-billion dollar market.

One of the more common approaches is to be long volatility, however, this can be very expensive as the VIX tends to trend and can trend against a long-only position. VelocityShares, a U.S.-based firm, offers volatility products as part of its tail-risk solutions, including six volatility ETPs that have twice-leveraged long and inverse positions on the S&P 500 VIX short-term futures index and the S&P 500 VIX mid-term futures index. According to Will Lloyd, Managing Director at VelocityShares, the inverse positions are critical—"being both long and short the VIX gets you the convexity that you need to effectively hedge tail-risk without the costs associated with being just long volatility."

He notes that the severe contango, or upward-slope of the VIX futures market is what makes it so expensive to buy and hold long positions. Lloyd and other VelocityShares principals Nick Cherney and Geremy Kawaller, wrote a paper[10] for the *Journal of Indexes* describing the consequences of this trend in detail. In it, they show that the VIX was in contango from mid-2009 to July 2011. However, coupled with the use of daily resetting leveraged and inverse products that exhibit positive convexivity, that cost can come down.

Lloyd also notes investors can get in and out quickly, "with futures you can liquidate pretty immediately, where as out-of-money put strategies often have 30-, 60-, or 90-day liquidation terms." However, he explains that the strategy needs to be more actively managed as exposures can vary based on the performance of the VIX futures index.

Ultimately, all men agree that buyers of tail-risk products need to go in with eyes wide open about the cost and structure of this type of hedge.

Movchan says these products are likely to remain in the consciousness of investors over the near term as global economic growth stays relatively weak. "Longer term, the big concerns we have in portfolio solutions are dealing with potential imbalances that have been built into the system as a result of central bank intervention since 2008."

## TAIL RISK HEDGES FOR RETAIL INVESTORS

Retail investors, which may look to managed futures mutual funds as a means of diversifying out of risk also have their own new tail risk mutual funds that operate on similar principals to the hedges outlined above. In 2012, Universa Investments launched two ETF products through Horizons Exchange Traded Funds Inc. and its affiliate AlphaPro Management Inc. which are now available to investors on the Toronto Stock Exchange. The firm uses its Black Swan Protection Protocol (BSPP) to provide unique tail risk hedging solutions to its client base.

"In marrying the hedge with what it is hedging we can better express the edge. It's actually even more about opportunistic offense, having the ammunition to buy when everyone else is panic-selling, than defense," explains Mark Spitznagel, of Universa.

For retail investors the product is slightly altered in order to work within a retail portfolio. A portion of the ETF will be invested in the same Black Swan Protection Protocol offered to the firm's hedge fund investors, while capturing the upside gains of the applicable stock index. As a result, the Black Swan ETF will have a slight drag relative to other ETFs accounting for the negative carry typically associated with tail risk hedges like the Protocol. However, during a black swan event, retail investors are likely to recapture some of that, just as a hedge fund investor would.

Investors that invest in the Black Swan ETF will also see any gains generated from Universa's strategy reinvested into the stock portion of the portfolio on an opportunistic basis, explains Howard Atkinson, president and CEO of Horizons ETFs. He notes that so far, demand from investors for the product has been consistent, reflecting an global investor landscape that is still reeling from 2008.

While Universa had the first mover advantage, two other firms—First Trust and VelocityShares have also filed for their own black swan ETFs. The First Trust CBOE VIX Tail Hedge Index Fund tracks the CBOE S&P VIX Tail Hedge Index and equities on the S&P 500. The VelocityShares Tail Risk Hedged Large Cap ETF will track the VelocityShares Tail Risk Hedged Large Cap Index, according to SEC filings for both firms. Both of these products rely on a VIX based approach to tail risk hedging which diverges from what is believed to be an options based approach used in the Protocol. The differences between these two approaches can be seen in detail, earlier in the chapter.

## DERIVATIVES

Earlier, we broke out how the rapidly growing OTC market led in no small part, to new regulations requiring central clearers for those instruments. While the creation of clearinghouses has had a chilling effect on the use of these instruments, they are still being used as part of trading strategies.

The use of credit default swaps (CDS) including those that are tied to sovereign bond debt remain one of the most popular instruments among investment advisors. Credit default swaps are essentially the insurance paid out on the default of a bond. CDS are a derivative instrument that transfers default exposure on fixed income investments to more than one party. The holder of a CDS contract pays on that contract until maturity of the underlying fixed income investment. If that investment defaults, the holder of the CDS contract will still get paid out. This accounts for their popularity as part of a hedging strategy. CDS have seen pressure from regulators however, especially because they can be tied to sovereign debt which sometimes defaults despite being risk free.

Other derivatives including those for currencies and commodities are also still seeing widespread use, and in fact some investors find comfort in the presence of central clearers. Institutions have been able to cut costs by doing away with shadow staff which validated these trades before the presence of clearinghouses. ETFs, which are available to retail investors, can also use derivatives as part of their funds. However, regulators have indicated that they will be keeping a close eye on the use of levered retail products like ETFs.

## SUMMARY

Each strategy will employ certain hedged overlays in order to mitigate downside risk or generate alpha. Understanding what instruments are involved in these strategies can help investors evaluate the performance of a given fund, and the relative ability of a given manager. Rules around each of these types of hedges are expected to continue to evolve over time as regulators seek to monitor and stem systemic risk or openly malicious trades. As new guidelines emerge, expect that new hedging tactics and perhaps even new instruments will also emerge. Hedge fund managers are trained to capture the dislocation of a given market, if they are able to see those dislocations, they'll build something to capture that.

## NOTES

1. "New Research Examines Quantitative Trend Following as an Equity Risk Hedge," *Opalesque Alternative Market Briefing*, www.opalesque.com/646534/New_research_examines_quantitative_trend_following_as_an653.html.
2. The BTOP50 is a benchmark of the top performing CTAs in the BarclayHedge universe, the index can be viewed here: www.barclayhedge.com/research/indices/btop.
3. "Tesla Falters in Texas, N.C. Fight Goes On," *Automotive News*, www.autonews.com/article/20130513/RETAIL07/305139962/tesla-falters-in-texas-n-c-fight-goes-on.
4. "Tesla Shorts Feel the Pain as Stock Price Gains 41%," *Opalesque Alternative Market Briefing*, www.opalesque.com/646474/Tesla_shorts_feel_the_pain_as_stock_price647.html.
5. Robert Battalio, Hamid Mehran, and Paul Schultz, "Market Declines: What Is Accomplished by Banning Short Selling?," Federal Reserve Bank of New York, www.newyorkfed.org/research/current_issues/ci18-5.html.
6. "Guest Article: A Short Note on Short Selling: Four Post Crisis Headwinds," *Opalesque New Managers*, www.opalesque.com/new-managers/206/guest-article-a-short-note-on.html.
7. "Guest Article—New Study Shows Small Equity Long/Short Managers Outperform Their Larger Peers over Five and Ten Year Periods," *Opalesque New Managers*, www.opalesque.com/new-managers/166/guest-article-new-study-shows-small.html.
8. Hayne E. Leland, "Who Should Buy Portfolio Insurance?," *Journal of Finance* 35, no. 2 (May 1980): 581–594. Papers and Proceedings Thirty-Eighth Annual Meeting American Finance Association, Atlanta, Georgia, December 28–30, 1979, www.jstor.org/stable/2327419.
9. Anna Katherine Barnett-Hart, "The Story of the CDO Market Meltdown: An Empirical Analysis," Harvard University, www.hks.harvard.edu/m-rcbg/students/dunlop/2009-CDOmeltdown.pdf.
10. "Portfolio Applications For VIX-based Instruments," *Journal of Indexes*, 2011, www.indexuniverse.com/publications/journalofindexes/joiarticles/10095-portfolio-applications-for-vix-based-instruments.html?showall=&fullart=1&start=9.

# About the Author

**Bailey McCann** is the U.S. editor for Opalesque, where she covers alternative investments for the daily *Alternative Market Briefing*. In November 2012 she also created and launched private equity coverage for the outlet with a monthly title—*Private Equity Strategies*. In addition to her work at Opalesque she is the founder and editor of CivSource, an online publication for state and local government professionals.

# About the Contributors

**Beverly Chandler,** Opalesque London, contributed to the flagship *Alternative Market Briefing* newsletter, and managed Asia coverage through the monthly title *Asia Pacific Intelligence*. Prior to her work at Opalesque, she was an in-house reporter with the GAIM, FundForum, and SuperReturn conferences.

**Benedicte Gravrand,** Opalesque Geneva, co-edits Opalesque's daily hedge fund publication *Alternative Market Briefing*, where she writes exclusive stories and special reports, and moderates some of Opalesque's roundtables. She is also the editor of Opalesque's *NewManager*, a monthly newsletter.

**Bruno Guillemin,** CAIA, Senior Analyst, Fundana SA, is an investment advisor to several Funds of Hedge Funds and directs around half of its new investments to Emerging Managers. The investment process typically involves allocating a small amount—day 1 or early-stage (within the first year after the fund's launch)—to new managers who have strong pedigrees.

**Charles T. Hage** is Director of Compliance at Mohican Financial Management, LLC. Mohican is a New York-based convertible arbitrage fund.

**Fraser McKenzie** is Managing Partner of 47 Degrees North Capital Management. 47 Degrees North is a specialist alternative investment firm, and a pioneer in early-stage hedge fund investing. It was selected as one of three successful candidates out of 97 applicants to manage the emerging hedge fund managers program at CalPERS.

**Mark Melin,** Opalesque Futures Intelligence, is a managed futures practitioner whose specialty is recognizing a trading program's algorithmic formula and mapping it to a market environment and performance driver. He provides analysis of managed futures investment performance and commentary regarding related managed futures market environment. A portfolio and industry consultant, he was an adjunct instructor in managed futures at Northwestern University/Chicago and has written or edited three books, including *High Performance Managed Futures* (Wiley 2010) and *The Chicago Board of Trade's Handbook of Futures and Options* (McGraw-Hill 2008). Mark was director of the managed futures division at Alaron Trading until they were acquired by Peregrine Financial Group in 2009, where he was a registered associated person (National Futures Association NFA ID#: 0348336). Mark has also worked as a commodity trading advisor himself, trading a short volatility options portfolio across the yield curve, and was an independent consultant to various broker dealers and futures exchanges, including OneChicago, the single stock futures exchange, and the Chicago Board of Trade.

**Nick Morrell** is Head of Operational Due Diligence and Chief Risk Officer at Fundana SA. Fundana is an investment advisor to several Funds of Hedge Funds and directs around half of its new investments to emerging managers.

# Additional Resources

For additional materials, including videos with some of the managers, please visit our website for this book: www.tactical-portfolios.com.

**Opalesque**
Opalesque is a leading news and information outlet for hedge funds and alternative investments.
www.opalesque.com

**Cambridge Associates**
Cambridge Associates is a global investment advisor that works with pensions and endowments.
www.cambridgeassociates.com

**Preqin**
A data provider for and about the alternatives investment industry, providing data on hedge funds, private equity, real estate and venture capital.
www.preqin.com

**eVestment**
eVestment provides data on performance, asset flows, and market trends on hedge funds, and other investments.
www.evestment.com

**CAIA**
The Chartered Alternative Investment Analyst Association provides aspiring and practicing industry professionals with accreditation and education.
www.caia.org

**AIMA**
The Alternative Investment Management Association provides educational information and professional development for investors and executives in alternatives investing.
www.aima.org

**TAAAPs**

The Alliance of Alternative Asset Professionals is a non-profit trade organization that provides educational information to investors and professionals.
www.taaaps.org

**HFA**

The Hedge Fund Association provides networking, education and support to the hedge fund industry.
www.thehfa.org

**MFA**

The Managed Funds Association is an alternatives trade association advocating for the public policy interests of the investment industry and providing educational information for investment professionals.
www.mangedfunds.org

**NFA**

The National Futures Association provides registration, education and outreach for those involved with or investing in futures.
www.nfa.futures.org

**Institute for Private Investors**

The institute provides networking and outreach among private investors, family offices. They also provide education to investors about the alternatives industry.
www.memberlink.com

# Index